THE JPS BIBLE COMMENTARY

ESTHER אסתר

The JPS Torah Commentary

GENERAL EDITOR   *Nahum M. Sarna*
LITERARY EDITOR   *Chaim Potok*

GENESIS   *Nahum M. Sarna*
EXODUS   *Nahum M. Sarna*
LEVITICUS   *Baruch A. Levine*
NUMBERS   *Jacob Milgrom*
DEUTERONOMY   *Jeffrey H. Tigay*

The JPS Bible Commentary

The Five Megillot and Jonah
GENERAL EDITOR   *Michael Fishbane*

JONAH   *Uriel Simon*
ESTHER   *Adele Berlin*

THE JPS BIBLE
COMMENTARY

ESTHER אסתר

The Traditional Hebrew Text with the New JPS Translation

Commentary by A D E L E   B E R L I N

THE   JEWISH   PUBLICATION   SOCIETY

PHILADELPHIA   2 0 0 1   /   5 7 6 1

Composition by El Ot Ltd. (English text) and Varda Graphics (Hebrew text)
Design by Adrianne Dudden
Manufactured in the United States of America

06 07 08 09 10   10 9 8 7 6 5 4

Library of Congress Cataloging-in-Publication Data

Bible. O.T. Esther. Hebrew. 2001
    Esther = [Ester]: the traditional Hebrew text with the new JPS
translation / commentary by Adele Berlin.
        p. cm. — (The JPS commentary)
    Hebrew and English.
    Includes bibliographical references.
    ISBN 0-8276-0699-0
    1. Bible. O.T. Esther—Commentaries. I. Title: Ester.
II. Berlin, Adele. III. Bible. O.T. Esther. English.
Jewish Publication Society. 2001. IV. Title. V. JPS Bible commentary.
BS1373.B47   2001   00-059074
222'.9077—dc21

GENESIS   ISBN 0-8276-0326-6
EXODUS   ISBN 0-8276-0327-4
LEVITICUS   ISBN 0-8276-0328-2
NUMBERS   ISBN 0-8276-0329-0
DEUTERONOMY   ISBN 0-8276-0330-4
Five-volume set   ISBN 0-8276-0331-2
JONAH   ISBN 0-8276-0672-9
ESTHER   ISBN 0-8276-06990

The publication of this book was made possible by a gift in honor of Esther Cohn Elson on the occasion of her 90th birthday by her children, grandchildren, and great-grandchildren.

To the memory of
Ruth Kraft Gumerman
Ruth Rice
Judy Licht

CONTENTS

PREFACE

The Book of Esther is, among Jews, one of the best-known and most enjoyed books of the Bible. The book's fame is due almost entirely to its connection with Purim. If we did not have Purim, with the reading of *Megillat Esther* as its centerpiece, Esther would languish in obscurity. In fact, it seems likely that Esther was included in the Bible because of the celebration of Purim. The converse is also probable: if we did not have the Book of Esther we would not have Purim, for Esther gives us the account of the origin of Purim and the reason for its annual celebration. Without the book, there would be little reason to perpetuate the observance of Purim. Whether the book preceded the festival or the festival the book, the two are now inextricably bound together. Esther is a joyous book for a joyous festival. It is my hope that this commentary will add to the joy and pleasure of reading the Book of Esther.

There are many excellent commentaries and studies, traditional and modern, on the Book of Esther. I have drawn extensively on the recent works by Frederic W. Bush, David Clines, Michael Fox, Amos Hakham, Jon D. Levenson, Carey A. Moore, and the commentary edited by Jacob Klein et al. in the series *'Olam Ha-tanakh*. My purpose is not to collect all previous interpretations but to present a coherent view of the book, emphasizing the literary qualities that give the book its distinctive character and message. My approach to the book's interpretation will stress two main points: (1) that the book is a comedy, and (2) that the author drew heavily on the literary motifs associated with Persia that were current at the time the book was written. Motifs about Persia survive almost exclusively in the Greek writings from the Persian period, and I will cite the Greek sources often for I find in them the key to understanding Esther. My purpose in providing these citations is to give the modern reader a sense of the world of storytelling from which Esther emerged, and to show what connotations specific themes and motifs might have had to an ancient reader.

While Esther should be seen as part of the broader literary world of the ancient Near East during the Persian period, it is, at the same time, a Jewish book reflecting Jewish experiences and aspirations. It drew on earlier biblical works and was itself included in the biblical canon. It is equally important, therefore, to note the particular aspects that reflect its biblical and Jewish origin and the ways that later generations of Jews interpreted it. So, in addition to reading Esther as an example of storytelling from the Persian period, my reading of it will also attend to Esther as a biblical book and as part of the canon explicated in the rabbinic tradition. These are the contexts that have influenced the book's place in Jewish life. As is inevitable, these contexts changed the way the book was read and changed the meaning of the story, so that the Book of

Esther as understood by Hellenistic Jews and by the rabbinic tradition is a different story from the one told in the Masoretic Text. Samplings of these postbiblical interpretations will be offered throughout the commentary.

I began work on this commentary while I was a Fellow of the Center for Judaic Studies at the University of Pennsylvania. I am grateful to the center, and its director, David Ruderman, for providing an ideal research environment. My thanks go to Sol Cohen for sharing his linguistic and textual knowledge, and to the staff of the library, who provided materials from near and far. I benefited from discussions with the 1997–1998 fellows and with other colleagues who were kind enough to take an interest in the work. Among these I am especially indebted to Linda Bregstein, Barry Eichler, Tikva Frymer-Kensky, Sy Gitin, Jacob Klein, Bernard Levinson, Gary Rendsburg, Jeff Tigay, and Ziony Zevit.

I was privileged to offer a course on Esther at the University of Pennsylvania during the fall 1998 semester. Thanks to the members of this class—Ami Butler, Paul Delnero, Leah Kaplan-Samuels, Stephen Sang-Bae Kim, Kevin McGeough, Deborah Posner, Matthew Rutz, Alvin Turner, Julie Wu, and Susan Zeelander—for their stimulating questions and comments.

I thank Michael Fishbane, editor of this series of commentaries, and Ellen Frankel, Editor-in-Chief and CEO of the Jewish Publication Society, for their invitation to participate in this project and for their guidance at many steps along the way.

I am grateful to Carol Hupping, Christine Sweeney, and Sarah Kornhauser for their skillful editorial assistance. My colleagues at Maryland continue, as they have for many years, to be supportive in innumerable ways. As in all things, my greatest thanks go to my husband, who is my first reader. His knowledge is broad, his critique gentle, and his encouragement unflagging.

A Note on Bibliography, Translation, and Transliteration

A bibliography of the works I consulted most often is provided and therefore in the notes I refer to these works by the author's name, or by the author's name and short title. When an author is cited without a page number, the reference is to that author's commentary on the verse under discussion.

Quotations from Herodotus are from R. Waterfield's translation of *The Histories*. Translations of other Greek sources are adapted from the Loeb Classical Library. Biblical translations are generally from The TANAKH (Jewish Publication Society) or are my own. The translations of the Septuagint Esther and apocryphal books are from the New Revised Standard Version, and that of the Alpha-text is from David Clines, *The Esther Scroll*.

Transliteration of the Hebrew Consonants

ʾ	alef
ʿ	ayin
b	bet
g	gimel
d	dalet
h	heh
v	vet, vav
z	zayin
ḥ	het
t	tet, tav
y	yod
k	kaf
kh	khaf
l	lamed
m	mem
n	nun
s	samekh, sin
p	peh
f	feh
tz	tzadi
k	kof
r	resh
sh	shin

Pronunciation Guide for Vowels

a	as in *farm*
ai	as in *eye*
e	as in *dent*
ei	as in *hay*
i	as in *hit* or *heat*
o	as in *hope*
u	as in *food*

ABBREVIATIONS

AB	Anchor Bible
ABD	*Anchor Bible Dictionary*
ANET	Pritchard, *Ancient Near Eastern Texts*
B.	Babylonian Talmud
BA	*Biblical Archaeologist*
BASOR	*Bulletin of the American Schools of Oriental Research*
Buber	*Sifrei De-'agadta'*
Bush	*Ruth, Esther*
CAH	*Cambridge Ancient History*
CBQ	*Catholic Biblical Quarterly*
CHI	*Cambridge History of Iran*
CHJ	*Cambridge History of Judaism*
Chron.	Chronicles
Clines	Clines, *The Esther Scroll*
Dan.	Daniel
Deut.	Deuteronomy
DSD	*Dead Sea Discoveries*
Eccles.	Ecclesiastes
EJ	*Encyclopaedia Judaica*
Esd.	Esdras
Exod.	Exodus
Fox	Fox, *Character and Ideology in the Book of Esther*
Gen.	Genesis
Hakham	*'Ester in Hamesh Megillot*
HAR	*Hebrew Annual Review*
HUCA	*Hebrew Union College Annual*
ICC	International Critical Commentary
JAOS	*Journal of the American Oriental Society*
JBL	*Journal of Biblical Literature*
JNES	*Journal of Near Eastern Studies*
Jon.	Jonah
Josephus	*Antiquities of the Jews*, Book 11
Josh.	Joshua
JQR	*Jewish Quarterly Review*
JSOT	*Journal for the Study of the Old Testament*

Jth.	Judith
JTS	*Journal of Theological Studies*
Judg.	Judges
KAT	Kommentar zum Alten Testament
Lam.	Lamentations
Levenson	Levenson, *Esther*
M.	Mishnah
Macc.	Maccabees
Mal.	Malachi
Mic.	Micah
Moore	Moore, *Esther*
Neh.	Nehemiah
Num.	Numbers
OP	Old Persian
Prov.	Proverbs
Ps.	Psalms
Sam.	Samuel
TDOT	*Theological Dictionary of the Old Testament*
Tob.	Tobit
VT	*Vetus Testamentum*
ZAW	*Zeitschrift für die alttestamentliche Wissenschaft*
Zech.	Zechariah

INTRODUCTION TO THE COMMENTARY: THE BOOK OF ESTHER AND ITS LITERARY WORLD

Why Was the Book of Esther Written?

Megillat Esther, the Book of Esther in the form that we have it in the Hebrew Bible, provides the story of the origin of Purim, the blueprint for its celebration, and the authorization for its observance in perpetuity.

The story itself is implausible as history and, as many scholars now agree, it is better viewed as imaginative storytelling, not unlike others that circulated in the Persian and Hellenistic periods among Jews of the Land of Israel and of the Diaspora. This story seems to have been known in several different versions, or to have gone through a number of different stages in its development before it was linked with Purim and incorporated into the Bible. As a Diaspora story—a story about, and presumably for, Jews in the Diaspora during the Persian period—it provides an optimistic picture of Jewish survival and success in a foreign land. In this it resembles other Diaspora stories such as the biblical Book of Daniel (chapters 1–6) and the apocryphal books of Judith and Tobit. But unlike those books, Esther lacks overtly pious characters and does not model a religious lifestyle. Esther is the most "secular" of the biblical books, making no reference to God's name, to the Temple, to prayer, or to distinctive Jewish practices such as *kashrut.* Yet Esther, of all the biblical books outside of the Torah, is the only one that addresses the origin of a new festival. For this reason, if for no other, Esther should be considered a "religious" book. Its main concern, the very reason for its existence, is to establish Purim as a Jewish holiday for all generations.

Megillat Esther establishes the Jewishness of the holiday by providing a "historical" event of Jewish deliverance to be commemorated and an authorization, through the letter of Mordecai, for the continued commemoration of the event. Just as the more ancient festivals are historicized and their observance is mandated by the Torah, so Purim is historicized and its observance is mandated by the *Megillah.* The Book of Esther serves as the authorizing document for Purim, a holiday that is not mentioned in the Torah. But the *Megillah*'s mandate differs from the Torah's in one crucial respect: it is careful not to say that God commanded the observance of Purim. In fact, God is nowhere mentioned in the book and his absence emphasizes the distinction

between the Torah and its festivals on the one hand and the *Megillah* and its festival on the other. The *Megillah* makes no suggestion that Purim is an ancient festival that had been forgotten or neglected. Purim is clearly a new festival, of recent origin.

The *Megillah* gives legitimacy to this first post-Torah festival in a mode that is quasi-traditional but at the same time quite contemporary. Following tradition, the book's explanation of Purim as a "historical" event to be commemorated harks back to the Torah's etiologies (stories of origin) for the well-established holidays. But, calling on contemporary practice, the form in which the holiday was instituted imitates the legal practice of Persia. Purim was legislated in much the same way that all Persian law was legislated—by means of a document written by the king or his authorized agent and circulated throughout the empire. This rhetorical strategy of calling upon both traditional and current forms must have made the etiology of Purim more compelling to ancient readers. In fact, the Book of Esther, more than anything else, is responsible for the continued celebration of Purim. It also opened the way for the establishment of later holidays that, like Purim, could be instituted without divine command if they commemorated an important event or served an important function in the life of the Jewish people.

Another successful rhetorical strategy is the combination of a serious theme and a comic style. The threat of the destruction of the Jews is no laughing matter, but the Book of Esther is hilariously funny. The raucous Persian court, with its lavish display of luxury and its pervasive drinking parties, is not the setting we expect for the impending annihilation of the Jewish people. The plot glories in revelry and bawdiness (and this may be the primary reason for the absence of God's name). The frivolity of the book's style—with its hyperbole, mockery, and comic misunderstandings and reversals—undercuts the gravity of its theme. Yet, for the Purim festival this setting, plot, and style are natural and fitting, part and parcel of the celebration of Purim. The tone of the book fits its purpose: a comic story for a carnivalesque holiday. I find in this comic style additional evidence that the purpose of the *Megillah* was to model and to authenticate the celebration of Purim. In the Greek versions of Esther, which de-emphasize Purim, the comic elements are diminished. The Hebrew Esther and the festival of Purim bring us a uniquely irreverent and joyously optimistic celebration of Jewish identity and Jewish continuity.

Esther as Comedy

One of the most frequently asked questions about the Book of Esther is: Are the events recounted in it true? In other words, is the book historically accurate? Arguing against the book's historicity is the fact that many things in the story conflict with our knowledge about Persian history or are too fantastic to be believable. The following points are among the most obvious.

We know of no Persian queen named Esther, or any Jewish queen of Persia, and we would not expect there to have been one. Queens came from the noble Persian families, not from ethnic minorities. Moreover, real kings don't choose queens from beauty contests. In fact, Esther enters the story more like a concubine, and only later emerges as a dignified queen. In contrast, Vashti, who was presumably a queen of proper ancestry and clearly in a high position at court, is treated like a concubine by Ahasuerus.

While Ahasuerus has been equated with Xerxes, no Persian king acted or would act the way Ahasuerus did. He is a king who cannot make the smallest decision without legal consultation, and leaves the big decisions to others altogether. Any resemblance to a real Persian king is purely coincidental.

To govern a country in which a law could never be changed would make governing impossible.[1]

A decree to annihilate the Jews is least at home in ancient Persia, an empire that is thought to have been relatively benevolent to the various ethnic groups within it, and is portrayed positively elsewhere in the Bible. This is the empire that permitted the Jews to return to Judah and rebuild the Temple, of which there is not a word in Esther.

The plot hangs on at least one particular hook that goes against all logic but which is crucial to the story: that Esther could keep her Jewish identity hidden while all the world knew that she was related to Mordecai and all the world knew that Mordecai was a Jew.

In contrast, those who defend the book's historicity point to the authentic information about the Persian court and its many customs and institutions, and the use of a number of Persian terms. But it is not simply a matter of weighing one side's proofs against the other side's, for, when we look carefully at the points for and against historicity, it turns out that the historically authentic material is in the background and setting, while the main characters and the important elements in the plot are much farther removed from reality. If this were a modern work, we would call it a historical novel, or historical fiction. While those terms may not be appropriate for the Bible, we can certainly recognize Esther as a form of imaginative storytelling, not unlike Jonah and Daniel, or Judith and Tobit in the Apocrypha. In fact, such storytelling was common in the Persian and Hellenistic periods, and even Greek historians such as Herodotus, whose writings are given more credibility as history, include imaginative tales in their works. The distinction between history and story, which is such an important issue for us, would not have engaged readers in the Persian period in the same way it does us. To the ancient reader an imaginative story was just as worthy, or even as holy, as a historically accurate one, so to declare Esther to be imaginative does not in any way detract from its value. The message of the Book of Esther and the significance of Purim remain the same whether or not the events of the book were actual.

Granting that Esther is an imaginative story, the next question is: What kind of story is it? What best describes the nature of the story and the way it was meant to be read? As shall soon become clearer, it is a comedy, a book meant to be funny, to provoke laughter. The Book of Esther is the most humorous of the books in the Bible, amusing throughout and at certain points uproariously funny.

The idea that Esther partakes of the comic spirit is not new. H. L. Ginsberg wrote in his introduction to Esther that "the Book of Esther may be described, if one stretches

a point or two, as a mock-learned disquisition to be read as the opening of a carnival-like celebration."[2] A longer explication of some of the humorous scenes was articulated well by Bruce W. Jones.[3] Yehuda Radday devoted a chapter to the humor in Esther;[4] Kenneth Craig authored a monograph on Esther as carnivalesque literature; and many others, among them Robert Alter, Jon D. Levenson, and Jack M. Sasson, have also recognized the pervasive humor, even bawdiness, of the book.

Despite the recognition of Esther's comic nature by many scholars, some readers may be surprised or even shocked by this idea. That is because the inclusion of a book in the biblical canon affects the way we perceive the book, or certainly the way it was perceived in premodern times and may still be perceived in traditional circles. The very fact that Esther is part of the Bible—a holy book with religious authority and religious teachings—forces us to make it fit the expectations we have about what the Bible is and what kinds of writing it contains. We expect a biblical book to be serious and its message to be congruent with the messages of other biblical books as they have been interpreted by the tradition. Moshe Halbertal has made this point most recently, with specific reference to Song of Songs and Esther. As he observes, the canonical status of Song of Songs deters us from reading it as an erotic love poem and compels the reading of it as a metaphor for the relationship between God and Israel. The same is true for Esther, which, Halbertal notes, "is not the canonization of a comedy about courtly life in a kingdom of Persia"—by which he means that Esther is in fact a comedy but that as part of the canon it was not seen as such in Jewish tradition. Halbertal concludes, "Paradoxically, then, the canonization of a work sometimes serves to suppress its most plausible readings."[5]

To restore its most plausible readings, to understand how the book was meant to be read, we must approach Esther as the comedy that it is. I want to press the point through a discussion of comedy because even commentators who recognize the comic nature of Esther do not take it into account sufficiently when they interpret the book. The comic aspects of the book are not incidental, merely to provide comic relief; they are the essence of the book. They define the genre of the book, and thus set the parameters according to which we should read it. We cannot appreciate the story fully unless we realize that it is meant to be funny. To be sure, it is not always easy to agree on what is funny, especially in an ancient or foreign work. Nonetheless, humor of various types is well-documented in ancient Near Eastern literature, including the Bible.[6] Most readers recognize the humor in Esther 6, when Haman realizes that he must honor the very person whom he wishes to disgrace, and in Esther 7, when the king reacts to seeing Haman fallen on Esther's couch. These scenes are not isolated touches of humor, but are among the most obvious in a book where comedy is the dominant tone.

Since we have no theoretical writings from ancient Israel about comedy, or about any type of literature, we must call upon later literary theory and apply it to the Bible as best we can. (Already I have taken the liberty of applying *comedy* to narrative, whereas in its narrowest definition it is limited to drama. This and related terms can be used for all forms of literature.) Several modern terms associated with the comic may be usefully

applied to Esther. They are not meant to serve as absolute definitions of Esther's genre or subgenre, and since their definitions grew out of very different literatures (ancient Greek and medieval and modern European and American literatures), we cannot expect a perfect fit with Esther. Nevertheless these terms and their definitions help to describe some of the parameters of comic literature and to suggest ways to understand the comic nature of the book. Comedy is the most general of the terms, and *farce* is even better, for it may be considered "the purest quintessential comedy.[7] Farce is

> a type of comedy designed to provoke the audience to simple, hearty laughter.... To do so it employs highly exaggerated or caricatured character types, puts them into impossible and ludicrous situations, and makes free use of broad verbal humor and physical horseplay.[8]

We will return to farce, for it best describes Esther, but first another term, *burlesque,* should be introduced. Burlesque is defined as "an artistic composition... that, for the sake of laughter, vulgarizes lofty material or treats ordinary material with mock dignity."[9]

The lofty material that Esther vulgarizes is the Persian empire and the Persian court. The normally sedate affairs of state, the carefully organized and controlled government structure, the legal system, the efficient postal system, the impressive accumulation of wealth indicative of a successful empire—all of the achievements most praiseworthy in the Persian empire are turned into a burlesque of Persian court life, caricatured by ludicrous edicts delivered by speeding messengers, a foppish royal court with an endless hierarchy of officials, and a wooden adherence to nonsensical laws. A major policy decision, the annihilation of the Jews, is made casually; but a small domestic incident, Vashti's nonappearance at a party, becomes a crisis of state, with all the bureaucratic trappings that can be mustered.

The term *satire* has also been applied to Esther, most recently by Ze'ev Weisman.[10] The line between farce and satire is hard to draw, and there are certainly elements of satire in the book, especially those directed at Persian court life. However, these elements are incidental. The book is not primarily aimed at criticizing the Persian empire or its lifestyle. After all, Ahasuerus emerges stronger at the end of the story than he was at the beginning, and Mordecai and Esther benefit handsomely from all that the Persian court has to offer and become two of its most elite members. It is better to understand the description of the Persian court as burlesque rather than as satire; its purpose is comedy, not critique.[11] The burlesque of the Persian court provides the setting for the farce. Burlesque also has the connotation of bawdiness, and as we shall see, the Book of Esther does not lack bawdiness, especially in chapter 1, the chapter in which court life is most on display.

The style associated with burlesque, farce, and other types of low comedy uses exaggeration, caricature, ludicrous situations, practical jokes, coincidences, improbabilities, and verbal humor. Farce often employs repetition—of scenes, events, and phrases—and inversions or reversals. Most of these features are prominent in Esther

and have been identified in the commentaries, but without the realization that they are characteristic of comedy or farce.

Another characteristic of farce is a misunderstanding in which two characters interpret the same event in different ways.[12] Classic examples of this type of misunderstanding occur in chapter 6, when Haman mistakenly assumes that the king is planning to honor him, not Mordecai, and in chapter 7, when Ahasuerus misunderstands or pretends to misunderstand why Haman has fallen on Esther's couch (see the Commentary to 7:8). The effect in both cases is extremely comic.

In farce, according to J. M. Davis,

> Type-characters are . . . quite unconscious of their limitations. They act and react blindly, driven by their rigidity. Although a type is certainly capable of congratulating himself on his cleverness or his good-fortune, he will lack self-consciousness. More often than not, the audience's position of privilege permits it to foretell a downfall that is concealed from the character himself.[13]

There is no better description of Haman, puffed up as he is with self-importance. He is absolutely certain that no one deserves as much honor as he does; and he is so lacking in awareness of his potential downfall that the author has supplied his advisors and his wife, Zeresh, to warn him that it will be caused by Mordecai.

In farce there is little concern with the subtlety of characterization. Farce tends to use exaggerated or caricatured character types. In Esther, all the characters are types: Ahasuerus is a caricature of a pampered and bumbling monarch, a ruler ruled by his advisors; Esther is a paragon of feminine heroism; Mordecai is the model of a wise courtier; Haman is the archetypal comic villain—a knave, but, in keeping with farce, not darkly evil. We are not meant to feel threatened by the comic villain—not even children are afraid of Haman—nor are we meant to sympathize with him when he meets his deserved end. He is doomed from the start and we enjoy watching his downfall.

While some of these characters show growth as the story progresses, and their various traits can be probed and described in a manner that makes them seem almost full-fledged characters (Fox has done this very successfully), they nevertheless remain types rather than full-fledged characters. This is not a defect in the narrative technique. The characterization in the book is intentional, cleverly done, and adds to the farcical humor. In fact, there is a striking resemblance to the stock characters in Greek comedy: the *alazon,* an imposter or self-deceiving braggart (Haman); the *eiron,* the self-deprecatory and understating character whose contest with the *alazon* is central to the comic plot (Mordecai); and the *bomolochos,* the buffoon whose antics add an extra comic element (Ahasuerus).

Understanding the Book of Esther as a comedy allows us to recognize that the threat to the Jews is not real. Comedies usually begin, notes M. Charney, with a startling pronouncement or an outrageous situation. Charney's description of the structure of comedy is so apt for Esther that it is worth quoting at length.

Curiously enough, comedies often begin with some climactic event, which may be more dire—or at least more convincing—than the actual climax of the work, especially since comic climaxes tend to be extremely melodramatic and implausible. We have some outrageous, arbitrary edict: all Syracusans discovered in Ephesus will be immediately put to death (as in Shakespeare's *The Comedy of Errors*). The reasons for the cruel law are left vague and unexplained, but, as good comic auditors, we accept what we are told without passing judgment. Comedy literally demands the willing suspension of disbelief....[14]

Although there may be more explanation for the edict against the Jews than for the edict against the Syracusans, Haman's edict is still preposterous, and goes against all that we know of the tolerance of the Persian empire. Nevertheless, we accept it as the motivation for the plot that follows, for "we must experience that feeling of dire climax and catastrophe with which many comedies begin."[15] As Charney says, the plot that follows is barely convincing, and the denouement—the scene in which Esther reveals Haman's wickedness to the king—is dripping with melodrama. ("Let my life be granted me as my wish.... Had we only been sold as bondmen..." [7:3–4].)

The plot is often unconvincing because one of the characteristics of farce is the rejection of rationality. "Farce enshrines the element of unreason."[16] So the logical impossibility that looms largest—that Mordecai's Jewish identity is publicly known while Esther's remains secret—suddenly ceases to be problematic and becomes one more piece in the highly improbable plot. In fact, the entire plot turns on a succession of unlikely events, like the selection of a queen in a beauty contest and a series of ridiculous but irrevocable edicts.

It is generally accepted that there is a strong link between comedy and carnival, going back to the origin of dramatic comedy, ancient Greece. Comic performances have been associated with popular carnival-like celebrations in medieval and Renaissance Europe.[17] In fact, the Greek word *komos,* whence "comedy" comes, signifies a riotous celebration. It is impossible to make a direct connection in the ancient Near East between performance and festival, for we cannot document any type of theatrical performance of the type known from Greece. There may, however, be a suggestive parallel. At a recent conference, the prominent Hittitologist Harry Hoffner described an unpublished Hittite ritual text in which, as part of the entertainment of the gods, the cook pours live coals on the head of the chief of the performers and then the chief of the performers strikes the cook on the head three times.[18] This sounds like a violent type of clowning, although we must await the further study of this text.

Certainly the celebration of Purim is carnival-like, with its drinking, costumes, Purim plays, and Purim carnivals. The *Megillah* itself sets the parameters for the celebration, and its later manifestations are completely congruent with the tone and genre of the book as well as with carnival celebrations known from many cultures. Carnival celebrations, best known from the Greek Dionysia, the Roman Saturnalia, and the English May Day (and in modern times Mardi Gras, Halloween, and New Year's Day), often contain elements such as eating, drinking, carousing, masks and disguises, parades and processions, and combat and mock battles. There is an air of wildness, boisterousness, and violence that is made acceptable, perhaps only barely

acceptable, because it is done within the bounds of a socially sanctioned festive occasion. Carnival permits the release of one's urge for violence and revenge in a way that channels the violence so that it is not actually destructive.

It is not a huge leap to see the Book of Esther as a festive comedy—that is, a comedy relating to the celebration of the carnival-like holiday of Purim, for the link with Purim is inherent in the book. I do not mean to suggest that the book was a script for a performance. Clearly, it is a narrative. It may be no accident, however, that the story has been acted out in generations of Purim plays. There is something about the book that lends itself to comic dramatization. (Perhaps it is the large amount of "stage direction" in terms of the positioning of characters. See below, "Narrative Artistry.") Esther may not be a play but it is surely carnivalesque literature. Its secret identities, gross indulgences, sexual innuendoes, and nefarious plot against the Jews are part and parcel of the carnivalesque world of madness, hilarity, violence, and mock destruction. Indeed, violence is very much a part of this world, and it is in this framework that we should understand the slaughter of the enemies of the Jews in chapter 9 (see the Commentary to chapter 9). The killing is no more real than anything else in the plot, and is completely in character with the story's carnivalesque nature.

The function of Greek comedy is nicely summed up by B. M. Knox, and is easily applied to our discussion.

> Comedy was the licensed clown of Athenian democracy; in its proper place and time its civic and religious duty was to release its audience from restraints and inhibitions . . . . For an hour or two at the end of the day comedy had license to turn the world upside-down. Its plots defy reality: . . . [they] are all events so utterly impossible that their presentation on stage constitutes no threat whatsoever to established institutions . . . . The proper function of comedy was not to advise but to be outrageous. It is the safety-valve of the emotional pressures generated by life in the polis and, like the reign of the Lord of Misrule in medieval England or the freedom granted to slaves at the Roman Saturnalia, it offers a utopian vision of revolution which serves to reinforce the solidity of the existing order.[19]

It is in this light that we should understand Esther. The largest interpretive problems melt away if the story is taken as a farce or a comedy associated with a carnival-like festival. The book sets out a threat to the Jews so that the Jewish audience can watch with glee and laugh with relief as it is overcome. The mad and threatening world of the beginning of the story fades into a happy ending where, for a brief moment, the Jews, through their two representatives, can play at wielding the highest power in the great empire to which they were in reality subservient and in which they were an insignificant minority. The story, like its accompanying festival, does what comedy and carnival are supposed to do: it confirms the belief that the power at work in the universe favors life and favors the success of the Jews. The Book of Esther affirms that all is right with the world and with the place of the Jews in it.

Narrative Artistry: Structure, Style, and Language

We find in the Talmud, B. Megillah 19a, the following discussion:

> From what point must a person read in the scroll in order to fulfill his obligation? Rabbi Meir says, "All of it." Rabbi Judah says, "From 'A Jewish man' (2:5)." Rabbi Yose says, "From 'After these things' (3:1)."

The Rabbis are posing a halakhic question pertaining to the sections of the scroll that must be recited on Purim (the halakhah is according to R. Meir). They are seeking to define the minimum required reading—presumably the minimum that constitutes the Purim story—and they do this through a midrashic interpretation of Esther 9:29, a verse used to infer the origin of the Scroll of Esther: "Queen Esther, daughter of Avihail, and Mordecai the Jew, wrote with full authority. . . ." The term "authority" (*tokef*) is interpreted by Rabbi Meir as referring to the authority of Ahasuerus (and hence the reading should begin when Ahasuerus is mentioned), by Rabbi Judah as referring to Mordecai's authority (and so one commences from the mention of Mordecai), and by Rabbi Yose as referring to Haman's authority (and so Rabbi Yose would begin when Haman enters the story). The Gemara even cites a fourth opinion that one may begin the reading of the *Megillah* from "On that night" (6:1).

Now the rabbis were not given to literary analysis, but in their desire to clarify what constitutes the essence of the *Megillah* they have hit upon three critical junctures in the story that in some sense may constitute its beginning: the prologue introducing Ahasuerus, around whom all the action will swirl; the introduction of the hero, Mordecai; and the introduction of the villain, Haman. It is clear to us, as it must have been to the Rabbis, that while the main plot does not begin until chapter 3, the events of chapters 1 and 2 are essential to the story, since they lay the groundwork for the main plot by setting the scene, paving the way for a new queen, introducing Esther into the palace, and presenting Mordecai as a loyal servant to the king.

If the first two chapters serve as prologues to the main action, parts of chapter 9 and chapter 10 serve as epilogues. Chapter 9 gives us the events of 14 and 15 Adar—the origin of Purim—and the explanation of how it was instituted as a permanent holiday. This takes us out of the story itself and into Jewish practice. It is the reason that the story was told; it gives the story significance. Chapter 10 returns us to the story, but after the main events have concluded. It tells us that the characters (or at least two of them) lived happily ever after and provides closure for the story.

Who is the hero of the story? It is difficult to choose just one hero because Esther and Mordecai share this role. The two work as a team, one initially from inside the palace and the other from outside, and then at the end, when both are at the heart of the government, they wield their authority in concert. To the extent that the plot revolves around the rivalry and enmity between Haman and Mordecai, Mordecai is the hero. However, it is in fact Esther who plans and carries out the actions that save the Jews, making her the true hero. Mordecai at first gives her advice, but Esther is not passive. In fact, it is she who designs the details of the strategy (see the Commentary

to 4:11). Mordecai tells her what to do but not how to do it. Going to the king unsummoned is really her idea, as is inviting the king and Haman to two parties. The denouncing of Haman is solely in Esther's hands and she performs brilliantly. She is rewarded with Haman's estate, which she shares with Mordecai. They both (with some confusion in the matter) authorize the institution of Purim. Mordecai alone is featured in chapter 10 as the protector of the Jewish community. Yet the book is known as the Scroll of Esther.

The story is structured on repetitions and reversals, climaxes and anticlimaxes. The audience's expectation is continually heightened only to be frustrated by yet another complication or delay, with the effect of increasing the tension and the humor. After Mordecai saves the king's life, we expect him to be rewarded, but it is Haman who is elevated to a high position. Mordecai's reward is delayed—saved for the delicious scene in which Haman's expectation is thwarted and he, in a wonderful reversal, must give to Mordecai the honor that he dreamed up for himself.

Similarly, Haman erects a stake upon which to impale Mordecai, but he must obtain the king's permission to use it. In seeking permission to have Mordecai impaled (a sign of maximum dishonor), he ends up honoring Mordecai with the highest honor. Later in the story, when Haman is impaled on the very stake he intended for Mordecai, the reversal is complete.

Another series of repetitions and delays turns on Ahasuerus's offer to Esther to make a request: "What is your wish and it will be done; what is your request, even to half the kingdom?" This is first said when Esther, risking her life, enters the king's presence unsummoned. There must have been an important reason for taking such a risk, as Ahasuerus perceives, but Esther deflects the question by inviting the king and Haman to a party. The sequence is replayed at the party, where again she delays her real purpose and invites them to another party. At the second party the question is posed yet again, and this time answered in a way that shocks both of the queen's guests. Furthermore, there is a fourth repetition of the question, in 9:12, after the first victory of the Jews in Shushan. Esther requests a replay of the victory, which she is granted. By this point, the question begins to sound like the king's automatic response whenever Esther comes before him. The fourth repetition is anticlimactic in the plot, but necessary for the etiology of Shushan Purim. It also adds to the humorous characterization of Ahasuerus, and to the notion that the battles between the Jews and their enemies are part of the carnival atmosphere. The quadruple use of the king's question emphasizes the feature of repetition through the doubling of scenes, and it underlines the main reversal of the story: the decree to annihilate the Jews is reversed to permit them to annihilate their enemies.

It cannot escape the reader that there are a lot of parties in the story—ten altogether. The parties, first of all, provide the setting and the tone of the book, which is one of feasting and revelry. This tone serves two purposes: to give a sense of Persian court life as it was often portrayed in the literature of the time when the story was written, and to mirror the tone of Purim, the holiday that grows out of the events of the story.

The parties also help to structure the scenes of the book. The book opens and closes with a series of banquets. At the beginning, Ahasuerus gives a banquet for the nobility from throughout the empire and then for the residents of Susa. This has its counterpart in the feasting of Purim at the end of the book, which is celebrated by the Jews throughout the empire on 14 Adar and by the Jews of Shushan on 15 Adar.[20] In 1:9, Vashti gives a banquet for the women; in 2:18, Ahasuerus gives a banquet for Esther. Ahasuerus and Haman party to mark the occasion of Haman's decree (3:15) while the Jews party when Mordecai's counter-decree is published (8:17). At the center of the plot are Esther's two banquets, the second being the climax of the story. Between these two banquets comes another climactic point—the reversal in which Haman must honor Mordecai.

More than just a structuring device, the banquet is the setting at which all the major events occur: Vashti loses her queenship at a banquet, Esther is made queen at a banquet, and, most important of all, Esther saves her people at a banquet. That most emblematic Persian institution, the banquet, or Table of the King (see the Commentary to chapter 1), is the occasion on which Jewish well-being is secured. How appropriate that the holiday commemorating Jewish deliverance in Persia features feasting and merrymaking, as if it were a re-enactment of the many banquets of the Esther story.

In literary terminology, the story of Esther is conveyed by "telling" rather than by "showing." In "showing," the characters talk and act, and the reader, seeing the characters in action, infers their motives and dispositions. In "telling," the author or narrator (in the Bible it is impossible to distinguish the two) describes and evaluates the qualities of the characters. This helps to keep the characters flat (as befits the comic genre). We hear only the narrator for most of the story; we do not hear the characters themselves. This does not mean that we get no picture of their inner lives; on the contrary, the narrator tells us, for instance, that the king was angry, that the king loved Esther, that Haman was filled with rage at Mordecai. But this is from the mouth of the narrator; we do not see Ahasuerus stomping or hear Haman cursing. In Esther's "telling" mode, the presence of the narrator looms large, so we have the sense that a story is being told. This, then, puts a psychological distance between the reader and the events of the story. The psychological distance adds to the sense that there is a lapse of time between the events and their narration.

The "telling" mode is congruent with the relatively lower incidence of dialogue and direct discourse that we find in Esther. The sparseness of dialogue means that we are more likely to have indirect speech, speech reported by the narrator, which we have on numerous occasions. For example, we do not have Mordecai's words to Esther telling her not to reveal her Jewishness; we have only the report that he told her this (2:10, 20). Other examples of indirect speech are found in 3:2 (Ahasuerus commanded everyone to bow to Haman), 3:4 (Mordecai had told the servants that he was a Jew), and 3:6 (they told Haman who Mordecai's people were). These cases of indirect discourse are used to supply information that the author chose not to present by "showing" because it would divert the reader from the focal point of the current scene. There is not, however, a

total absence of direct discourse in Esther. When dialogues occur they serve, as they do elsewhere in the Bible, to highlight the important scenes: the decree against Vashti in chapter 1; Haman convincing the king to authorize the decree against the Jews in chapter 3; Esther and Mordecai planning in chapter 4. And certainly dialogue is used with excellent effect in the climactic episodes in chapters 6 and 7. For the most part, though, the ratio of narration to direct discourse is higher in Esther than in other biblical narratives.[21]

Related to the paucity of direct speech is the absence or minimization of the wording of edicts and letters. Only the gist of the edict regarding Vashti is given; Haman's decree against the Jews, the centerpiece of the plot, is never quoted directly, although its content is summarized and much is made of its official writing and publication throughout the empire; and the wording of the Purim letters of Mordecai and Esther is not recorded. In contrast, Ezra and Nehemiah quote documents at length. Daniel 3:4–6 and 6:26–28 contain short decrees while 6:7–10 resembles Esther in that we have the advisors' "draft" of the edict, the writing of the edict, but not the actual edict in the words of the king. The Greek Additions to Esther supply the contents of Haman's decree in the form of a letter from Artaxerxes and the contents of the counter-decree in another letter.

Another feature that tends toward the psychological distancing of the reader is the extensive use of the passive voice and passive constructions. Examples are "let it be written" (1:19); "Esther was taken" (2:8, 20); "the matter was investigated and found to be true" (2:22); "it shall be granted to you" (5:3 and passim); "we have been sold" (7:4); "to be avenged from their enemies" (8:13); "to be executed" (9:1); "these days are recalled and observed" (9:28). The effect of so many passive constructions is to create the impression that things happen on their own, without human or divine agency: Persian bureaucracy grinds on, the king takes little responsibility for his actions, and God is not present on the surface of the text.[22]

The story has a well-developed sense of place and setting. It is not just a matter of describing the lavish Persian decor, which is so essential to the plot, but of conveying information at every turn about the physical location of the characters. We know where Vashti was when she refused to appear before the king, we hear about the movement of the women in the harem, we are very conscious in chapter 4 that Esther is inside the palace and Mordecai is outside, we see Esther as she enters the inner court in 5:1 and Haman in the outer court in 6:4. In chapter 6, Haman moves from his home to the palace to the public square then back to his home and is then whisked away to the party. In chapter 7, the king exits and re-enters, and Haman stands and falls. The staging in this chapter is crucial for the comic effect. All this attention to the physical positioning of the characters makes the book seem like a play.

The physical movement of the characters keeps the story moving, quickening its tempo. This fast tempo is characteristic of farce, and it has the effect of making the actions seem abstract and automatic, and consequently less real.[23] The quick pace and lack of reality are most evident in the hurried movement from one scene to another and

in the speed with which important decisions are made. Vashti is instantly deposed; the decree against the Jews is made with no thought on the part of the king; Haman is whisked off to Esther's party and later is summarily impaled. While the rapid decision making may be poking fun at the pseudo-efficiency of the Persian court and legal system, when observed along with the abrupt physical movement, its literary effect is to speed up the pace of the story, and transport the reader into an arbitrary and unreal world.

When it comes to the language of Esther, the medium is the message. The language, like the story, is full of exaggeration and contributes to the sense of excess. There are exaggerated numbers (127 provinces, a 180-day party, a 12-month beauty preparation, Haman's offer of 10,000 talents of silver, a stake 50 cubits high, 75,000 enemy dead) and long lists of unpronounceable names (the eunuchs, the advisors, the sons of Haman). The language is flowery ("What is your wish? It shall be granted to you. And what is your request? Even up to half the kingdom, it shall be fulfilled"). Also, the syntax is bulky, with many relative clauses intervening ("If of Jewish stock is Mordecai, before whom you have begun to fall, you will not overcome him; you will surely fall before him"). The rule for vocabulary, as for drinking, seems to be "the more the better." There are lots of "alls" ("all the people who lived in the fortress Shushan," "every palace steward," "all the provinces," "all the women," "all the Jews," "all the king's servants") and the story never uses one word if it can use two. Dyadic expressions may consist of the same word used twice ('ish va-'ish, "every man"; *medinah u-medinah*, "every province"; 'am va-'am, "every people") or of synonyms joined together ("officials and courtiers," "the vast riches of his kingdom and the splendid glory of his majesty," "relief and deliverance," "light and gladness, happiness and honor"). One example of how this type of repetition may pile up is 8:17, whose literal translation is: "In every province and province and in every city and city wherever the king's command and decree arrived, there was gladness and joy among the Jews, a feast and a holiday." This type of repetition, combined with the appearance of the same phrase at various points in the story ("what is your wish . . . what is your request," "the king's scribes were summoned") makes for a highly repetitive style, which goes well with the repetition of scenes and events (parties, writing and sending of edicts) that figure so prominently in the story.

Certain words recur often, like keywords, sounding out the themes of the story: *party, law, honor, royal*. There is also a sprinkling of Persian words (*partemim*, "nobles"; *'ahashdarpanim*, "satraps"; *dat*, "law"; *pitgam*, "edict"), which lend authenticity, but are also for showing off, adding to the snobbery of the court.

Jack Sasson has noted that the narrator of Esther adopts the style of an archivist, recording the dates of various incidents, providing genealogies for the main characters, flaunting his knowledge of the workings of the Persian empire, imitating Persian nomenclature, and making a reference to the Chronicles of the Kings of Media and Persia.[24] There is merit to this observation, for the book is in some ways fashioned on the pattern of the Book of Kings, which can also be seen as an archivist style. But, while

the Book of Kings may have served as a model, Esther's attempt to sound like a historical work is tongue in cheek and not to be taken at face value. The author was not trying to write history, or to convince his audience of the historicity of his story (although later readers certainly took it this way). He is, rather, offering a burlesque of historiography. He is imitating the writing of history, as he knew it from the earlier books of the Bible and perhaps also from the Greek historiographers (whose motifs about Persia he shares). The archival style, like the verbal style, makes the story sound big and fancy, official and impertinent at the same time—and this is exactly the effect that is required for such a book. All these stylistic features reinforce the sense that the story is a farce. They lend an air of comic burlesque to the description of the Persian court and to all that happens in it.

Greek Storytelling about Persia

No book is an island. All literary works reside in a universe populated by other literary works, and it is in the context of these other works that authors write and readers read. Part of the modern reader's difficulty in reading an ancient work is that the ancient literary context is not fully known. What were the narrative conventions? What were the then-current "bestsellers"? Which works were revered as authoritative? In other words, what literary conventions and literary works might have shaped the Book of Esther? A surprisingly large number of themes, motifs, and other narrative features that are found in Esther are also found in other biblical and apocryphal books—before, during, and after the time that Esther was written—and also in Greek writings from the Persian period. These writings form the literary context in which Esther is best understood as a literary work. The Greek writings are an especially interesting case.

Many scholars have remarked on the accuracy of the Persian background in Esther, and have looked to Greek historiographical writings to prove it, for these are among the most voluminous sources for the Persian period. In fact, their works are so voluminous that for lack of anything of comparable mass, and because they were taken as objective fact, they have long been regarded as the standard against which the accuracy of Esther is to be measured. And so, when Esther agrees with Herodotus or Xenophon, Esther was deemed to have accurate information about Persian life. In many cases Esther *does* agree with the Greek authors, but there is something more interesting than historical accuracy at work here. That "something" is literary rather than historical. Esther should be seen as part of the same literary context from which the Greek writings emerged. Esther and the Greek works share a set of literary motifs and stereotypes relating to Persian court life.

The seeds of the literary comparison between Esther and the Greek works were planted by the famous historian Arnaldo Momigliano who observed in 1965 that:

No doubt many features of the Books of Judith and Esther can be explained in terms of international storytelling with a Persian background; and the same is true of several stories in the first Books of Herodotus, in Ctesias and, up to a certain point, in the *Cyropaedia* of Xenophon.[25]

Shortly after Momigliano's paper, Elias Bickerman (1967) pointed out several instances of shared motifs and shed light on Esther from his vast knowledge of the classical texts.[26] In the years that followed, more shared motifs and themes were noted and discussed by a growing number of scholars.[27]

Beginning in the late 1980s and continuing today, classicists and Persianists have been revisiting the Greek historiographical texts from the perspective of postmodern cultural studies. The main question posed to those texts has changed. No longer is it: What can we learn about Persian history from the Greeks? Now it is: What was the Greek view of the Persians and why did they hold that view? For our purpose, the "what" is more important than the "why." The simple answer is that the Greeks portrayed the Persians—and mostly that means the Persian court—as indulgent, decadent, and effeminate. There was much emphasis on Persian luxury, palace bureaucracy, and an extensive hierarchy including slaves. The Persians were, in the eyes of the Greeks, an inferior power in decline. Part of this perceived inferiority was undoubtedly a result of the failed Persian attempts to conquer Greece, but much of it lay in the basic differences between Greek and Persian culture. Two differences that arise often in the Greek texts, and that seem especially relevant to Esther, are the views of kingship and the place of women (especially royal women) in society.

Until now, we have been speaking of the Greek historians, most of whom were east Greeks, from Asia Minor, who lived and wrote during the Achaemenid period (539–330 B.C.E.) under Persian sovereignty. (The author of Esther, too, probably lived somewhere in the Persian empire during this period.) More recently, Christopher Tuplin has investigated references to Persians in the works of Greek dramatists, philosophers, and orators. These authors were Athenians, further removed from Persia, and have less to say about the Persians, but even so, their portrayal of Persian life is not much different from that of the historiographers. Among the Persian practices that Tuplin finds in Athenian writings, and that are most relevant to Esther, are the use of Persian or Persian-sounding, but actually fake, names; references to tribute, law, *proskynesis* (bowing down), impalement, the King's Eye, the good road system, eunuchs, and *paradeisos* (royal gardens); much emphasis on Persian wealth and luxury, heavy eating and drinking, drinking from goblets of glass and gold; and the Great King priding himself on his wealth. Tuplin presents the following composite picture of Persia, as seen in the writings from Athens:

> They...possess a large empire...whose only (other) physical, floral or faunal characteristics are extremes of heat and cold, mountains, citrus fruit, camels, horses, peacocks, cocks, (perhaps) lions for hunting, *paradeisoi*, road systems measured in parasangs and travelled by escourted ambassadors and official messengers....There is great wealth.... Persians are liable to pride, hauteur and inaccessibility....They enjoy a luxurious life-style

(exemplified by clothing, textiles, food and drink, tableware, means of transport, fans and fly-whisks, furniture) in a positively organized, regimented fashion: but the Queens are sexually virtuous and sometimes energetically warlike....Their polity is defined by a tyrannical ideology and systems of deferential behaviour and hierarchical control which deny equality[,]...value mere power and are inimical to the principle of Law—except that there have been "good" Persian kings to whom some of this does not apply. Eunuchs will be encountered; and impalement or crucifixion is employed as a punishment.[28]

This composite Greek picture of the Persians is remarkably similar to the one in Esther, which also features luxury, bureaucracy, drinking, a postal system, *dat* (imperial law), bowing down, eunuchs, impalement, and a sexually virtuous queen. The author of Esther is not alone in the way that he describes Persia. Esther's image of Persia is stereotypical. Even the use of burlesque in the portrayal of Persia is found among the Greeks, but for a slightly different purpose and with a sharper edge to it.

Behind a stereotype is often a fair measure of reality. In comparison with the Greeks, and even with other places throughout the Persian empire, the Persian court *was* luxurious, hierarchical, fond of drink, and so forth. But the point is not that Esther's portrait of Persia is realistic, but that it is *conventional*. The author of Esther used conventional literary motifs to portray Persia—the same motifs that the Greek historiographers, dramatists, and philosophers used. The author of Daniel did so, too, and had similar stories in other languages survived from this period we would not be surprised if they, too, shared these motifs. If a story has a Persian setting, these are the trappings to use to give it local color. Actually, many of the customs and institutions that characterize Persia were not Persian inventions, but were inherited from the Assyrians and the Babylonians (ornate palaces, banquets, reclining on couches, bowing down to monarchs, impalement). But they became associated with Persia because Persia was the dominant power at the time that this type of storytelling came into vogue. To the extent that this view of Persia was pervasive throughout the Persian empire and beyond, there is no reason to assume that the author of Esther lived in Susa or even in Persia proper. He could have lived anywhere in the Persian empire or even in Greece (although Greece is unlikely). To the extent that this view is the product of the late fifth and fourth centuries—the period of most of the Greek works—it lends support for dating Esther in the Persian period. (See below, "When and Where Was the Book of Esther Written?")

To understand that Esther is full of commonly used motifs is to see Esther in a new light, both in terms of the exegesis of individual episodes and in terms of the question of the book's date and provenance, and for these reasons I have incorporated into the commentary many Greek excerpts that illustrate the shared motifs. The classical authors upon whom I will draw are

Herodotus, ca. 480–420 B.C.E..

Xenophon, ca. 428–354 B.C.E.. His most relevant work is *Cyropaedia.*

Ctesias, late fifth century B.C.E.. He was a Greek physician who served at the court of Artaxerxes II. He wrote the *Persika,* a work that survives only in quotations in other Greek works.

Aeschylus, 525–456 B.C.E.. His relevant drama is *The Persians*.
Aristophanes, ca. 450–385 B.C.E. His relevant comedy is *Lysistrata*.

Later authors who drew extensively on earlier works about Persia are

Plutarch, ca. 50–120 C.E., who wrote in Greek.
Quintus Curtius Rufus, first century C.E., who wrote in Latin.
Diodorus of Sicily (Siculus), first century C.E., who wrote in Greek.

It is not only a question of identifying the common motifs, but also of understanding how they are being used. This is not a simple matter. While the Book of Esther portrayed the Persian court in the same stereotypical manner that we find in the Greek writings, the Bible in general and Esther in particular do not necessarily share the Greek attitude toward Persia. For the Bible, Persia was, in comparison to Babylonia, a beneficent and tolerant empire. For the Greeks, the Persians were an imperial power that hoped to conquer them through a series of wars. Moreover, Greek culture and society were very different from Persian culture and society, and the Greeks disdained it even as they were fascinated by it. The Greeks had no king, no court hierarchy, and a much more spare lifestyle, and, while they despised the idea of the Persian monarchy, they could not but be impressed by its power and opulence. The Jews, having once had their own monarchy and having lived under the sovereignty of empires, did not find the idea of the monarchy alien. Greek attitudes toward Persia, though they make a fascinating study, cannot be detailed here. Suffice it to say that, while at some points the biblical view of Persia coincides with the Greek view, at other times it diverges. When it comes to literary motifs, we will find that, for example, the Book of Esther adopts for the purpose of its plot the Greek abhorrence of bowing down to humans, but it does not cast this motif as a critique against the lack of democracy in the Persian empire. Likewise, the plot contains sexual impropriety but it is used to provoke a belly laugh, not a snicker of contempt. The motifs are the same, and to know how these motifs are understood by the Greeks helps us to interpret Esther. However, Esther does not have the sardonic tone that accompanies many of these motifs in the Greek writings.

This tone of derision to which I refer is illustrated most clearly and unambiguously in Quintus Curtius, *History of Alexander* 6.6.1–9. The passage provides a capsule of the Persian lifestyle adopted by Alexander the Great. The elements that are included are familiar from many Greek writings, and are also featured in Esther: bowing down to the king, wearing a diadem, wearing Persian garb, sealing letters with a royal signet ring, and having a large number of concubines. Quintus Curtius also includes plenty of editorial comment that is representative of the Greek judgment of Persian court life; he finds Alexander's practices to be "corrupted by luxury and foreign customs."

It was in fact at this time that Alexander gave loose rein to his passions, and changed continence and self-control, eminent virtues in every exalted fortune, to haughtiness and wantonness. Regarding his native customs and the discipline of the Macedonian kings,

wholesomely restrained and democratic, as too low for his grandeur, he strove to rival the loftiness of the Persian court, equal to the power of the gods; he demanded that the victors over so many nations in paying their respects to him should prostrate themselves upon the ground, and gradually sought to accustom them to servile duties and to treat them like captives. Accordingly, he encircled his brow with a purple diadem, variegated with white such as Darius had worn, and assumed the Persian garb. . . . In fact, he used to say that he was wearing the spoils of the Persians; but with them he had assumed also their customs, and insolence of spirit accompanied the magnificence of his attire. The letters also which were to be sent to Europe he sealed with the device of his former ring; on those which he wrote to Asia, the ring of Darius was impressed. . . . Three hundred and sixty-five concubines, the same number that Darius had had, filled his palace, attended by herds of eunuchs, also accustomed to prostitute themselves.

Quintus Curtius, who held Greek values as his standard, does not approve of Alexander's "Persian" court. In contrast, the Persian court in the Book of Esther, where there is no conflict with Greek values, is a much more congenial place—drunken and bungling to be sure, but a place where good triumphs over evil and the Jews over their enemies.

The Persian Period: A Brief Overview

The Persian (Achaemenid) period begins in 539 B.C.E. when, under the leadership of Cyrus, the Persians conquered the Babylonians and became heirs to their empire. It ends with the death of Darius III in 330, shortly after the conquest of Alexander. We have a body of disparate sources—Persian, Elamite, Greek, Akkadian, Aramaic, and biblical—for this period. They do not provide as complete a picture as we have for the Assyrian and Babylonian empires, but, through a judicious combination and re-evaluation of these sources, modern historians continue to piece together an increasingly nuanced picture of the Persian empire. (See especially the works of P. Briant, A. Kuhrt, and H. Sancisi-Weerdenburg.) Our knowledge about Jewish life in the Persian empire, however, especially outside of Judah and Elephantine, remains sketchy at best. There were Jewish communities in a number of other places, most notably in Babylonia and Susa, and presumably elsewhere, but we know little about them.

The founder of the Persian empire was Cyrus (ruled 550–530 B.C.E.). After having gained control of the Medes, he captured Babylon in 539 B.C.E.. He made his capital at Pasargadae. Cyrus instituted a policy toward the various peoples of the empire that has often been considered benevolent. He and the kings who followed him respected local languages, traditional laws and religious practices, and some governmental structures, permitting them to coexist within the centralized Persian system of government. This was not, however, done out of love for the various peoples in the empire; it was, rather, a politically wise policy intended to secure the loyalty of the conquered peoples, and it was for the most part quite successful. The Jews benefited from it by being able to return to Judah and rebuild the Temple. It is not surprising, then, that the Bible portrays Cyrus in a very positive light, as the deliverer of Israel from the hands of the

Babylonians. The Greek historians, too, see Cyrus in a favorable light—as a father figure and a fine political leader.

Cyrus had probably planned a campaign against Egypt (the Jewish returnees in Judah, loyal to Persia out of thankfulness for this privilege, would be a strategic factor), but it was his successor, Cambyses (530–522 B.C.E.), who actually carried it out. By 525 B.C.E., the Persian empire had almost reached its fullest extent; it included the ancient kingdoms of Media, Lydia, Babylonia, and Egypt—all incorporated into the Persian empire as satrapies.

The Persian empire, like the empires before it, was not immune to rebellions on its fringes and intrigues at its center. Cambyses was called back to the capital to put down an uprising, but died en route. A dynastic struggle ensued, from which Darius (522–486 B.C.E.) emerged as the new king. He was faced with considerable opposition early in his reign, but proved capable of overcoming it; he went on to become, after Cyrus, the most noteworthy of the kings. He achieved military victories and annexed the Indus valley; with this annexation the empire reached its greatest extent. Darius is best known for constructing a new capital at Persepolis and probably designated Susa as the winter capital (Babylon also had a winter palace and Ecbatana a summer palace). Persepolis and Susa were the most lavish of the royal courts and symbolized Achaemenid power and majesty. Darius also reorganized the empire. He centralized the government and systematized the collection of taxes and tribute. Native Persians were installed as satraps and they paid annual tribute directly to the Persian king. A network of royal roads provided a physical link, aiding communication from the capitals, the collection of tribute from the provinces, and the movement of military forces wherever needed. The wealth of the central government grew, as did its control over all parts of the empire. Another of Darius's innovations was "the law of the king," imperial law—another measure of central control. The king dominated this imperial system. At the same time, the older policies respecting local traditions remained in effect, for they continued to serve the objectives of the empire.

It was during the reign of Darius that the military engagements with Greece escalated—the First Persian War and the defeat at Marathon was in 490 B.C.E.—and they continued under Xerxes (486–465 B.C.E.). The Persians suffered a number of setbacks in these military campaigns. From the Greek perspective (and it is largely the Greek perspective that has survived), the reign of Xerxes ushered in the period of Persian decadence and decline. While this is a biased view, and may be exaggerated, modern historians speak of a period of consolidation and the beginning of stagnation following Darius. The empire did not expand further and actually lost some territorial control as a result of defeats at the hands of Greece. A rebellion had broken out in Egypt shortly before Xerxes came to the throne, and one in Babylonia shortly afterward. Xerxes put both rebellions down with force, destroying the temples in Babylonia and carrying off the statue of Marduk; this marked a deviation from the usual policy of religious tolerance. Xerxes led a major invasion into Greece in 480–479 B.C.E. and was defeated. The king devoted himself to the enhancement of his capital at Persepolis and to his harem. It is in the time of Xerxes (or Artaxerxes, if we follow the

Septuagint) that the story of Esther is set. Given the many motifs and themes that Esther shares with the Greek writings, it is not strange that its setting should be one that the Greeks would find appropriate for a slightly off-color comedy about a bumbling king, concerned with the display of wealth and women.

The last kings of the Persian empire were Darius II (424–405 B.C.E.), Artaxerxes II (405–359 B.C.E.), Artaxerxes III (359–338 B.C.E.), Arses (338–336 B.C.E.), and Darius III (336–330 B.C.E.). Their reigns were occupied by a complex chain of events involving Greece and the western satrapies. Loss and gain, war and peace, alternated until Alexander's military conquest brought the Persian empire to an end and inaugurated a new era of Greek dominance in the ancient Near East.

Esther as a Diaspora Story

Esther is a story about Jews living in the Diaspora, and in this it resembles several other books from the late biblical and early postbiblical period. The Book of Daniel, chapters 1–6, very similar in parts to Esther, also features a Jewish courtier who achieved outstanding success at the court of a Persian (and a Babylonian) king. The apocryphal Book of Judith, from the Hellenistic period, is set in a fictional Jewish community besieged by a foreign enemy. Judith, like Esther, features a woman who saves her people from destruction. The Book of Tobit, also in the Apocrypha, tells of the adventures of a pious Jew and his family, descended from the tribe of Naphtali and exiled to Nineveh by the Assyrians. All of these books are entertaining fictional narratives that present models of successful behavior for Jews living in the Diaspora. They are designed to promote pride in Jewish identity and solidarity within the Jewish community and with Jewish tradition. They reflect a situation in which Jews were a minority in a larger society and where it fell to the individual Jew, not the state, to ensure Jewish continuity. All the stories except Esther stress Jewish piety and commitment to Jewish values and rituals. The "secular" nature of Esther—its lack of God's name, prayer, *kashrut,* traditional modesty, and endogamous marriage—sets it apart from other Jewish Diaspora stories, and from other books of the Bible as well. But in its general tone and contents, Esther is properly classified among the Diaspora stories that circulated in the Persian and Hellenistic periods.

The Book of Esther also partakes in the category of stories about wise courtiers. This theme, recently discussed by L. Wills, was widespread in the ancient Near East and is also found in the biblical stories of Joseph and Daniel.[29] The most famous extrabiblical example is the Book of Aḥiqar. This story was probably not Jewish in origin but was popular among Jews. The earliest extant version of it was written about 400 B.C.E. in Aramaic and discovered at the Jewish colony in Elephantine. Aḥiqar was not a Jew, but the character of Aḥiqar found his way into the Book of Tobit (set in Assyria like the Aḥiqar story), where he is a Jew and a relative of Tobit.

Aḥiqar was a wise scribe and counselor in the court of the Assyrian kings Sennacherib and Esarhaddon. Since he had no son, he adopted his nephew, Nadin,

whom he instructed in wisdom so that the nephew could some day be his successor. Nadin did find a place at court but dealt treacherously with Aḥiqar, accusing him of treason and forging letters in his name. Aḥiqar was sentenced to death. The official in charge of the execution, however, had once been saved by Aḥiqar and so he returned the favor, sparing Aḥiqar and executing another person in his place. Shortly afterward, the Pharaoh of Egypt issued a challenge to the king of Assyria. If the Assyrian king could send someone to Egypt to construct a palace between heaven and earth, the Egyptians would send tribute to Assyria; if not, Assyria must send tribute to Egypt. The king of Assyria had thought that Aḥiqar was dead, but when he discovered, to his joy, that he was alive, he sent him to Egypt to meet the challenge. Aḥiqar accomplished his mission, brought back tribute, and then saw to it that Nadin was punished for his treachery.

While the story of Aḥiqar is not a Diaspora story, the theme of the wise courtier in a foreign court occurs in Jewish Diaspora stories and in the "diaspora" stories of other peoples. L. Wills points out that there were Ionian stories composed under Lydian domination about wise Ionian courtiers in the Lydian court, and Lydian stories composed under Persian domination about Lydians advising Persian kings. In all three cases, says Wills, "the ruled ethnic perspective court legend is used to the same effect: to assert the wisdom and statecraft of the cultural hero of the ruled ethnic group." He goes on to make the point that

> They also do not seem merely to provide a "role model for success" in the diaspora . . . although this function should not be totally excluded. Instead, they generally serve to affirm the value and identity of the ruled ethnic group . . . .[30]

In other words, as we have intimated above, Esther, like other Jewish Diaspora stories, strengthens the ethnic pride of Jews under foreign domination; and one of the ways that Diaspora stories achieve this is through the use of the theme of the wise courtier in the foreign court.

There is another important dimension of Jewish Diaspora stories that has not been adequately noted. These stories not only provide models for Jewish success and Jewish pride in foreign lands; they also provide answers to the critical question of how a Jewish community in exile can see itself vis à vis the Israel of the Bible. One of the ways to accomplish this is to relate the Diaspora stories to the biblical stories that were already accepted as traditional by Diaspora Jews. I see a strong, though not always direct, effort in Esther to stress Jewish identity and continuity with the biblical history of Israel. This is done through various thematic and verbal references to earlier parts of the Bible. Mordecai was exiled with King Jeconiah (Jehoiachin), which not only gives him a good Jewish pedigree but also links him with the narrative at the end of the Book of Kings. A frequent refrain in the Book of Kings, "are they not written in the book of chronicles of the kings of Israel/Judah" is echoed in Esther 10:2: "are they not written in the book of the chronicles of the kings of Media and Persia." The story of Esther (as we will explain at greater length below in "Esther's Links with Other Biblical Books")

alludes to the Joseph story and to the story of Saul and Agag. For, like the sons of Jacob, the Jews of Persia have a "brother" who will help them succeed in a foreign land; and, like Saul, they are engaged in the never-ending battle with Amalek.

In fact, many Diaspora stories draw on biblical themes, images, and language. The Book of Judith uses the theme of the Jael and Sisera story; the Book of Tobit harks back to the marriage practices of the patriarchs in Genesis. Other postexilic narratives, not usually called Diaspora stories, also place their heroes outside of the borders of Israel and link themselves with earlier parts of the Bible. Ruth, whose opening chapter is set in Moab, has strong connections with the story of Judah and Tamar in Genesis 38. Jonah, a story about a prophet sent on a mission to a foreign city, Nineveh, is patterned on the stories of earlier prophets and takes its name from one of them (2 Kings 14:25). While all of these books have more specific messages as their focus, they all share, through their allusions to earlier biblical stories, a strong tie to the traditions of preexilic Israel.

Esther's Links with Other Biblical Books

Just as the Book of Esther was written and read in the context of extrabiblical works of its own time, so it was also written and read in the context of the traditional literature of the Jewish community. The author of Esther and his audience were familiar with parts of the Bible: the Torah and most of the Prophets and probably with some of the Writings as well. In fact, during the exilic and postexilic periods (586 B.C.E. and thereafter) there was great attention to what came to be thought of as Scripture. It is in the Persian period, under the guidance of Ezra, that the Torah was declared authoritative for the Jewish community who returned to Judah. It is likely that the Former Prophets took their shape also sometime during the exilic period. This collecting and editing of traditional writings and their acceptance by the Jewish community marks the beginning of the process of canonization. Along with it went the writing of new works, which would later be included in the biblical canon.[31] So it is quite natural that the author of a new work such as Esther would wish to connect his work to earlier biblical books, and I believe he accomplished that in the ways outlined below.

This link with the Bible is especially important in a Diaspora story, for it ties the fate of the Diaspora community to the story of biblical Israel. The Book of Esther presents a tale of Persian Jewry, and by extension all exiled Jewry, as a continuation of the story of Israel, with the same type of enemies and heroes, and the same patterns of danger and deliverance. Esther, no less than Ezra and Nehemiah but of course in a different fashion, picks up the story of Israel where the Book of Kings left off, with the exile of Jehoiachin to Babylonia, signaling the end of Judean independence and the beginning of the exile (2:6). But instead of continuing the story from the point of view of the return to the Land of Israel, as most of the late biblical books do, Esther maintains the point of view of the community in exile, the Diaspora community (as does Daniel).

Esther has an additional need to interact with the earlier biblical books, especially the Torah, since it is innovating a holiday not mentioned in them. Esther is, as it were, imitating the Torah by authorizing the holiday of Purim.[32]

The Joseph Story. There are noticeable similarities between the story of Joseph and the story of Mordecai and the two stories have often been compared, even as early as rabbinic times.[33] Both Joseph and Mordecai rose to high positions in the court of a foreign king, and both used their positions to help their families or people. Parts of the Book of Esther may have been modeled on the Joseph story, for there are a number of thematic and verbal similarities. The descriptions of public honor, to Joseph in Gen. 41:42–43 and to Mordecai in Esther 6:11 and 8:2, both include dressing in special garb, riding, a proclamation, and the transfer of the king's ring. Verbal and syntactic similarities appear at other points in the story, even when the themes are unrelated. Genesis 39:10 and Esther 3:4 both say: "when she/they continued to speak/tell...day after day, but he did not listen to her/them." Other comparisons are found in Gen. 44:34 and Esther 8:6; Gen. 43:14 and Esther 4:16; Gen. 41:34–37 and Esther 2:3–4. Several motifs appear in both stories: the main action is set at a foreign court; the heroes suffer a decline in their fortunes and then overcome their problems and rise to prominence; eunuchs plotting against the king are the vehicle through which the hero renders a service to the king; a banquet scene where the true identity of the host or hostess is revealed; punishment by impalement. These and other similarities should not blind us to the large differences in the stories, yet it seems clear that there is some relationship between them. At the very least, they share features associated with stories of Jewish courtiers at a foreign court (as does Daniel), and this may be an ancient genre of storytelling. But the many verbal similarities suggest a more direct relationship. It seems, although we cannot know for sure, that the author of Esther drew on the Joseph traditions, if not on a written text, and that he intended for his readers to understand that the success of Jacob's family in Egypt would be repeated for the Jews of Persia.

The Exodus. Some scholars, most notably G. Gerleman, have seen a connection between Esther and the Exodus narrative. While the connection is not as strong as that between Esther and the Joseph story, both Esther and Exodus recount the escape of the Israelites or Jews from a dangerous enemy and the origin of a holiday to celebrate that escape. Passover is not mentioned in Esther, but Haman's decree was promulgated on the thirteenth day of the first month (3:12), that is 13 Nisan, just one day before the eve of Passover. Midrash Leqaḥ Tov, in its comment on 4:17, dates Esther's fast to 13, 14, and 15 Nisan, thereby making the beginning of Passover a fast day. Ahasuerus's sleepless night (6:1) was on "the night of watching" (Exod. 12:42), that is, the night of the Exodus. And Haman was impaled on 16 Nisan, during Passover.[34] This tradition, which occurs in bits and pieces in other midrashim, is perhaps most familiar from references in the *piyyutim* at the end of the Passover seder: *'az rov nisim,* by Yanai, mentions that among the events that happened on the night of Passover was the writing of Haman's edict (*sin'ah natar 'agagi ve-katav sefarim ba-lailah*) and the king's

sleepless night (*'orarta nitzaḥakha 'alav be-neded shenat lailah*); Eliezer Kalir's *piyyut*, *'ometz gevurotekha*, notes that on Passover Esther called for the three-day fast *(kahal kinsah hadasah tzom...)* and Haman was impaled on a stake fifty cubits high *(ro'sh mi-beit rasha' maḥatzta be-'etz ḥamishim)*. Later generations linked Pharaoh and Haman together with later tyrants who sought the harm of the Jews. The famous Spanish-Jewish poet Judah ha-Levi (ca. 1075–1141) drew an analogy between the escape of the Israelites at the Red Sea and the Purim story in his poem, *'adon ḥasdekha bal yeḥdal*, which was incorporated into the Morning Service in the Sephardic liturgy on the Sabbath preceding Purim.[35] Indeed, Midrash Leqaḥ Tov anticipated this connection in its comment on 3:7, when Haman cast his lot. The biblical verse begins: "In the first month, which is the month of Nisan," about which Leqaḥ Tov says: "The month during which miracles were performed for our fathers, in Egypt, at the sea, and at the Jordan."[36] Clearly, in the rabbinic tradition, the deliverance of the Jews in the Book of Esther is seen in terms of the deliverance of the Jews from Egypt.

1 Samuel 15. A more obvious link is made with 1 Samuel 15, the story of Saul and Agag, the Amalekite king. Mordecai is descended from the same genealogical line as Saul, and Haman is an Agagite, and so the story implies that these main characters are continuing an ancient rivalry between Saul and Agag and an ancient enmity between Israel and Amalek. The notice, on several occasions, that the Jews of Persia were permitted to take booty from their enemies but did not, further calls attention to the fact that Saul permitted the taking of booty when he was commanded to destroy totally all that belonged to Amalek. It is as if the Jews in Mordecai's day are finally correcting the deficit that cost Saul his kingship. The loss of Vashti's queenship, which was to be given "to her comrade who is better than she" also reminds us of 1 Sam. 15:28, where Samuel informs Saul of the loss of his kingship in the same terms. Yet, while this connection seems to be implied, the *Megillah* does not actually mention Saul by name, and does not mention Amalek. It is enough to mention Kish, the father of Saul, and Agag, the only name of an Amalekite king we have (also mentioned in Num. 24:7—it has even been suggested that "Agag" is a title like "Pharaoh"). "Agag" immediately evokes "Amalek" and all that the term connotes. Amalek, a descendent of Esau, is the prototypical enemy of Israel (and unknown from extrabiblical sources)—an enemy from the time of Moses with whom the Lord will be at war throughout the ages (Exod. 17:14). In a somewhat oxymoronic way, Amalek must be remembered forever and its name blotted out (Exod. 17:14 and Deut. 25:17–19). The story of Esther manages to both remember and to blot out Amalek. Through the story of Esther, the Jews of Persia are, by implication, the heirs of the ancient and never-ending battle with Amalek, and thereby assert their continuity with the history of Israel. If Amalek is the prototypical enemy, then Agag is the prototypical enemy leader, the Darth Vader of biblical historiography. By making Haman an Agagite, the story makes him a personification of the forces opposed to Israel.

Jewish tradition has long emphasized the Amalekite connection. Josephus mentions Haman's Amalekite lineage specifically. Rabbinic exegesis includes it at

various points. In the synagogue, on the Sabbath preceding Purim, Shabbat Zakhor, Deut. 25:17–19, and 1 Samuel 15 are read. On the morning of Purim, the reading is Exod. 17:8–16, the battle between Israel and Amalek. In contrast, in the Greek versions Haman is not an Agagite, so the Amalekite dimension of the story is lost.

The Book of Kings. Amos Frisch, who discusses the resemblances between Esther and Kings, notes that there are especially strong links between Esther and the beginning and end of the Books of Kings.[37] At the beginning of 1 Kings, David is advised by his servants to find a young virgin to warm him. A search is made throughout Israel and a beautiful girl is found. The theme and language are close to Esther 2, where Esther, like Abishag, is discovered as a result of an empire-wide search for a beautiful virgin, as suggested by the royal servants.

There is a more general similarity in plot structure between Esther and 1 Kings 1–2. A rival for the throne, Adonijah, emerges; while not exactly a Haman-figure, he plays a similar role in the plot. The queen, Bathsheba, speaks to the king against him, as Queen Esther speaks to Ahasuerus against Haman. Bathsheba was advised by Nathan much as Esther was advised by Mordecai. Neither Bathsheba nor Esther seem to have had recent visits to the king for sexual purposes, and must gain an audience with him specifically to deliver their messages. In the end, the king (David/Ahasuerus) chooses the "right" person to honor—Solomon in Kings and Mordecai in Esther. The honoree rides on the king's animal. The "wrong" contender is killed, and the putative reason has to do with the contender's desire to have the king's queen or concubine. There are several verbal similarities, the most outstanding being the use of the root *n-ś-ʾ* for the elevation of the wrong contender (1 Kings 1:5; Esther 3:1) and the king's solicitous question to the queen, *mah lakh,* "what's the matter" (1 Kings 1:16; Esther 5:3).

The connection between the account of Jehoiachin's exile in 2 Kings 24:11–15 and Esther 2:6 is well known. It is as if Mordecai is being written into 2 Kings 24:14. Finally, Esther 10:2 sums up its "chronicle of events" with the words: "all the deeds of . . . are they not written in the book of the chronicles of the kings of Media and Persia." This is an imitation of the oft-used phrase throughout Kings, referring the reader to fuller sources in the Chronicles of the Kings of Israel and the Chronicles of the Kings of Judah.

What should we make of these similarities to Kings? One may be tempted to conclude that the author of Esther is trying to make his story sound *historical,* thereby according it more authority (Fox, 150). But, as I mentioned before (see "Narrative Artistry"), I prefer to conclude that the author is trying to make his story sound more *biblical.* He is imitating the framework of the Books of Kings—starting near the beginning of the reign of a specific king and ending with a reference to the rest of the deeds of that king in the official annals—and using some of the themes and motifs found in Kings, because he is modeling his story, to some extent, on the traditional writings of the Jewish community. It is this resemblance to traditional texts, rather than its historicity, that would give Esther more authority, as well as more familiarity, to the Jews of the Persian period.

Daniel 1–6.   Of all the biblical writings, the stories in the first six chapters of Daniel are closest to the story of Esther, and are often compared to it. These stories are set in the court of the king of Babylonia or Persia and feature a Jewish courtier who overcomes religious or ethnic obstacles to become a high-ranking member of the royal court. The two books share many specific details. The description of the royal court, with a king surrounded by advisors, luxurious vessels and trappings, and a royal signet ring. The Jewish heroes (Daniel and his friends and either Esther or Mordecai) have both Hebrew and vernacular names; are described as beautiful or handsome; are among those exiled from Judah; sit at the king's gate; gain the favor of those who are in charge of their care; and are at the end elevated to high positions at court. The heroes are slandered by villains who plan to kill them, but the villains are killed by the means that they had designed for the heroes. Shared motifs include an order to bow down; communicating with peoples in their various languages; edicts that cannot be changed; banquets with wine drinking; an exaggerated number of satrapies; hero dressed in purple; the king's sleepless night. There are also linguistic similarities between Esther and Daniel 1–6, even though Daniel 2–6 is in Aramaic. These stories all probably originated in the same period. The later chapters of Daniel and the compilation of the book as a whole date from the Maccabean period, so we cannot say that Esther was imitating scriptural writings in this case. Both Esther and Daniel 1–6 are examples of a type of fictional storytelling that was popular during the Persian period.

Other Books from the Persian Period.   There are other biblical books from the Persian period that have been compared to Esther, although their resemblance is less close. Ezra and Nehemiah are historiographical accounts of the return of the Jews to Judah. The prophets Haggai, Zechariah, and Malachi add the prophetic dimension to the accounts of Ezra and Nehemiah. Chronicles reviews all of biblical history, or at least the genealogical line, from Adam until the edict of return of Cyrus. All of these books model themselves, even more closely than Esther does, on earlier biblical writings, for they are in the same genre as the Books of Kings and the books of the classical prophets. The genre of "story," relatively short fictional story, is also exemplified by Ruth and Jonah, both dated by most scholars to the Persian period. The plots, styles, and settings of Ruth and Jonah differ greatly from Esther, but they all have in common that the central character is a Jew or Israelite in a foreign land. Ruth and Jonah show us a different kind of postexilic storytelling. They are more about individuals than about the Jewish people, and so less amenable to being called "Diaspora stories."

S. Talmon has argued for a link between Esther and biblical Wisdom Literature, calling Esther "a historicized wisdom tale."[38] Talmon's thesis provides an explanation for the omission of specifically Israelite religious practice, for this is a feature of Wisdom Literature also. Likewise, both Esther and Wisdom Literature tend to be anthropocentric. The differences between these two types of literature, however, outweigh their similarities.[39] Wisdom Literature mentions God often, and holds the fear of God as its first principle. National concerns loom large in Esther, whereas they are absent or minimal in Wisdom Literature. Wisdom Literature is didactic in tone and

purpose, while Esther is not. Closer to being "historicized wisdom tales" are two nonbiblical narrative compositions with the theme of the wise courtier in the foreign court that contain teachings or instructions: the *Book of Aḥiqar* and the *Instruction of Onkhsheshonq*. These compositions may be considered under the rubric of Wisdom Literature, as well as under the rubric of "wise courtier." But the Book of Esther does not include the kind of sapiential teachings found in these two works, and, for the reasons just mentioned, Esther seems distant from Wisdom Literature. It seems to me that the absence of the divine name and Jewish religious practice is better explained by the nature of the story and the holiday of Purim—a comedy for a carnivalesque festival.

When and Where Was the Book of Esther Written?

Most scholars now date the writing of the Book of Esther to the late Persian or early Greek period, roughly between 400–200 B.C.E.. (An older view saw it as the product of Hellenistic or Maccabean times.) To put the dating in a broader context, here are the dates generally given for some other biblical and apocryphal books.

> Ruth and Jonah: Persian period;
> Isaiah 40–66: 550–500 B.C.E.;
> Haggai, Zechariah, Malachi: 500–300 B.C.E.;[40]
> Ezra-Nehemiah: 400–300 B.C.E.;
> Chronicles: 400–300 B.C.E.;
> Ecclesiastes: dated by most scholars to about 250 B.C.E., but C. L. Seow has recently proposed an earlier date, 450–350 B.C.E.;[41]
> Tobit: 225–175 B.C.E.;
> Daniel as a whole is dated in the Maccabean period (ca. 164 B.C.E.), but Chapters 1–6 may go back to the fourth or third centuries B.C.E.;
> Judith: about 100 B.C.E..

For the reasons discussed below, I would place the writing of Esther earlier in the accepted period rather than later, about 400–300 B.C.E., after the reign of Xerxes and before the Hellenization of the East in the wake of Alexander.

Linguistic analysis shows the language of the book to be Late Biblical Hebrew (like the books of Ezra, Nehemiah, Chronicles, and some of the later prophets), with some Mishnaic Hebrew features. Typical of the Hebrew of the Persian period is the use of late vocabulary, words like *birah,* "capital, fortress"; *keter,* "crown"; *'igeret,* "letter"; *malkhut* instead of *mamlakhah* for "kingdom." There are loanwords from Aramaic, like *yekar,* "honor," and from Persian, like *dat,* "law." Late syntactic features include an increased use of the infinitive construct for other forms of the verb (as in 1:17 and 9:14); reversed order for names and epithets ("Esther the queen" instead of "Queen Esther"); and the presence of elliptical sentences that lack a specific subject or verb (1:2).[42] The use of the Babylonian names for the months (Adar, etc.) is also a late linguistic feature. The language of Esther is recognizably late, even though it has an archaizing tendency, to make it sound more like earlier parts of the Bible.

Several phrases hint that the story was written some time after the events that it purports to recount, that is, after the time of Xerxes I (485–465 B.C.E.), but that could still be during the Persian period. To the extent that Esther is a burlesque of the Persian court, it makes sense to date the story to the Persian period, for a burlesque would be less effective after the Persian empire ceased to exist. The worldview portrayed, in which the Jews are ultimately safe and successful in the Diaspora, suggests a time before the Maccabean revolt (in 167 B.C.E.). The book does not evince any antagonism toward Hellenistic culture, as one would expect if it had been written in Hellenistic times. The strongest argument for dating it to the Hellenistic period is Haman's description of the Jews in 3:8, which contains the elements typical of Hellenistic anti-Jewish rhetoric. But as P. Schäfer has shown, and as I discuss in the Commentary to 3:8, these elements can be traced back to the third and perhaps the fourth century B.C.E., in the Persian period.

Because the story is set in Susa, many scholars have assumed, either naively or for lack of a better alternative, that it was written in Susa, or at least in Persia. There is no evidence to support this, nor is there evidence to disprove it. Earlier scholars who dated the book to Maccabean times were more likely to find its provenance in Palestine or Egypt. If it is, indeed, a Diaspora story from the Persian period, it could have been written in any Jewish community, more likely a Diaspora Jewish community, but it is not possible to identify its place of origin.

The proposed date for Esther coincides with the flowering of the Greek works on Persia, composed in the fifth-fourth centuries B.C.E. (a few later authors, like Plutarch, Diodorus, and Quintus Curtius, drew extensively on the earlier Greek authors). Indeed, the author of Esther seems to have been very familiar with the kinds of stories and motifs that occur in the Greek writings about Persia during the Persian period, and that may have been conventional literary fare at that time. While I am not suggesting that the author of Esther read the Greek stories, only that the Greek writers and our author drew on a similar collection of narrative motifs, the similarities between them raise intriguing questions of literary history that relate to the book's place of origin and to the larger question of the relationship between Greek literature and the Bible. How widespread were the motifs associated with Persia that are reflected in Esther? How widespread was knowledge, direct or indirect, of the Greek writings about Persia? Many of the Greek historiographers were residents of Ionia (Asia Minor) and lived under Persian rule. Greeks were found in many places throughout the Persian empire, including Babylonia and even at the Persian court at Susa. Evidence of commerce with Greece, if not actually Greek settlements, is found in Palestine well before the Persian period and continues throughout.[43] It would seem that there was ample opportunity for other peoples to become acquainted with Greek thought and literature well before Alexander, and for the Greeks to become conversant with the stories of the many peoples of the East. The Greeks did not pretend to have invented the stories they told about the Persians; they collected them from informants who had first-hand knowledge. So there is every reason to think that these stories and motifs were commonly known throughout the East, and that the author of Esther could have

drawn on them easily. The fact that they were preserved primarily by the Greeks (who gave them their own distinctive twist) is an accident of literary history, for we do not have an extensive narrative literature from anywhere else during the Persian period.

When Was Esther Included in the Canon?

The date of the canonization of the Book of Esther is obviously related to the date of the canonization of the *Ketuvim* section of the Bible as a whole, and on this there is not a consensus among scholars. It is now agreed that canonization was a gradual process that occurred over many years, not a one-time act by a group of rabbis, but exactly when the process was completed or when during its progression the Book of Esther was accorded canonical status is difficult to ascertain. The main evidence brought to the discussion are the rabbinic sources that mention the status of Esther. (Esther is among a small group of books—also including Ezekiel, Proverbs, Song of Songs, and Ecclesiastes—about which there are disputes in rabbinic literature.) The passages most relevant to Esther are the following:[44]

> B. Baba Batra 14b–15a, which contains a tannaitic comment (second century C.E.) listing the Scroll of Esther among the biblical books, in the Hagiographa, between Daniel and Ezra.

> B. Megillah 7a:
> R. Simeon b. Yohai (135–170 C.E.) says: Ecclesiastes is among the lenient decisions of the School of Shammai and among the stringent decisions of the School of Hillel, but [all agreed that] Ruth, Song of Songs, and Esther defile the hands.

> B. Megillah 7a:
> Rab Judah (250–290 C.E.) said in the name of Samuel (220–250 C.E.): The Scroll of Esther does not defile the hands. Are we to infer from this that Samuel was of the opinion that the Scroll of Esther was not composed under divine inspiration? How can this be, seeing that Samuel has said that the Scroll of Esther was composed under divine inspiration? It was composed to be recited but not to be written.

> B. Sanhedrin 100a:
> Levi ben Samuel (290–320 C.E.) and R. Huna ben Hiyya (290–320 C.E.) were repairing the mantles of the scrolls at R. Judah's (250–290 C.E.) academy. On coming to the Scroll of Esther, they said: This [Scroll of Esther] does not require a mantle. He [R. Judah] reproved them saying: Such behavior smacks of irreverence.

At issue is the meaning of the term "defiles the hands." Some scholars, notably S. Z. Leiman, R. Beckwith, and M. Broyde, argue that this term does not refer to the canonical status of the book, but rather to whether it was divinely inspired. These scholars conclude that Esther was canonized by the middle of the second century B.C.E., and that the entire canon of the Hebrew Bible was closed at this time. Most recently, Menahem Haran has added his voice to this group advocating an early date for canonization. Haran's interpretation of "defiles the hands" is, however, somewhat different;

he concludes that it has to do with the ability of the physical scrolls to acquire and transmit impurity, rather than with their inspired status. A scroll could become defiled by a person with unclean hands, and anyone who read from it on a public occasion might have unclean hands (there was no way to check). Hence, deduces Haran, when the School of Shammai says that certain books do not defile the hands, this implies that they did not acquire impurity because they were not read publicly on the Sabbath or holidays.[45]

These rabbinic passages, then, have no bearing on the date of canonization. The fact that there are many other rabbinic statements and halakhot (legal rulings) pertaining to the observance of Purim shows that the Rabbis accepted the festival without question.[46] And if they accepted the festival of Purim, they must have accepted the book that authorized it.

Another view is espoused by scholars who argue that the term "defiles the hands" does, indeed, refer to canonical status. In their opinion, the process of canonization continued at least until the first century C.E., and they find doubts about its canonical status among the Rabbis as late as the third century C.E. This view tends to be an older, more established one, and it remains to be seen if it will give way to the re-definition of "defiles the hands" and the view of an earlier date for canonization.

For scholars who date the composition of the Book of Esther to the Greek period (especially the Maccabean period), an early date for its canonization is obviously difficult. Since I date the book's composition to the early fourth century B.C.E., and assume that Purim was an accepted Jewish festival by that time, a second-century B.C.E. date for the canonization of Esther is completely acceptable, even preferable.

One place where the Book of Esther was not considered canonical was Qumran. No copy of Esther has been found at Qumran (it is the only book of the Bible not attested at Qumran), and by now it is agreed that the community at Qumran did not preserve this book. Shemaryahu Talmon has recently demonstrated that the people at Qumran alluded to phrases from Esther in their other writings and therefore must have known the Book of Esther even though they did not preserve it.[47] Sidnie White Crawford has examined the so-called Proto-Esther texts from Qumran and has argued persuasively that these are fragments of a literary genre that can be termed "tales of the Persian court," a genre to which Esther belongs. They are not, however, fragments of the Esther story, although they may be sources upon which the author of Esther drew.[48] We may conclude, then, that the Qumran community knew of the Book of Esther, and had in their collection of texts stories of a similar genre, but that they rejected the Book of Esther itself.

A few scholars have suggested that the rejection of the book was based on theological grounds—the absence of the divine name and religious observance, and the marriage of a Jewess to a pagan king. A more likely reason is that the book was not accepted because Purim was not accepted. C. A. Moore (xxi) does not think Purim was rejected because it was not mentioned in the Torah, since the Qumran community celebrated other non-Torah holidays, but he raises the possibility that it was rejected because of its pagan origins.[49] Roger Beckwith deduced ingeniously that neither Esther

nor Purim was accepted because to do so would conflict with the Qumran calendar.[50] The sectarians at Qumran had adopted a 364-day calendar (different from the calendar of mainstream Jewry), which originated in the middle of the third century B.C.E., before Esther was in the canon of Palestinian Jewry. In this calendar there are exactly fifty-two weeks in the year, so that a specific date in the month will always fall on the same day of the week. According to the Qumran calendar, 14 Adar would always be on the Sabbath. To accept Esther after this calendar had gone into effect would cause a serious inconsistency, since one of the principles governing the calendar was that no dated event in the Bible could fall on the Sabbath, lest it be construed that biblical figures were performing work on the day when work was forbidden. A related principle was that no holy day could fall on the Sabbath (except for week-long holidays). So there would be a double problem with Esther and Purim: (1) the Jews of Shushan, according to the Qumranic calculation, would have violated the Sabbath when they fought against their Persian enemies on 14 Adar; and (2) the Qumran community would find problematic the celebration of a holiday that fell on the Sabbath, as Purim always would in their calendar. Interestingly, while rabbinic Judaism had no problem with holidays falling on the Sabbath, the celebration of Purim may be viewed as incompatible with Sabbath observance. In fact, according to the Jewish calendar now in use, 14 Adar can *never* fall on the Sabbath.

The canonical status of Esther among Christians is an equally complex question. Since the church did not have Purim in its liturgical calendar, Christians did not have the compelling reason that Jews had to accept the book. But since the Christian canon of the Old Testament derived from the Hebrew Bible, and Esther was part of the Hebrew Bible, one would expect to find Esther among the canonical books in Christian Bibles. That is true today, but it was not always so everywhere in the early Christian centuries. The evidence—lists of canonical books of the church fathers, councils, and synods—shows that in the West, Esther was usually included in the canonical lists, but in the East it was often omitted. Even when it was present, its status may have been marginal as it occupied the last place on a number of the lists. Esther was often mentioned in conjunction with the books of the Apocrypha, especially Judith.[51]

Purim

Purim is the only Jewish holiday that is mentioned in the Bible but not in the Torah, and our only information about its origin comes from the Book of Esther. In fact, one of the main purposes of the book, if not its main purpose, is to explain how Purim came into being. The book provides an etiology for the festival—an explanation of how Purim originated—and gives an authoritative reason for its perpetual celebration. Now etiologies do not precede the entities that they explain, but rather offer an explanation for what already exists. So we may conclude that Purim existed, in one form or another, before the book was written, or at least before the Purim passages in chapter 9 were written.

What do we know about the origin of Purim? Because of the similarity between Purim and other ancient carnival-like festivals and/or festivals occurring around the same time of the year—near the vernal equinox or near the end of the calendar year (the Babylonian and Persian year ended in Adar)—scholars have attempted to discover the origin of Purim in one or another of these ancient festivals.[52] Because the Book of Esther is set in Persia, many scholars have looked to Persia for Purim's origin, finding it in the Persian Farvardigan, the Festival of the Dead (whose name sounds somewhat like "Purim"), or in the Persian New Year. Other scholars preferred Babylonia as the place of origin, because of the large Jewish community living in Babylonia during the Persian period, because the term *pur*, "lot," whence "Purim," derives from Babylonian, and because it had been popular to associate the names of Esther and Mordecai with the Babylonian deities Ishtar and Marduk. A Greek origin had also been proposed by H. Grätz in 1886 but was rejected by Paton in 1908 and was never considered seriously again.[53] A Greek origin, however, may be no less likely than any other, especially given the fact that the Book of Esther has in common with Greek literature its use of many motifs and a comic form. The Greeks had a festival called the City or Great Dionysia, which took place in March-April for four days (later three days). The festival was the occasion for the tasting of new wine, revelry, and masquerading, and beginning in 486 B.C.E. included the performance of comedies (the Greek word *komos*, from which "comedy" derives, means "revel, a riotous celebration"). The actors in these comedies wore grotesque masks and phallic appendages, and the dancers had deliberately vulgar choreography.[54]

All of these possible origins are suggestive, but none is provable. There were many late winter or early spring holidays, some of them carnivalesque, in the ancient world as in the modern one (compare Mardi Gras), and one or more of them may have been adopted by Jews and, in the course of time, become a Jewish festival.

Rather than speculate on Purim's pagan origin, we might do better to ask: When did Purim become a *Jewish* holiday? Unfortunately, this question is no easier to answer because our sources for Jewish life during the Persian period are meager. The dating of the observance of Purim is obviously related to the date of the Book of Esther (ca. 400–200 B.C.E.) and to the date of its canonization (perhaps as early as the second century B.C.E.), for the book would not have been written in its current form or preserved without the popular acceptance of Purim. This suggests that Purim was being celebrated by around the third century B.C.E., but we have no evidence to confirm it.

We have firm evidence for the Jewish observance of Purim in the Hellenistic period. Our earliest reference is in 2 Macc. 15:36 (written 104–63 B.C.E.), which mentions "the day of Mordecai" on 14 Adar. A second piece of evidence is the colophon to the Septuagint Esther, which reads: "In the fourth year of the reign of Ptolemy and Cleopatra, Dositheus, who said that he was a priest and a Levite [or: priest, and Levitas], and his son Ptolemy brought to Egypt the preceding Letter about Purim, which they said was authentic and had been translated by Lysimachus son of Ptolemy, one of the residents of Jerusalem." The Ptolemy and Cleopatra referred to are usually dated to 114–113 B.C.E. or to 78–77 B.C.E.[55]

By around the end of the second century B.C.E. we can speak of the Jewish celebration of Purim in the Land of Israel (although not at Qumran) and in Egypt. We are still left with a gap between the Book of Esther's putative origin of Purim in Susa at the time of Xerxes (fifth century B.C.E.), and even between my third century B.C.E. estimate of its origin, and its documented observance several centuries later in communities far to the west. By the Roman period, the time of our rabbinic sources, Purim was firmly entrenched. *Megillat Ta'anit,* a first century C.E. tannaitic work containing a list of the days on which fasting is prohibited, lists 14 and 15 Adar as Purim. Later rabbinic sources, especially the Mishnah and the Gemara, provide many details about the observance of Purim and we can conclude that by the early centuries C.E. Purim was firmly established in rabbinic Judaism.

The name "Purim" calls for comment. This is the name that the Book of Esther uses, although the reason for the name—after Haman's casting of a lot (3:7; 9:24)— seems forced because the casting of the lot is not central to the plot of the story. This is more likely a "false etymology" of the type common in the Bible, in which the similarity of sounds is used to link a name with an explanation in the accompanying narrative (for example, Moses' name in Exod. 2:10). This has led some scholars to propose other derivations for the word "Purim" but they are not convincing. The reference in 2 Macc. 15:36 calls the holiday "the day of Mordecai" and does not mention "Purim." The Greek versions use terms that sound like "Purim" but are not identical with it: the Septuagint 9:26–29 calls it *phrourai* ("guards"), echoed also in Josephus, and the Alpha-text (another Greek version of Esther; see below, "The Greek Versions and Josephus") uses *phourdaia.*[56] All this suggests early uncertainty about the name of the holiday. Rabbinic texts, beginning with *Megillat Ta'anit,* use "Purim."

There is also uncertainty about the date of Purim, even in the Book of Esther itself, or at least about where it was celebrated on 14 Adar and on 15 Adar. Chapter 9 recounts a second day of fighting in Shushan, which was most likely added to the story to account for the fact that the holiday was observed there on 15 Adar, and on 14 Adar everywhere else (9:17–18). But then 9:19 assigns 14 Adar to Jews of unwalled towns, implying that Jews of all walled cities observed the holiday on 15 Adar (as was the practice as defined by the later rabbinic literature). The Septuagint has the Jews of Susa congregating on 14 Adar but celebrating on 15 Adar, and the Jews of the countryside (that is, outside of Susa) celebrating on 14 Adar. Earlier, in 3:7, the Septuagint has Haman's lot fall on 14 Adar, instead of 13 Adar.[57] The Alpha-text records the dates for Phourdaia as 14 and 15 Adar, without explaining that there was a different date for different locations. It is reasonable to conclude from this confusion that Purim originally may have been celebrated on 14 Adar in some communities and on 15 Adar in others, and that the Book of Esther is trying to justify and regularize this practice.

The essential features specific to the observance of Purim, as described in rabbinic sources, are the reading of the *Megillah,* the Purim banquet, the sending of gifts, and the giving of gifts to the poor. The last three are specified in the *Megillah* itself. And, while the *Megillah* does not state that it should be read, its reading has become the

centerpiece of the observance of Purim. M. Fox has a wonderful explanation for why this is so.

> The public reading of the Scroll is not ordained in the book itself, yet the reading is rooted in the book's ideology. The only festival practice the author envisaged was festivities which replicate the Jews' rejoicing of year 12 [the time of the events of chapters 8 and 9]. The Jews of subsequent generations, rather than commemorating something that happened to their ancestors, celebrate their ancestors' *experience* . . . . It was an accurate extension of the author's intention when the rabbis took an imperative implicit in the text—"read me"—and made that the prime commandment of the festival.[58]

The tone of the Purim celebration—the boisterousness and frivolity of a topsy-turvy world—is captured in the talmudic statement that on Purim one should get so drunk that he can no longer distinguish between "Cursed be Haman" and "Blessed be Mordecai" (B. Megillah 7b). This tone, like the reading of the scroll, stems from the tone of the book itself; and, indeed, many of the components of the celebration of Purim derive from the story. Not only do we re-enact the rejoicing of the Jews of Persia, as Fox so well put it, but we re-enact the book in a broader sense. We do so in a literal way through Purim skits and plays. No less an enactment of the story, we eat and drink and carouse on Purim just as Ahasuerus did in his royal court. As for masquerades, they are at home in other carnivalesque occasions (e.g., Halloween and Mardi Gras), but they are also a natural outgrowth of the Book of Esther, where we find Mordecai's changes in costume—from wearing sackcloth, to being arrayed in the king's robe, to dressing in his own multicolored royal outfit—and the theme of concealed and confused identities (Esther's Jewishness is concealed, Haman thinks he is the man the king will honor). In celebrating Purim we relive the carnivalesque aspects of the book. The ways of observing Purim begin with and derive from the Book of Esther.[59]

Purim shares many features with other carnival holidays (Halloween, Mardi Gras, April Fool's Day, and New Year's Day in the United States and Yom ha-'Atzma'ut [Israeli Independence Day] in Israel). These carnival days differ one from the other, but in all of them there is a certain gaiety, levity, and disregard for norms of propriety. In his discussion of Purim, H. Fisch opines that it is not an actual carnival but a symbolic carnival.[60] J. Rubenstein, using the anthropological model of Victor Turner, concludes that Purim is a time of liminality, an "in-between" time when the normal structures of society do not pertain. Both of these scholars sense that in Purim, and, we might add, in other carnival celebrations as well, there is not a complete breakdown or reversal of norms (as many discussions of carnival would have it), but a symbolic or partial reversal of norms. To me this signifies the *miming* of a reversal, imitating or pretending to turn society's norms on their head, knowing all the while that it is just pretend. In carnival the world of make-believe takes the place of the real world. Costumes and masks, excessive drink, noise, rowdiness, and even (mock) violence are some of the common manifestations that symbolize both the aura of make-believe and the permissible reversing of the rules of society. It may not be unreasonable to suggest that the manner in which *dat,* "rule, law, custom," is constantly being called upon in the

Book of Esther is another sign of the carnivalesque spirit of the book, for the rules are themselves capricious and silly, their publication is exaggerated, and immutable laws are easily changed. True, the motif of law is at home in all types of storytelling about Persia, but it is additionally useful here, in the world of carnival, where law is disregarded and custom is flouted. It is not the Persians that are being made fun of; it is the rule of law. Inscribed in the book is the idea that rules are meant to be broken.

The type of psychological release that is accomplished by carnival and that is embodied in Esther and in Purim, as well as the plot of the book in which the Jews overcome their enemies, lends itself to other occasions when a celebration of community survival was called for. Various Jewish communities during the Middle Ages and the Early Modern period instituted a *Purim katan,* "a minor Purim," imitating the observance of Purim on a date that commemorates their deliverance from destruction.[61]

The Greek Versions and Josephus

Esther presents us with an unusual opportunity to study the early growth and interpretation of a biblical story. In addition to the Masoretic Text (the accepted Hebrew text of the Bible), two Greek versions of the story survive: the version preserved in the Septuagint, also known as the B-text, and a shorter Greek version, known as the Alpha-text or A-text (sometimes referred to as the Lucianic recension, or L).

Current scholarly interest in Jewish literature of the Greco-Roman period and in the history of biblical interpretation has spurred a number of recent studies of the Greek versions and comparisons of the two Greek versions with each other and with the Masoretic Text.[62] These studies shed light on what the basic outlines of the earliest form of the story might have been before it reached the form in which we have it in the Masoretic Text, and how the story was reshaped in its different textual versions. The complicated textual development that produced the three extant versions need not occupy us here. Our concern is the Masoretic Text, so we need to understand that this text was probably based on a Hebrew story that has not been preserved but that was similar to our Hebrew Esther. In its pre-Masoretic form, it was not the story of the origin of Purim; the emphasis on Purim was added by the author of the Masoretic Text, who reshaped the story as an etiology for Purim. We do not know whether the original Hebrew story contained religious language. Some people think that it did, and that the author of the Masoretic Text took out the references to God and religious observance. Others think that the original story lacked religious language and that it was added only later, by the author of the Septuagint. In either case, the absence of religious language in the Masoretic Text is completely appropriate, if not absolutely necessary, given that it is a farce associated with a carnivalesque occasion.

The major differences between the Masoretic Text and the Greek versions are the six Additions. These Additions were once an integral part of the Septuagint but when Jerome (fourth century C.E.) translated the Greek Bible into Latin (the Vulgate), he

observed that these passages had no equivalent in the Hebrew text of his time. Doubting their authenticity as divinely inspired scripture, he relegated them to the end of his translation. They remain canonical for the Roman Catholic and the Eastern Orthodox Churches. Protestants declared them uncanonical and placed them in the Apocrypha, under the title "Additions to Esther." The Additions make little sense at the end of the book since they are out of context, so some modern Christian Bibles have reinstated them into their appropriate positions within the story.

Addition A, which stands at the beginning of the story, contains a dream of Mordecai foreshadowing destruction, and Mordecai's discovery of a plot against the king. Addition B, which follows 3:13, contains the wording of the edict against the Jews. Addition C, which follows 4:17, is the prayer of Mordecai and the prayer of Esther, asking for deliverance. Addition D, which follows Addition C, is an account of Esther's appearance before the king. It is longer and more dramatic than the account in the Masoretic Text. Addition E, which follows 8:12, gives the contents of the edict on behalf of the Jews. Addition F, which comes at the end of the story, after 10:3, is the interpretation of Mordecai's dream, relating it to the events of the story.

The Greek versions also include the religious elements so obviously absent in the Masoretic Text—the name of God and prayer. The name of God occurs not only in the Additions, but at several other points in the story. There are a number of other differences in the details of the story and in the way the story is told. For instance, Haman is not an Agagite; Purim does not receive as much emphasis; and Esther is characterized differently.[63]

The Greek versions, especially the Septuagint, have a different tone and reflect a different view of the Jewish characters from the Masoretic Text. David Clines, who believes that the religious elements were originally absent and were added in the Septuagint, has perceptively argued that the Septuagint added the religious dimension in order to "assimilate the Book of Esther to a scriptural norm."[64] That is, the Septuagint sought to make the book sound more biblical, more like the Books of Ezra, Nehemiah, and Daniel, where God's presence is felt in the events that unfold and where the characters engage in religious activities (praying and invoking God's name). Mordecai's dream and its interpretation is also similar to what we find in Daniel. And, thirdly, the inclusion of the contents of the edicts also resembles the practice in Ezra, Nehemiah, and Daniel, which include what purports to be verbatim copies of Persian documents. We have discussed above how the Masoretic Text of Esther sought to fashion itself, in part, on the model of earlier biblical writings; now we see that principle carried further, for different effect, in the Septuagint.

But "assimilation to a scriptural norm" does not account for all the differences between the Masoretic Text and the Septuagint. There are other differences that reflect the Septuagint's Hellenistic worldview as opposed to the earlier worldview of the Masoretic Text. The Hellenistic world was one in which, according to R. Frye, religious identity had replaced ethnic identity.[65] That may explain even further why the Jewish characters are more religious, for it is religious practice that defines one as a Jew. Take the practice of circumcision. No mention is made of it in the Masoretic Text of

Esther, but in the Septuagint at the end of chapter 8 we read: "And many of the Gentiles were circumcised and became Jews." Now circumcision is an ancient biblical practice, and was practiced by other peoples beside Israel; but in the Hellenistic world, circumcision was taken to be the distinctive sign of (male) Jewish identity. It was, along with the observance of the Sabbath and *kashrut* (especially the prohibition on the eating of pork), the most outstanding mark of the Jew in relation to other religions or nationalities.[66] In the same vein, we find Esther, in her prayer in Addition C, saying "I abhor the bed of the uncircumcised and of any alien" and that "Your servant has not eaten at Haman's table, and I have not honored the king's feast or drunk the wine of libations." The Septuagint has made Esther into a pious Jewess of the Hellenistic (early rabbinic) period, who disdains marriage with a non-Jew, eats only kosher food, and does not drink wine used for libations to pagan gods *(yein nesekh)*.

The Septuagint reflects Hellenistic times in another way—in its literary style and tone. On occasion, it seems to move in the direction of the style of the later Greek novels, with emotional and psychological dimensions that are absent in the Masoretic Text. This is most obvious in Addition D, when Esther goes to the king uninvited. She entered, adorned with majesty, leaning on the arms of her two maids. Her heart was frozen with fear, and the bedazzling sight of the king, in full array, covered with gold and precious stones, was terrifying. Then,

> Lifting his face, flushed with splendor, he looked at her in fierce anger. The queen faltered, and turned pale and faint, and collapsed on the head of the maid who went in front of her. Then God changed the spirit of the king to gentleness, and in alarm he sprang from his throne and took her in his arms until she came to herself. He comforted her with soothing words.

This is the stuff of Greek romances (and modern ones, too), and it is in utter contrast to the sparseness of the Masoretic Text at this point in the story. So, we may conclude that the Septuagint is, on one hand, more biblical than the Masoretic Text, but on the other hand it is more Hellenistic, both in respect to Jewish identity and practice and in respect to Hellenistic storytelling.

This description of how the Septuagint reshaped the story should make clear that it is a form of early biblical interpretation. The relationship between it and the Masoretic Text is not simply that of an original Hebrew text and its translation, although even a translation is a form of interpretation, since the translator must decide on the meanings of words and verses in order to translate them. But besides that, the Septuagint's translation of Esther has the added complication of diverging rather more from the Masoretic Text than do its translations of other biblical books. Of the 270 verses in the Septuagint, 107 find no parallel in the Masoretic Text.[67] The Greek translation, and presumably the Hebrew that lay behind it (which must have been different to some extent from the Hebrew of the Masoretic Text), shows that the form of the story of Esther was once more fluid, and the possibilities for interpreting it were correspondingly more flexible, than had been previously realized. As more and more scholars are coming to see, the early fluidity of the Hebrew text and the variety of ways that the

story was retold, in Hebrew or other languages, belong to the history of early Jewish biblical interpretation. The Septuagint is a window onto how Greek-speaking Jews of the early pre-Christian centuries read and understood the story of Esther.

Josephus's paraphrase of the Esther story in *The Antiquities of the Jews,* Book 11 Chapter 6, also in Greek, may be considered a third Greek account, or interpretation, written somewhat later (in the first century C.E., about a century after the Septuagint). Drawing on the Septuagint and on the Jewish exegetical works of his time (probably the Targum), Josephus retells the story in a way that served his own agenda. As L. Feldman points out, in *The Antiquities* Josephus tries to show the biblical precursors of the themes and personalities that he discussed in his *Jewish War.*[68] As a Jewish apologist, he sought to make Jewish values appear congruous with Greco-Roman values. He was especially concerned with combating the anti-Jewish stereotypes of his time and showing the Jews as tolerant of other religions, and therefore omits or minimizes details in the story that might make the Jews seem misanthropic or intolerant. For instance, he makes a strong point of identifying Haman as an Amalekite (the term is not used in the Masoretic Text or in the Septuagint) so that he can attribute Haman's hatred of the Jews to a family feud or personal grudge, rather than to the Jews' distinctiveness or misanthropy or to an eternal Jewish-gentile conflict.

Josephus's concern for law and order is manifest in his portrayal of Ahasuerus (who is in general more positive than in the Masoretic Text) as extremely law-abiding. Ahasuerus could not take Vashti back because the law forbade it. Vashti's refusal to appear before the king is attributed to a law that forbade women to be seen by strangers. Mordecai refused to bow to Haman because the laws of his own people forbade it. In other words, the motif of the Persian legal system, which in the Masoretic Text takes on elements of parody, is used and amplified by Josephus in a more serious and positive manner so as to conform with the Greco-Roman esteem for law and legal systems.

Like the Septuagint, Josephus adds romantic and dramatic elements to the story. His treatment of the scene in which Esther approaches the king unbidden is similar to the Septuagint's. Later, when Esther reveals that Haman is the enemy, Ahasuerus runs out of the room hastily because he is so perturbed. Upon returning, he calls Haman a "wretch, the vilest of mankind."

The many differences between Josephus and the extant versions of the story raise the question of whether there were different texts of the story in circulation that have not survived. Whether or not there were, it is clear that surrounding the Esther story there was, from early times, a body of interpretive lore that found its way into the Greek versions and Josephus, and, as we shall see, into rabbinic exegesis as well.

Rabbinic Interpretation

The Rabbis, like the author of the Septuagint, molded Esther to their own needs. But while the Septuagint's author was free to rewrite parts of the story, the Rabbis had a

fixed text from which they could not depart. Their "rewriting" was done in the form of midrashic exegesis on the text of the Masoretic Text. If, as we suggested above, the Septuagint made the story more biblical and more Hellenistic, then rabbinic interpretation made the story more biblical and more rabbinic.

There is a large body of midrashic interpretation on the Book of Esther.[69] The Babylonian Talmud contains a midrashic exposition of the entire book in B. Megillah 10b–17a (the only midrashic exposition of an entire biblical book to be incorporated into the Talmud).[70] There are two Aramaic translations of Esther, Targum Rishon and Targum Sheni.[71] They are among the most expansive of the *targumim,* and it is stretching a point to call them translations; they are better labeled midrashim. A number of midrashic collections have been preserved, including Esther Rabbah, Abba Gorion, Panim Aherim (two versions), Leqaḥ Tov, Midrash Megillat Ester, and Aggadat Ester.[72] Pirke de-Rabbi Eliezer, chapters 49–50, also contains material on Esther, as does Yalkut Shimoni. Midrash Shoḥer Tov, a midrash on psalms, also contains material on Esther in the chapter on Psalm 22. Seder Olam Rabbah devotes Chapter 29 to Esther. While these works span centuries, and, as one would expect, there are many differences among them, they share what E. Segal calls an "infrastructure of thematic and narrative assumptions" such that we can speak of a common exegetical tradition, which, according to Segal, probably took shape in the tannaitic period or before (first or second century C.E.—around or slightly after the time of Josephus).[73] Thus, the midrashim preserve a very old perspective on the story of Esther.

Like midrash in general, the midrashim on Esther seek to weave a particular passage, character, or episode into the fabric of the entire Bible and to make the meaning of the passage congruent with the values and practices of rabbinic Judaism. As part of Scripture, and as the authoritative text for Purim, the Book of Esther must be meaningful for a traditional Jewish community. The midrashim accomplish this by embellishing the text with fanciful episodes and dialogues that read between the lines, as it were—drawing the characters in sharper relief than the Bible does and constructing a literary and religious world around the text that is quite different from the world of the Masoretic Text's story. The midrashim are unabashedly anachronistic and delightfully fanciful. While the modern reader may look with indulgent amusement at some of the midrashic interpretations, we should understand how they make the text come alive within the framework of rabbinic Judaism. And, while it is unlikely that the Rabbis viewed Esther as a comedy, many of their comments add to the fun of reading the story.

Among the embellishments of the midrash are the vilification of Ahasuerus and Vashti. It was during the time of Ahasuerus that work on the rebuilding of the Temple was forbidden and it was on the advice of Vashti, who was the granddaughter of Nebuchadnezzar (the Babylonian king who destroyed Jerusalem), that the king had the work on the Temple brought to a halt. The golden vessels used for drinking at the king's party had been stolen from the Temple in Jerusalem. (Notice how these comments also bring the Book of Esther closer to the Books of Kings, Ezra, Nehemiah, and Daniel.) Mordecai and Esther, in contrast, are made more pious than in the Masoretic

Text. Neither would eat the food nor drink the wine served in the palace (compare the Septuagint, Addition C, which has Esther abstain from food and wine) and both observed the Sabbath. Additional concern with Jewish religious practice surfaces a number of times, for example, in Targum Rishon's comment at the end of chapter 8, where the Jews, besides feasting and rejoicing, were given permission to study Torah, observe Sabbaths and holidays, circumcise their sons, and put on phylacteries.

The Rabbis did not shy away from making prurient comments, which add to the negative characterization of the "villains" (and to the lewd enjoyment of the story): Vashti's party for the women was in the king's bedroom; she was ordered to appear naked before the king; and she was to be executed naked; Haman's daughter dumped the contents of a chamber pot on her father's head (see the Commentary to 6:12).

An example of how the midrash extends and enhances the text of the Masoretic Text in a way that seems to bring out its implicit meaning is the comment on how Haman arrayed Mordecai:

> Haman took the apparel and the horse and went to Mordecai. (Haman) said to him: Arise and put on the purple of the king. (Mordecai) said to him: Villain! Do you not know that for three days I have been wearing sackcloth and ashes, sitting in the ashes, because of what you have done to me? Now take me to the bath-house and afterwards I will put on the purple of the king. And he washed him and dressed him. (Haman) said to him: Mount and ride on the horse. He said to (Haman): On account of the affliction of the fast I have no strength to mount and ride on the horse. What did Haman do? He bent down, and Mordecai put his foot upon his neck, and he mounted and rode on the horse.[74]

In the scene that the midrash constructs, Haman is a greater villain and fool than in the biblical story, and is degraded even more. (According to Panim Aḥerim, there was no attendant in the bath-house so Haman had to scrub the bath himself.) The midrash makes explicit the dishonor that Haman must have felt he was receiving, and gives the clever Mordecai a more active role in bringing this dishonor upon him. This midrash is funny in its own way and has its own type of bodily humor. It is carnivalesque in its own right—a fitting complement to the carnivalesque story that it interprets.

Selections from the midrashim are interspersed throughout the commentary that follows. They obviously do not reflect the plain sense of the biblical story, but they enrich the reading of the story in an imaginative way.

Esther and Biblical Women

The question of what the Book of Esther has to say about women is a natural one in light of feminist interest in the Bible, but, despite the burgeoning literature on feminist biblical interpretation, surprisingly little detailed analysis has been written on Esther as a whole.[75] The way one views issues pertaining to gender will naturally be influenced by the type of feminist criticism one engages in (and there are many different types), and the methodologies for biblical criticism one espouses (here, too, there are many types).

My commentary aims at understanding the Book of Esther in its original setting in the Persian period and in the early Jewish communities that interpreted it—the Greek-speaking communities that produced the Greek versions and the rabbinic communities that bequeathed us their midrashim. Accordingly, I have not posed questions about the roles of women versus men, the relationships of sex and power that are in play in the story, and similar questions that reflect modern feminist ways of reading. I have also not attempted to relate Esther to the history or sociology of women in the Persian period. This is a study that should be done, and there is a growing body of relevant information, but it is beyond the scope of this commentary.[76] Nevertheless, a few comments about Esther and other women in biblical literature are in place here.

There are certainly a number of important, even heroic, women in the Bible: Eve, Sarah, Rebecca, Rachel, Tamar, Miriam, Deborah, and Abigail, to name the more famous ones. But, as it has been noted some years ago, while women like these may stand in the spotlight for a scene or two, the stories in which women appear are usually about men.[77] It is the male heroes, and few of them at that, who are the focal point of the great narrative block from Genesis through Kings: the patriarchs, Joseph, Moses, the kings. But when it comes to late biblical and apocryphal books, especially those that resemble fiction, the situation changes. Instead of one long continuous narrative we have shorter, self-contained narratives, and in a number of them women are the central characters. Most obvious is the Book of Ruth, now dated by most scholars to the Persian period, in which Ruth and Naomi completely eclipse the male characters. The Story of Susanna, part of the Additions to Daniel in the Apocrypha, also features a woman in a central role, standing against the men of the establishment, although her ultimate vindication comes from Daniel. Most heroic is Judith, in the apocryphal book by that name. Judith, using her brains, her feminine wiles, and her physical strength, single-handedly kills the enemy of Israel and saves her people. Esther is like Judith in that she, too, is responsible for saving her people from the enemy, but Esther does so in concert with Mordecai. The tendency to feature women in sustained roles continues in the pseudepigraphal book Joseph and Asenath and in the Greek romances. The point is that in terms of the prominence and potency of women characters, the Book of Esther is part of the late biblical and postbiblical trend to feature women characters in important roles, whether alone or together with male heroes.

It is not my purpose to analyze the female characters in the book, or the male characters either. I will, though, make a few points in what follows about how some of them may be interpreted.

Vashti is not meant to be a major character but her function is important nonetheless. She, like Orpah in the Book of Ruth, serves as a contrast to the main female character. Orpah was not wicked or inconsiderate; in returning to her family she followed Naomi's instructions and did the sensible thing. Ruth's actions stand out as extraordinary against this background.

But in what terms should the contrast between Vashti and Esther be made? Some would juxtapose Vashti's strength and assertiveness against Esther's passiveness and docility; but I think to do so misreads both women. Vashti, like Orpah, represents the

norm, the expected reaction in the situation in which these women find themselves. Of course Vashti should have refused to come at the king's call; his invitation was inappropriate and insulting. Her refusal was neither a sign of her stubborn disobedience (as her detractors would have it) nor of her independence or liberation (as her defenders see it). She simply did what any right-thinking queen would do. She tried to preserve her dignity in the face of a group of drunken men who had lost theirs.

Vashti's actions (a separate party for the women, her refusal to appear before the men) establish the standard for sexual behavior at court, which is violated by the king, overreacted to by his courtiers, and used by Esther for her own ends. The scene introduces the tone of bawdiness, which continues throughout the story and is a feature of its farcical nature. More important, it paves the way for Esther's entrance into the story and into the court. Without Vashti there would be no Esther. Vashti's point of view is never given. She does not speak, not because the author "silenced" her, but because the plot requires that we see her only through the eyes of men. Her absence—both her voluntary and her involuntary absence—is the most powerful aspect of her characterization. Her absence hovers over the plot: when Ahasuerus misses her and gets a new queen; when Esther dares to enter the king's inner court uninvited (an inversion of Vashti's refusal to appear when invited); and when the king accuses Haman of a sexual advance against Esther (the king is suddenly protecting the honor of the queen—he did the opposite to Vashti).

A woman with an even smaller role is Zeresh, the wife of Haman, who makes two brief appearances in 5:10–14 and 6:13. In the first case she and Haman's friends propose the impalement of Mordecai and in the second she and Haman's advisors predict Haman's downfall before Mordecai. In these vignettes the rivalry between Mordecai and Haman is encapsulated: Haman wishes to disgrace Mordecai but he will be disgraced by Mordecai. Zeresh and the friends are more clever than Haman, and more prescient. By comparison, Haman looks dull and inept.

Esther is clearly the star of the show, a role she shares with Mordecai. She emerges from two positions of weakness, as a ward of Mordecai and as a member of the king's harem. Both are very feminine roles, and they cast the woman as a dependent of men. Esther uses both positions to good advantage. To the extent that she "overcomes" the limitations of these positions of weakness she is heroic, not because she is a "liberated woman" seeking independence and autonomy, but because she moves from a low status to a high status. It is a form of the Cinderella motif. (Another low-status role for a woman is that of a prostitute, but this would hardly work in this plot.) By making her a "sex object" locked in the harem, and the surrogate daughter of Mordecai, the author is not trying to diminish the character of Esther; he is, rather, paving the way for her rise to the heights of Persian court life and to the ultimate model of a Diaspora Jewess who saves her people.

The similarities between the story of Esther and the story of Joseph are well known, but it is usually Mordecai who is compared with Joseph, since both are wise courtiers to a foreign king. But in chapter 2 it is Esther who resembles Joseph. In her harem "prison" she immediately finds favor in the eyes of the attendant Hegai, as did Joseph

in Gen. 39:21, and then in the eyes of others even up to the king, who rewards her with the highest possible position.

How passive is Esther vis à vis Mordecai? The common perception that Esther simply carried out Mordecai's instructions, even somewhat reluctantly, is shown to be mistaken when one reads closely. As I explain in the Commentary to chapter 4, Esther deserves credit for initiating the details of the plan that Mordecai advocated only in the most general terms. Mordecai told her to go to the king to plead for her people, but he did not tell her when or how to do it. It is Esther who plans and executes the strategy for informing the king and revealing the enemy. She engineers it beautifully, with narrative tension and dramatic flair. Her plan and its denouement form the bulk of the second part of the main plot; and Mordecai is absent throughout it.[78]

Who gets the credit for saving the Jews? Chapter 9, which presents many difficulties in interpretation, also shows confusion about the respective authority of Esther and Mordecai (especially at the end of the chapter, in the writing of the second Purim letter). In some measure they seem to share power, but at other times Mordecai overshadows or replaces Esther. It is here that one suspects that the role of a woman could not quite accommodate what was needed in the book. Not that a woman could not save her people! Women have been saving or preserving their people, in one way or another, throughout the Bible, and most obviously in the (slightly later) Book of Judith. But the purpose of chapter 9 is to verify the initiation of a new holiday, and that, it would seem, could not be authorized by a woman alone. To sum up, Mordecai and Esther are co-heroes, each contributing in ways that are congruent with their gender roles in the world of biblical narrative in the Persian period.

Notes to the Introduction

1. Fox, 22.
2. Ginsberg, 83.
3. Jones, "Two Misconceptions."
4. Radday and Brenner, 295–313; see also 71–72.
5. Halbertal, 26. Francis Landy makes a similar point in "Humour as a Tool for Biblical Exegesis" in Radday and Brenner, 102.
6. See Foster, and Radday and Brenner. Whedbee, *The Bible and the Comic Vision* has a definition of the comic that may be too broad to be meaningful in our discussion.
7. Charney, 97.
8. Abrams, 26.
9. *The Random House Dictionary of the English Language,* second edition, 1987.
10. Weisman, 139–63.
11. The distinction between satire and farce suggested by Davis (*Farce,* 86) is helpful: "[T]he comic spirit of farce is one which delights in taboo–violation, but which avoids implied moral comment or social criticism."
12. Davis, 62. This type of misunderstanding is not limited to comedy; it can be used in tragedy as well.
13. Davis, 63.
14. Charney, 76.
15. Charney, 80.
16. Davis, 23.
17. See Barber, *Shakespeare's Festive Comedy* and Bakhtin, *Rabelais and His World.*
18. Hoffner, "Text, Artifact, and Image: Revealing Ancient Israelite Religion."
19. Knox, 285–86.
20. Berg, *The Book of Esther,* 32.
21. Levenson, 1.

22. G. Cohn in Hakham, 11, notes that many of the passive phrases may be appropriately indirect because they are used in reference to royalty.

23. See Bentley, xx.

24. Sasson, 335.

25. Momigliano, *Essays in Ancient and Modern Historiography,* 27.

26. Bickerman, *Four Strange Books,* 181, 183, 193, 198, 200, 220. Bickerman also notes the similarities with motifs in other literatures.

27. For example, Grottanelli; Heltzer, "Mordekhai and Demaratos"; Hofmann and Vorbichler.

28. Tuplin, *Achaemenid Studies,* 164.

29. Wills, *The Jew in the Court of the Foreign King.*

30. Wills, *The Jew in the Court of the Foreign King,* 68.

31. For the dating of some of the later books of the Bible see below, "When and Where Was the Book of Esther Written?"

32. See above, "Why Was the Book of Esther Written?" and the Commentary to 9:31. A number of rabbinic comments bear on the relationship of Esther and of Purim to the Torah: "Forty-eight prophets and seven prophetesses prophesied to Israel and they neither took away nor added anything to what is written in the Torah except the reading of the Book of Esther" (B. Megillah 14a); "Moses told us that no prophet should add anything to the Law from now and henceforth; and yet Mordecai and Esther desired to create and establish a new institution" (J. Megillah 1:5, 7a); "In the world to come all the other parts of the Prophets and Writings will lose their worth and only the Torah of Moses and the Book of Esther will retain their value" (J. Megillah 1:7, 70d). (These passages are collected and translated in Rubenstein, 275–76.)

33. For recent comparisons see Berg, *The Book of Esther,* 123–42, and Gan, "Megilat 'Ester."

34. Buber, 103. The strong connection between Passover and Esther was called to my attention by Leah Kaplan-Samuels.

35. Jarden, 276. See also Gaster, *Purim and Hanukkah,* 81.

36. Buber, 98.

37. Frisch, "Bein megilat 'ester." Jeremiah Unterman also notes many of the same features in an unpublished paper entitled "The Influence of Kings on Esther."

38. Talmon, "'Wisdom' in the Book of Esther."

39. See Fox, 142–43, for a critique of Talmon's position.

40. Haggai and Zechariah 1–8 are dated to the first part of this period and Zechariah 9–14 and Malachi to the latter part.

41. Seow, 38.

42. Bergey, *The Book of Esther* and "Late Linguistic Features in Esther." A summary is found in A. Sáenz Badillos, 112–29.

43. See the articles by Waldbaum for the archeological evidence.

44. These passages are translated and discussed in Leiman, 106–7.

45. Haran, 201–75, especially 202–5, 225–26, 230–35.

46. For a summary of Purim in rabbinic sources see Tabory, *Mo'adei Yisra'el,* 323–67.

47. Talmon, "Was the Book of Esther Known at Qumran?"

48. White Crawford, "Has *Esther* Been Found at Qumran?"

49. Moore, *Daniel, Esther, and Jeremiah,* 160.

50. Beckwith, 291–94.

51. See Beckwith, 295–97 and Moore, xxv–xxix, for more details.

52. Summaries of the older theories of Purim's origin are supplied in Paton, 77–94 and of more recent ones in Rubenstein, 248–49.

53. Paton, 83–84. His rejection was due in part to his dating of Esther to the Maccabean period, when he assumed that the Jews would reject anything of Greek origin.

54. See B. M. Knox, "Athenian Religion and Literature."

55. Bickerman, "The Colophon."

56. Josephus omits Haman's casting a lot. Dorothy, 224, cites the variants of the name in the Septuagint manuscripts. He raises the possibility that these divergent spellings may attest different translations in different communities from a term that was originally Aramaic.

57. The Masoretic Text has its own problems connected with the date on which the lot fell. Haman's lot falls on the month of Adar, according to 3:7, but no date is given there. The date of 13 Adar appears only in 3:13.

58. Fox, 152. See also Fisch, "Reading and Carnival."

59. For a wealth of information on Purim customs see Goodman, 321–422, and Rubenstein, "Purim."

60. Fisch, "Reading and Carnival," 69.

61. See *Encyclopedia Judaica* 13: 1395–1400 and Goodman, 14–37.

62. See the works of Clines, Day, De Troyer, Dorothy, Fox, *The Redaction of the Books of Esther,* and Jobes.

63. For a discussion of the characterization of Esther in the Masoretic Text and the Greek versions see Day, *Three Faces of a Queen.*

64. Clines, 169–74.

65. Frye, "Minorities in the History of the Near East."

66. See Schäfer, 93–105.

67. *ABD* V, 1101.

68. Feldman, 539. See 500–38 for a discussion of the Book of Esther. See also Feldman's article on Josephus in *ABD* III, 981–98.

69. For bibliography see Walfish, *Esther in Medieval Garb,* 245 note 63. For an English compilation see Ginzberg, IV, 363–448.

70. The critical edition in English is Segal, *The Babylonian Esther Midrash.*

71. See the editions and translation by Grossfeld.

72. Buber, *Sifrei De-'agadta',* contains Abba Gorion, Panim Aḥerim (versions A and B), and Leqaḥ Tov. Midrash Megillat Ester is in Horowitz, 417–75. Buber, *Aggadat Ester.*

73. Segal, *The Babylonian Esther Midrash,* I, 20.

74. Friedlander, 404; variations on this pericope occur in Panim Aḥerim and elsewhere.

75. See the works by Bal, Beal, Brenner, Day, Gendler, LaCocque, *The Feminine Unconventional,* Lubitch, Niditch, "Short Stories," and White, "Esther: A Feminine Model for Jewish Diaspora." Fox, 205–11, reviews and critiques the pre-1991 feminist readings of the Book of Esther. He calls the author of Esther "something of a protofeminist" and observes that this is the only book in the Bible "with a conscious and sustained interest in sexual politics" (209).

76. For example, see Brosius, Sancici-Weerdenburg, "Exit Atossa," and T. Eskenazi, 25–43.

77. Bird, "Images of Women in the Old Testament," in Ruether, 41.

78. For more on Esther's role as an active character, see Fox, 199–202.

THE COMMENTARY TO
ESTHER

Wine and Women

Chapter 1 serves as the prologue to the story. A prologue is not part of the main plot or action, but it is certainly part of the story and is essential for setting the scene and motivating the plot. Chapter 1 sets the tone of the book, and it is a tone of excess, buffoonery, and bawdiness. It portrays the Persian court in all its decadent lavishness, and, with a hint of mockery so at home in burlesque, it paints a picture of a bumbling king and his overly ambitious courtiers. Most important, it paves the way for Esther's entrance into the story through the Vashti incident.

Chapter 1 also foreshadows the types of actions and reactions that will figure prominently in the main plot. The scene in which the king is so easily persuaded to issue a ridiculous edict, published posthaste, prepares us for the main plot, when we again see the king casually giving approval for an unreasonable edict against the Jews and revving up his extensive communications network to publicize it. A sense of this chapter's foreshadowing, and also of the reversals on which the plot is constructed, is neatly encapsulated in the midrashic identification of "that Ahasuerus" (1:1):

> Ahasuerus who put his wife [Vashti] to death on account of his friend [Memucan, who is identified with Haman], is the same Ahasuerus who put his friend [Haman] to death on account of his wife [Esther]. (Esther Rabbah 1.1 and Targum Sheni)

Wine: Party Time in Persia   (vv. 1:1–8)

Through elaborate description of detail, the reader is taken into the Persian court, known in the ancient world for its opulence. After the notice of the time and place, the description moves to the banquets, whose main purpose seems to have been, as far as our story is concerned, to provide an opportunity for the king to display his wealth. We are apprised of the guest list and shown the banquet hall. The description of the hall is a marvel of texture and color, as it guides the reader's eyes from ceiling to floor: draperies and columns, couches, and mosaic floor, all of the finest materials. Then the narrative focuses on the drinking vessels—the Persian equivalent of china and crystal—equally exquisite. From the drinking vessels it is but a small step to the wine, and here we move closer to the action, for it was when he was happy with wine that the king gave the order that set in motion the events of the story.

The description of the setting is atypical of biblical narrative, not because the Bible lacks physical descriptions, but because it does not generally use them to set a scene. Descriptions like those of Solomon's Temple and Ezekiel's vision of the "chariot," which bear some similarities to our passage, constitute main narratives, not introductions to main narratives. The Temple is described in 1 Kings 6–7 step by step as it was built because the narrative is about the building of the Temple. Similarly, the prophet's vision is the main topic of Ezekiel 1 and vividly recounts Ezekiel's first prophetic experience.

The opening description in Esther is more typical of late biblical and apocryphal books of the Persian and Greek periods, and of some Greek romances from a slightly later period (which often describe banquet scenes). It may be compared with the opening of the Book of Judith, which also begins with a notice of the regnal date and proceeds to a detailed description, replete with measurements, of the fortifications of Ecbatana.

As in Judith, the description in Esther contains many numbers—perhaps more than one would expect: the number of provinces and the number of days of each banquet. At first, these numbers may seem to lend a sense of historical precision, but upon reflection they appear inflated and may be more accurately interpreted as contributing to the tone of excess and exaggeration that permeates the chapter. Their placement at the ends of their verses (in the Hebrew) emphasizes their magnitude. The language of the chapter, heavy with duplication, interrupting and turning back on itself, adds to the desired effect of excess.

The decor that makes an impression on the reader of Esther is very similar to the Persian accoutrements that impressed the classical authors. They speak often of gold and silver furniture and furnishings, sometimes ornamented with gems, and cups of gold and silver. Horse trappings, weapons, and armor were also gold or gilded. What most impressed the classical authors was the Persian textiles, many of which the Persians themselves considered valuable enough to be kept in the royal treasuries.[1] The classical authors mention, among other objects, purple-dyed rugs; hangings embroidered with gold thread; hangings with animal patterns; purple garments with gold embroidery; garments studded with jewels or gold beads; and brilliantly colored clothing.

The Greeks were also impressed by Persian banquets, which were in their eyes one of the outstanding traits of Persian social life that stood in marked contrast to Greek life. Greek descriptions of these banquets are quite similar to the Book of Esther's, with an emphasis on the quantity and luxury of the dinnerware and the food and drink consumed (they mention glass vessels in addition to gold and silver ones, and a variety of meats).

Persian banquets had a precedent in Assyrian banquets, one of which is described in an inscription of Ashurnasirpal II. From it we see that Ahasuerus was not the only king to indulge in big parties. On the occasion of the dedication of his palace at Calah, Ashurnasirpal II made a banquet consisting of large amounts of meat, fowl, fish, eggs, bread, beer, vegetables, condiments, and other delicacies (described in detail, with the quantities noted). He goes on to say:

> I treated for ten days with food and drink 47,074 persons, men and women, who were bid to come from across my entire country, (also) 5,000 important persons, delegates from the country Suhu ... 16,000 inhabitants of Calah from all ways of life, 1,500 officials of all my palaces, altogether 69,574 invited guests from all the ... countries including the people of Calah. I provided them with the means to clean and anoint themselves. I did them due honors and sent them back, healthy and happy, to their own countries.[2]

Persian banquets are more than just fancy dinner parties. By virtue of their large guest lists, menus, and furnishings, they represent the diversity of the empire, its wealth, and the king's control over it. The king's table was supplied by food from provinces throughout the empire, as a form of gift or tribute (in Greek texts, banquets and tribute are mentioned side by side). Not all the food was eaten at the dinner; large quantities were given to the guests to take home, or were distributed to the army and officials as a form of payment. In this way, tribute from the provinces was redistributed. The royal banquet, then, was an important economic and political institution.[3] Satraps and governors had similar banquets in their home provinces. Compare Neh. 5:14–18.

1 It happened in the days of Ahasuerus—that Ahasuerus who reigned over a hundred and twenty-

א וַיְהִ֖י בִּימֵ֣י אֲחַשְׁוֵר֑וֹשׁ ה֣וּא
אֲחַשְׁוֵרֹ֗ושׁ הַמֹּלֵךְ֙ מֵהֹ֣דּוּ וְעַד־כּ֔וּשׁ שֶׁ֖בַע

1. *It happened in the days of* This phrase, seeming to set the story in a precise time in the Persian period, lends a quasi-historical air to the book. But, although it seems perfectly natural to open a narrative in this manner, it is actually relatively rare. Biblical narratives commonly begin with "it happened" but omit "in the days of." On the other hand, prophetic writings are often introduced as having occurred "in the days of King X." Actually, the opening is more like the opening of a folktale, with the aura of "Once upon a time, in the days of the great and glorious Ahasuerus, King of the vast Persian empire . . . ."

A common midrashic explanation (e.g., Targum Sheni) of the phrase notes that three other narratives open with these words: "It happened in the days of Amraphel" (Gen. 14:1), "It happened in the days of Ahaz" (Isa. 7:1), and "It happened in the days when the judges judged" (Ruth 1:1). The Rabbis, seeking significance in this particular usage, find that the sound of the word *vay-hi* signals trouble and woe.

Ahasuerus The name is usually identified with Persian *xšhayāršhā*, Xerxes, although the Septuagint and the Peshitta read Artaxerxes. The historical Xerxes I reigned from 486–465 B.C.E. and Artaxerxes I from 465–424 B.C.E.. Modern historians credit the historical Xerxes with substantial administrative and military accomplishments, although he was defeated by the Greeks in a series of battles between 485–479 B.C.E..

However, it would be a mistake to equate the Ahasuerus of Esther with a historical figure. Ahasuerus is no more a real historical personage than the obviously pseudo-historical "king of Nineveh" in Jonah or "Darius the Mede" in Daniel. These impossible royal personages are indicators of a fictional mode.[4] But even when the names and titles are real, the portrayal of the characters bearing those names may not be, for historical personalities take on fictive personas in literature. In Greek sources, Xerxes is portrayed as cruel, corrupt, and decadent; he is the image of the Asiatic despot as he ushers in the decline of the Persian empire. It is no accident, of course, that the Greeks portrayed him in this way, for he was the king who fought against Greece in an unsuccessful attempt to conquer it. The Greek attitude toward Xerxes is complex and ambivalent: he is the enemy and "the other," representing a culture antithetical to Greek culture; at the same time he is a worthy opponent, master of a world empire, and there is a certain fascination with him and his court . The Jewish experience with Xerxes was quite different from the Greek, but to the extent that the literary motif of Xerxes circulated widely throughout the Mediterranean world, the Jews could have adopted it for their own purpose, as they did so many other motifs.[5]

If the author of Esther was looking for a character to play the role of a Persian king of great power and great ineptitude, he could not do better than Xerxes in his literary incarnation. Ahasuerus is portrayed in this chapter and throughout most of the book as a figurehead who is concerned with the trappings of power but who, in reality, exercises little leadership or authority. He emerges as a comic and somewhat pathetic figure, easily manipulated by his courtiers—inept but not evil.[6] The Rabbis, who regularly rewrite biblical characters so as to exaggerate either their virtue or wickedness, equate Ahasuerus with the Ahasuerus of Ezra 4:6 and accuse him of preventing the completion of the Second Temple.[7] The king is a much more evil character in rabbinic sources.

that Ahasuerus who reigned A parenthetical comment that interrupts the main clause, pinpointing with more detail the description of the king. It is not a question of identifying which Ahasuerus this is (as if there were other kings by the same name), but rather of delineating the extent of his sovereignty.[8] This was an Ahasuerus who reigned

seven provinces from India to Ethiopia. ²In those
days, when King Ahasuerus occupied the royal throne

וְעֶשְׂרִ֥ים וּמֵאָ֖ה מְדִינָֽה׃ ² בַּיָּמִ֖ים הָהֵ֑ם
כְּשֶׁ֣בֶת ׀ הַמֶּ֣לֶךְ אֲחַשְׁוֵר֗וֹשׁ עַ֚ל כִּסֵּ֣א

over an enormous empire. The clause also gives the sense that the narrator is at some
distance in time from the events of his story.

from India to Ethiopia The extent of the great Persian empire, from east to west.
(In the Hebrew, this phrase precedes the notice of the number of provinces.) The province
of India (Persian, Hi[n]dush; Hebrew, Hodu) was added to the empire by Darius, the
predecessor of Xerxes. Compare the Darius inscriptions from Persepolis, which open: "Says
Darius the king: This is the kingdom/kingship which I hold, from the Saka beyond Sugda to
Kusha, and from Hi(n)dush to Sparda." The extent of the empire is described by mentioning
the provinces at its four corners, northeast to southwest and southeast to northwest. Kusha
and Hi(n)dush, therefore, represent the southwestern and southeastern limits of the
empire. Kusha (Hebrew, Kush; English, Ethiopia) is the land south of Egypt. Hi(n)dush
is located in the Indus valley, in the modern province of Sind, in southern Pakistan.

The same mode and purpose of describing the extent of the empire is found in
Xenophon, *Cyropaedia* 8.8.1:

> That Cyrus's empire was the greatest and most glorious of all the kingdoms in
> Asia—of that it may be its own witness. For it was bounded on the east by the
> Indian Ocean, on the north by the Black Sea, on the west by Cyprus and Egypt,
> and on the south by Ethiopia.

The Bible's phrase "from India to Ethiopia" echoes in part the Persian and Greek
manner of describing the empire. At the same time it is at home in biblical style, for the
pattern "from *x* to *y*" to show extent is common throughout the Bible (for example, "from
Dan to Beersheba" in 1 Sam. 3:20). See also 1:5 and 3:13.

a hundred and twenty-seven provinces There is confusing and seemingly
contradictory information in the Persian, Greek, and biblical sources about the terminology for the subdivisions of the Persian empire and their number. Persian royal
inscriptions, seeking to show the expanse of the empire, list the provinces (Persian *dahyu,*
plural *dahyava*). These *dahyava,* numbering between twenty and thirty-two, represent
ethnogeographic districts and are not administrative units. Herodotus 3.89–96 lists twenty
satrapies organized in the time of Darius for purposes of administration and taxation, but
most scholars do not view these satrapies as synonymous with the Persian *dahyava.* The
Greek equivalent of *dahyu* is *ethnos,* and Herodotus mentions that several *ethnoi* were
combined for taxation purposes into one satrapy. The Persian term for satrap, rendered in
Hebrew as *'ahashdarpan* (OP *xshathrapavan*), occurs in Dan. 6:2 (where the number of
satraps is given as 120) and in Esther 3:12 and 8:9.

The term *medinah* represents a district within a satrapy; that is, a province.⁹ *Medinah* is
roughly synonymous with *dahyu* and *ethnos,* but see below at verse 22.

Whether or not the number 127 (as in Esther and also 1 Esd. 3:1, imitating Esther) or
120 (as in Daniel) corresponds to an actual number of provinces, the large number may
have become a convention in Jewish writings. Here it adds to the impression of the
vastness of the empire and the tone of exaggeration.¹⁰

2. In those days This phrase returns the reader to the main clause in verse 1. It
also adds to the impression that the narrator is removed in time from the story. This sense
of distance is reinforced by the explanatory phrases in 1:8 and 1:13.

occupied the royal throne The phrase is redundant and has been interpreted in
several ways. Since there were four Persian capitals—Susa, Ecbatana (Hamadan), Babylon,
and Persepolis—the phrase may indicate that the king was now in residence in Susa.

in the fortress Shushan, ³ in the third year of his reign, he gave a banquet for all the officials and courtiers—

מַלְכוּתוֹ אֲשֶׁר בְּשׁוּשַׁן הַבִּירָה: ³ בִּשְׁנַת שָׁלוֹשׁ לְמָלְכוֹ עָשָׂה מִשְׁתֶּה לְכָל־שָׂרָיו

Several traditional and modern commentators have suggested that the phrase means that the king sat securely on his throne, after having put down uprisings in Egypt. Or, the phrase may be seen as simply another example of the repetition that characterizes the book's style. The literary effect of the phrase is to reinforce the notion of royalty. The term *m-l-k,* "to rule" appears four times in the first three verses, emphasizing the royal reign of Ahasuerus. Ironically, this king was ruled by his courtiers.

In a more fanciful vein, several rabbinic midrashim explain that Ahasuerus wished to sit upon the throne of Solomon, the vicissitudes of which are recounted at length. Since Ahasuerus was unable to do so, he commissioned his architects to fashion one like it. They failed to duplicate the throne but produced an inferior one. Their work took two years, and in the third year Ahasuerus sat on his new throne. The midrashim elaborate on the theme of the throne, describing its jeweled inlays and the six steps leading up to it, with lions and eagles (or other animals) on each step. The Purim Panel in the third-century C.E. synagogue at Dura Europus illustrates the steps (although there are fewer than six) with lions and eagles. (The paintings at Dura often reflect the midrash.)

the fortress Shushan   Susa. Once the capital of Elam and then conquered by Cyrus in 539 B.C.E., Susa was chosen by Darius I (521–485) as the site of the main administrative capital of the Persian empire and the king's winter residence (or spring residence; cf. Xenophon, *Cyropaedia* 8.6.22). In the Greek sources, Susa is the only reported destiny of Greek embassies and, in the eyes of the Greeks, is the hub of the Persian empire.[11]

Darius built a fortified royal city to the west, on an acropolis, while to the east lay the unfortified lower city where the populace resided. The two parts of the city were separated by a canal. This bifurcation is reflected in the terminology in Esther, where "the fortress Shushan" refers to the royal city and "Shushan" or "the city of Shushan" refers to the lower city. The Hebrew term for fortress, *birah,* is related to Akkadian *birtu.*

The palace complex, along with its courtyards and gardens, dominated the royal city. The Foundation Charters at Susa (inscriptions on tablets deposited in the foundation of Darius's palace buildings) describe its construction and record the importation of materials (expensive woods, precious stones, gold, silver, ivory, and ebony) and skilled craftsmen from all parts of the empire. The palace was intended to be an impressive sight, and the description in Esther shows that it was, indeed, perceived as a magnificent edifice.

Being the administrative center of the empire, orders went out from Susa to the provinces and reports from the provinces came to Susa. Many government embassies would come from distant provinces on official business.

3.   The occasion for the banquet is not specified. Ibn Ezra prefers to see it as the celebration of the king's marriage to Vashti, presumably by analogy with 2:18, the party for the coronation of Esther. The Septuagint also regards it as a marriage feast. Herodotus 9.110 notes that the Persian king celebrated his birthday each year with an elaborate dinner at which gifts were distributed. Perhaps this was not literally his birthday, but a fixed date on which he commemorated his coronation.[12] It is also possible that the king was celebrating the inauguration of a new capital, as, for example, Ashurnasirpal II celebrated his new capital at Calah with a lavish feast.[13]

The Persian palaces at Persepolis and Susa had large assembly halls (Persian: *apadana*) separate from the royal residence that were used for receiving embassies from throughout the empire. Reliefs depicting these assemblies—representatives from different provinces bearing gifts—decorated the walls. These reliefs may be correlated with the Greek

the administration of Persia and Media, the nobles and the governors of the provinces in his service. ⁴ For no fewer than a hundred and eighty days he displayed the vast riches of his kingdom and the splendid glory of his majesty. ⁵ At the end of this period, the king gave a banquet for seven days in the court of the king's palace garden for all the people who lived in

וַעֲבָדָיו חֵיל ׀ פָּרַס וּמָדַי הַפַּרְתְּמִים וְשָׂרֵי הַמְּדִינוֹת לְפָנָיו: ⁴ בְּהַרְאֹתוֹ אֶת־עֹשֶׁר כְּבוֹד מַלְכוּתוֹ וְאֶת־יְקָר תִּפְאֶרֶת גְּדוּלָּתוֹ יָמִים רַבִּים שְׁמוֹנִים וּמְאַת יוֹם: ⁵ וּבִמְלוֹאת ׀ הַיָּמִים הָאֵלֶּה עָשָׂה הַמֶּלֶךְ לְכָל־הָעָם הַנִּמְצְאִים בְּשׁוּשַׁן הַבִּירָה

descriptions and together they both show that the royal table was of central significance in the political ideology of Persia. The number of guests could be very large, according to some Greek sources. It was a mark of high status to be seated at the king's table. Indeed, the groups of guests mentioned in this verse constitute the elite of Persian society.

administration of Persia and Media   The word *ḥeil* here refers to the free men in Persia and Media proper (not in the other provinces). They had special privileges and were given grants of land by the king. The Persian term is *kara*. Compare the use of *ḥayil* in *'ish gibor ḥayil,* "a man of substance" in Ruth 2:1 and *'eshet ḥayil,* "a wife appropriate for a man of substance" in Prov. 31:10.

Others interpret *ḥayil* as the officers of the army. They, too, were included in the distribution of provisions from the king's table, whether or not they were actually seated among the guests.

Persia and Media   Persia and the Media were originally separate kingdoms, although ethnically related. They were united in the person of Cyrus I, who had both Median and Persian ancestry. Persia and Media comprised the core of the Persian Achaemenid empire. This is the usual order for the names although sometimes the order is reversed.

nobles   Hebrew *partemim* is borrowed from Persian *fratama.*

governors of the provinces   Local leaders of the provinces and districts were recognized by the crown and were permitted to retain their authority, serving under the satraps, who were usually Persian. The reliefs in the assembly halls identify the governors and representatives from various provinces in the empire by their distinctive dress.

4.   A true case of conspicuous consumption. The party lasted for six months (often compared with the 120 days of feasting in Jth. 1:16) and the display of wealth is mentioned twice. It is difficult to know whether this is intended to give authentic flavor to the story or to poke fun at the decadence of Ahasuerus's court. Greek sources also note the lavishness of Persian banquets.

5.   After the first banquet there was a shorter one, lasting a week, for the residents of the royal city. Excavations at Susa have confirmed that there was a lightly populated residential area in the royal city. The Rabbis take pains to note that only Jews disloyal to their tradition attended this banquet (where nonkosher food and wine were served) and that Mordecai and his associates were not among them.

in the court of the king's palace garden   The party was not inside the palace but in the court of the garden where there was a *bitan,* a colonnaded pavilion used as a banquet hall. The word *bitan* derives from the Akkadian *bitānu,* for the practice of having a garden and a pavilion on the palace grounds originated with the Assyrians.¹⁴ This party was held outdoors to accommodate the large crowd, and the furnishings described in the next verse were in the court. (Compare the smaller banquet in 7:7–8 held in the pavilion.) According

the fortress Shushan, high and low alike. ⁶ [There were hangings of] white cotton and blue wool, caught up by cords of fine linen and purple wool to silver rods and alabaster columns; and there were couches of gold and silver on a pavement of marble, alabaster, mother-of-pearl, and mosaics. ⁷ The drinking-ware was golden beakers, beakers of varied design. And there was

לְמִגָּד֖וֹל וְעַד־קָטָ֑ן מִשְׁתֶּ֛ה שִׁבְעַ֥ת יָמִ֖ים
בַּחֲצַ֕ר גִּנַּ֥ת בִּיתַ֖ן הַמֶּֽלֶךְ׃ ⁶ ח֣וּר ׀ כַּרְפַּ֣ס
וּתְכֵ֗לֶת אָחוּז֙ בְּחַבְלֵי־ב֣וּץ וְאַרְגָּמָ֔ן עַל־
גְּלִילֵ֥י כֶ֖סֶף וְעַמּ֣וּדֵי שֵׁ֑שׁ מִטּ֣וֹת ׀ זָהָ֣ב וָכֶ֗סֶף
עַ֛ל רִֽצְפַ֥ת בַּהַט־וָשֵׁ֖שׁ וְדַ֥ר וְסֹחָֽרֶת׃
⁷ וְהַשְׁקוֹת֙ בִּכְלֵ֣י זָהָ֔ב וְכֵלִ֖ים מִכֵּלִ֥ים

to Josephus's version of the story, the king had a tent pitched, supported by gold and silver pillars, with curtains of linen and purple, so that tens of thousands of guests could be seated. This is perhaps influenced by the Tent of Xerxes, described in Herodotus 9.82. This tent was taken into battle against the Greeks and left to Mardonius when Xerxes fled. It was lavish in its size and appointments, with gold and silver and gaily-colored tapestries, gold and silver couches, tables, and banquet service.

Persian royal gardens were often cited by the Greeks as one of the signs of Persian luxury. They used the term derived from Persian—*paradeisoi* (whence the word "paradise"). Esther does not employ this term (although it occurs in Eccles. 2:5; Neh. 2:8; Song 4:13), but the same setting is intended. These gardens, whose history began under the kings of Assyria, were large parks with trees, wild animals, and sources of water. Targum Rishon elaborates on the theme by describing the garden as being planted with fruit-bearing trees and spices half overlaid with gold and with a setting of gems covering them. The colorful decorations described in verse 6 were pictured as jewels hanging from the trees.

high and low alike   Hebrew: "from the greatest to the least." This party was for all the residents and was not limited to the elite, as the first party was. The phrase is not unusual and signifies the totality of people, but in this context it may also hint at the consciousness of social hierarchy, a trait that the Greeks associated with the Persians.

6.   The Hebrew text employs several rare terms, adding to the exotic effect. Compare 8:15.

butz ve-'argaman   *butz* means "fine white linen" and is here combined with *'argaman* in a hendiadys meaning "fine purple linen."

7. golden beakers   Another opportunity to display opulence. The Persians were known in the Greek writings for their use of glass and metal drinking vessels. According to Ctesias, those favored by the king would receive gold and silver vessels, and those not favored would receive earthenware vessels. Compare also Dan. 5:2 when Belshazzar, under the influence of wine, displayed the treasures his father had looted from the Temple and used the golden goblets as drinking vessels. Our story makes no reference to the Temple or any religious impropriety; Ahasuerus is merely acting in the way of wealthy foreign monarchs.

beakers of varied design   The variety is another indication of luxury since it suggests the work of many artisans from different places with different techniques. It is known that craftsmen from throughout the empire, each an expert in the techniques of his locality, were brought together in the royal workshops. The Achaemenids were especially accomplished in their metal and glass products. Or, the vessels may have been gifts sent to the court from far-flung provinces.

Many of the midrashim interpret this expression to mean that no one used the same cup twice. A more fanciful midrashic explanation, taking *shonim* as "different, changing," is that the beakers were different from the other royal vessels because they had been taken

royal wine in abundance as befits a king. ⁸ And the rule
for the drinking was, "No restrictions!" For the king
had given orders to every palace steward to comply

שׁוֹנִ֔ים וְיֵ֥ין מַלְכ֖וּת רָ֑ב כְּיַ֖ד הַמֶּֽלֶךְ׃
⁸ וְהַשְּׁתִיָּ֥ה כַדָּ֖ת אֵ֣ין אֹנֵ֑ס כִּי־כֵ֣ן ׀ יִסַּ֣ד
הַמֶּ֗לֶךְ עַ֚ל כָּל־רַ֣ב בֵּית֔וֹ לַעֲשׂ֖וֹת כִּרְצ֥וֹן

from Solomon's Temple; and in the presence of the Temple vessels, the Persian vessels lost
their brilliance and turned to lead (or conversely, that the Temple vessels changed their
appearance to lead).

there was royal wine in abundance, as befits a king Persian parties were famous
for their sumptuous repasts and especially for their consumption of wine. Persian wine-
drinking is described by Herodotus (1.133).

> They are extremely fond of wine, and they are not supposed to vomit or urinate
> when anyone else can see. Although they have to be careful about all that, it is
> usual for them to be drunk when they are debating the most important issues.
> However, any decision they reach is put to them again on the next day, when they
> are sober, by the head of the household where the debate takes place; if they still
> approve of it when they are sober, it is adopted, but otherwise they forget about it.
> And any issues they debate when sober are reconsidered by them when they are
> drunk.

The quality and quantity of the wine is part of the display of wealth. Moreover, the
emphasis is on wine here and in the next verse for under its influence the king will soon
issue a command that will set the entire plot in motion.

8. the rule for the drinking Hebrew *dat,* "rule," is a Persian loan-word (*data,*
"law") used throughout the book in reference to royal decisions and decrees, and in the
broader sense of practice or custom. The Septuagint adds "not" before "rule," because
according to some interpretations the normal rule or custom was not followed. That may
mean that the wine normally reserved "by royal law" for the exclusive use of the king was
served to the guests.¹⁵ The phrase *ha-shetiyah ka-dat 'ein 'ones* is then better translated "As
for drinking according to the rule, no one enforced it."

no restrictions I prefer the interpretation just given—that the drinking of the
royal wine was not restricted to the king; but most commentaries take this as a reference to
the amount of wine: each man could drink as much or as little as he liked. Modern
interpreters generally emphasize that each person could drink his fill, there being no limit
to the amount of wine served. Ancient and medieval exegetes, and some moderns, tend to
see it in reverse: the usual practice was for the guests to drink whenever the king drank, or
to be obligated to drink continuously, whereas on this occasion each man could set his own
limit.

each man's wishes There is a certain irony in the juxtaposition of "law" and
"complying with each man's wishes."¹⁶ Indeed, the concern with Persian law becomes an
ironic topos throughout the book, through the pretext of legalities that are then
subverted.

The autonomy of each man, paramount at the party, is, in Memucan's view, under
attack when Vashti refuses to make an appearance.

with each man's wishes. ⁹In addition, Queen Vashti   ‫אִישׁ־וָאִישׁ: 9 גַּם וַשְׁתִּי הַמַּלְכָּה עָשְׂתָה‬

Women: The Vashti Incident   (vv. 1:9–22)

This scene has an aura of debauchery and lewdness, although it is not as explicitly bawdy as some of the rabbinic exegetes made it seem. The Greek authors, who also tell more risqué stories than Esther, supply us with several episodes that incorporate themes of which the Vashti incident partakes. They will help us understand why the king summoned Vashti and why she refused to come. I have identified four relevant themes, which I call: (1) Nice queens don't go to drinking parties; (2) How to show off your wife's beauty to other men; (3) Persian lechery; (4) The chaste concubine—or, just say "No."

(1) Plutarch, in his "Advice to Bride and Groom," says:

> The lawful wives of the Persian kings sit beside them at dinner, and eat with them. But when the kings wish to be merry and get drunk, they send their wives out and send for their dancing girls and concubines. They are right in what they do because they do not concede any share in their licentiousness and debauchery to their wedded wives. (*Moralia* 140 B 16)

Indeed, there are other Greek references to the fact that ladies of the nobility did not drink with their men. That is why Vashti held a separate party for the women. It seems clear that the ancient reader would have known that Ahasuerus's summons was improper. Perhaps he wouldn't have invited Vashti had he not been merry with wine.

(2) Ahasuerus summoned Vashti in order to display her beauty to all the men at the party. This has reminded several exegetes of the Candaules story, told by Herodotus (1.8). Candaules was so taken with the physical beauty of his own wife that he wanted others to see it. So he coerced one of his bodyguards, Gyges, to see the wife as she was undressing, in a way that she would not know that someone was observing her. But she found out and was furious at having been shamed in this way. She got her revenge by forcing Gyges to choose between killing Candaules or being killed himself. He chose to save his own life.

The motif of seeing a naked woman is not explicit in the Vashti incident, although some indecency may be implied. The Midrash, leaving nothing to the imagination, supplies the missing nudity by explaining that when Ahasuerus ordered Vashti to come wearing the royal crown, she was not to be wearing anything else.[17]

(3) A tale closer in tone and substance to the Vashti episode is the tale of Amyntas, a Macedonian who was hosting Persian messengers from the victorious Darius. It is recounted by Herodotus (5.18).

> After the meal, over the wine, the Persians said, "Macedonian ally, in Persia it is customary for us to bring in our concubines and wives to join us at the close of important meals. You have made us so very welcome, you are entertaining us so lavishly,...let's see you observe this custom of ours."
>
> "My friends from Persia," Amyntas replied, "that is not the way we do things here: we keep men and women separate. But since you are our masters, if that's what you want, you shall have it." And with these words Amyntas sent for the women.
>
> The women came in response to his summons and sat in a row opposite the Persians. When the Persians saw how beautiful the women were they told Amyntas that what he had done was quite stupid; it would have been better, they

said, for the women not to have come in the first place than to come and not sit next to them, but opposite them where they were a torment to the eyes. Amyntas had no choice but to tell the women to go and sit next to the Persians. As soon as the women did so, the Persians, who were exceedingly drunk, began to touch their breasts, and one or another of them would even try to embrace them.

Amyntas's son was not about to let the Persians get away with this indecent and insulting behavior. In the sequel, he urges the drunken Persians to rest for awhile and let the women go out and freshen up. He promises that the women will rejoin them soon, but in the interim, he substitutes smooth-chinned Macedonian warriors, dressed in women's clothing, with hidden daggers. The "women" take their seats beside each Persian, and as soon as the Persians begin to lay hands on them, the warriors dispatch their guests with their daggers.

The scene in Esther shares the voyeuristic tone of the first part of the Greek tale. It is a scene in which a gathering of rich drunken men want to get a look at the queen. The Persians in Esther also seem lecherous, but more subtly so. The scene in Esther is burlesque in both the literary and the common definition (as discussed in the Introduction). While there are obvious differences in the stories, the Greek, too, may contain burlesque elements as it pokes fun, both at the Macedonians, whom Herodotus considered country bumpkins who did not know Persian ways, and at the Persians, who do not recognize men in drag.

On the surface, this story appears to contradict the distinction Plutarch made between wives and concubines. But the Amyntas story seems calculated to portray the Persians as deceitful victimizers of Greek women, whether they be concubines or wives, and the cause of shame to their host. The presence of "wedded wives" makes the Persians' behavior all the more indecent, for it goes against their own custom. Notice that Herodotus does not report the practice concerning wives in his own words, but through words put into the mouths of the deceitful Persians. In biblical poetics, the words of a character may not always be as reliable as the words of the narrator, and this may also be true in Herodotus. In Esther, too, a (wedded) wife is invited to the men's drinking party with the same overtones of impropriety.

(4) The chaste concubine is, of course, an oxymoron, but Plutarch (*Artaxerxes* 26.2) presents just such a case.

> Once when Cyrus was at supper she [a concubine named Aspasia] was led in to him along with other women. The rest of the women took the seats given to them, and when Cyrus began to sport and flirt and jest with them, they showed no displeasure at his friendly advances. But Aspasia stood by her couch in silence, and would not obey when Cyrus called her; and when his chamberlains tried to lead her to him, she said: "Indeed, whoever lays his hands upon me shall rue the day." The guests therefore thought her a graceless and rude creature. But Cyrus was delighted, and laughed, and said to the man who had brought the women: "Can you not see at once that this is the only free and unperverted woman you have brought me?" From this time on he was devoted to her, and loved her above all women, and called her The Wise.

The similarity to Vashti's refusal is obvious, increasing our sense that Ahasuerus was treating Vashti like a concubine (Fox). This theme may also resonate in chapter 2, where Esther stands out from the other concubines-to-be, and where we have the phrase "the king loved Esther more than all the women" (2:17).

The Vashti incident incorporates the same motifs found in the Greek stories: drinking parties, voyeurism, improper sexual advances, and general Persian licentiousness. It is a

gave a banquet for women, in the royal palace of King Ahasuerus.

מִשְׁתֵּה נָשִׁים בֵּית הַמַּלְכוּת אֲשֶׁר לַמֶּלֶךְ אֲחַשְׁוֵרוֹשׁ: ס

¹⁰ On the seventh day, when the king was merry with wine, he ordered Mehuman, Bizzetha, Harbona,

¹⁰ בַּיּוֹם הַשְּׁבִיעִי כְּטוֹב לֵב־הַמֶּלֶךְ בַּיָּיִן אָמַר לִמְהוּמָן בִּזְּתָא חַרְבוֹנָא בִּגְתָא

vulgar scene, exactly fitting for a farce. It mocks propriety even more than the Greek stories by making the object of male desire a queen, and then again by having her refuse to come. The chapter reeks of drunken indulgence, royal incompetence, and sexual innuendo, made more hilarious by lists of eunuchs and advisors with funny-sounding names and a compulsive concern for law and etiquette under the most ludicrous circumstances. Law and bureaucracy, also part of the Persian stereotype, are combined with wine and women for comic effect.

The reaction on the part of the king's advisors is out of all proportion to Vashti's offense and does not provide an obvious remedy for it. To put it bluntly, the danger they see in Vashti's refusal is preposterous. It is best understood as part of the comedy with sexual innuendo that permeates the scene. As they rush ostensibly to preserve the honor of the king, the advisors express more of their own sexual anxiety than concern for damage control. The advisors are not worried that Vashti's example will provoke other Persian *subjects* to disobey the *king;* they are afraid that all the Persian *women* will scorn their *husbands.* This must have the same sexual nuance that the king's invitation had: other wives will be unavailable when their husbands want them just as Vashti was unavailable when Ahasuerus called for her. The advisors are trying to ward off a sexual strike by Persian women (and this is another theme found in Greek literature of the Persian period—in Aristophanes' comedy *Lysistrata*). They are as concerned about themselves as they are about the king.

9. the royal palace Hebrew: *bet ha-malkhut.* This probably refers to a public reception hall or throne room, as in 5:1. The men's party was outside in the garden.

The Book of Esther uses the word *malkhut* in two ways: as the Late Biblical Hebrew equivalent of *mamlakhah,* "kingdom," and as a noun meaning "royal." The second usage often occurs as the last part of a construct chain, in an adjectival sense: *yein malkhut* (1:7); *keter malkhut* (1:11); *devar malkhut* (1:19); *levush malkhut* (6:8); *kise' malkhuto* (5:1); *'osher kevod malkhuto* (1:4). It means "royal," in the sense of official, public, or governmental. *Bet ha-malkhut* would then mean something like "the royal hall." I would distinguish it from *bet ha-melekh,* the palace, which was a compound containing both public and private areas, including the *bet ha-nashim* and the *bet ha-malkhut. Bet ha-melekh* might signify the entire compound or any part of it.

In B. Megillah 12a, R. Abba bar Kahana[18] notes that Vashti made the party in the king's palace rather than in the women's quarters, or harem (*bet ha-nashim,* cf. 2:3), and suggests that both Vashti and Ahasuerus had immoral intentions.[19]

10. On the seventh day, when the king was merry with wine The last day of the last party. Surely by then the king had had much to drink. While the drinking motif is stereotypically associated with the Persians by the Greeks, the Bible has its own shameful associations with drunkenness, for example, Noah (Gen. 9:21–25) and Lot (Gen. 19:30–38).

he ordered Mehuman... The names of the servants are Persian-sounding, and there have been attempts to equate them with known Persian names, although whether they are authentic is not clear. Greek dramatists would sometimes give their Persian characters names that sounded Persian but were not authentic names, and perhaps the

Bigtha, Abagtha, Zethar, and Carcas, the seven eunuchs in attendance on King Ahasuerus, [11] to bring Queen Vashti before the king wearing a royal diadem, to display her beauty to the peoples and the officials;

וַאֲבַגְתָא זֵתַר וְכַרְכַּס שִׁבְעַת הַסָּרִיסִים הַמְשָׁרְתִים אֶת־פְּנֵי הַמֶּלֶךְ אֲחַשְׁוֵרוֹשׁ: [11] לְהָבִיא אֶת־וַשְׁתִּי הַמַּלְכָּה לִפְנֵי הַמֶּלֶךְ בְּכֶתֶר מַלְכוּת לְהַרְאוֹת הָעַמִּים וְהַשָּׂרִים

author of Esther did the same. The mention of these seven tongue-twisting names, like the names of the ten sons of Haman, provided an added touch of comedy.[20] Seven eunuchs are listed here and seven ministers are mentioned in verse 14. The effect of all this quasi-authentic detail, like the exotic terms describing the decor in verse 6, adds to the picture of exaggerated luxury, and in this case, of a large bureaucracy. The king is surrounded by servants and advisors, all named and labeled, and he can do nothing without them.

Fox calls the summoning of the eunuchs a "phony ritual, created for the nonce, to show that in this court, everything, even an invitation to the queen, is thick with pomp and circumstance." Indeed, we can picture the troop of eunuchs, in dress uniform, marching in step to fetch the queen.

11. Just as the king has displayed his wealth, so he wishes to display his queen, who is part of his wealth. Just as the royal wine is not reserved exclusively for the king, so the king's wife is not kept for his eyes alone.

Vashti Vashti gets mixed billing in rabbinic midrash. She is given a genealogy that links her with Nebuchadnezzar. Since he is the Babylonian king who destroyed the Temple, this would normally be a negative characterization, but Targum Rishon credits him with merit for having clothed Daniel in purple. Vashti is bidden to appear before the king naked, according to the rabbis. This is suitable punishment, according to some, because she caused the Jewish women to work naked on the Sabbath. Others view her refusal to appear naked before the men at the party as virtuous.[21] Modern readers, especially feminists, tend to view her positively, as a woman who resisted male domination and was victimized by it. The biblical Vashti can be interpreted as a character with an independent spirit and a desire to maintain her dignity in the face of her husband's loss of his own dignity.[22] But in keeping with the stereotypical characterization of the book, it may be best to see Vashti simply as another type—the strong-willed royal woman—a type that is also found in Greek writings about the Persians.

a royal diadem Hebrew: *keter malkhut.* A mark of belonging to the royal household. Ahasuerus puts the royal diadem on Esther's head in 2:17; in 6:8 the horse has a royal diadem. In Persian sculptures and seals, there are female figures wearing turreted or dentate crowns (a flat crown edged by a row of small triangles).[23] The king wore a higher dentate crown. It would seem that this is what is meant by *keter*. Greek sources, however, speak of the king's turban-like headdress encircled with a jeweled band, called a "tiara." There is confusion in the Greek sources between *kitaris/kidaris* (apparently a borrowing from *keter*) and *diadema*. The word *keter* is a late word in Hebrew and appears in the Bible only in Esther. Its etymology is uncertain. Most recently, Salvesen (45) concludes that it is Semitic, not Persian as previously thought, and that it refers to a headband worn widely in the Persian empire, with a distinctive fabric or color reserved for royalty. Note that in 8:15, when Mordecai wears a "crown of gold," the term is 'atarah, not keter.

The midrashim make the point that Vashti was to appear wearing nothing but the royal diadem, that is, she was to be naked. Esther Rabbah comments on this verse in a manner that highlights the impropriety, making it sound more like the Greek stories about Candaules and Amyntas.

for she was a beautiful woman. 12 But Queen Vashti refused to come at the king's command conveyed by the eunuchs. The king was greatly incensed, and his fury burned within him.

13 Then the king consulted the sages learned

אֶת־יָפְיָ֔הּ כִּי־טוֹבַ֥ת מַרְאֶ֖ה הִֽיא׃
12 וַתְּמָאֵ֞ן הַמַּלְכָּ֣ה וַשְׁתִּ֗י לָבוֹא֙ בִּדְבַ֣ר
הַמֶּ֔לֶךְ אֲשֶׁ֖ר בְּיַ֣ד הַסָּרִיסִ֑ים וַיִּקְצֹ֤ף הַמֶּ֙לֶךְ֙
מְאֹ֔ד וַחֲמָת֖וֹ בָּעֲרָ֥ה בֽוֹ׃
13 וַיֹּ֣אמֶר הַמֶּ֔לֶךְ לַחֲכָמִ֖ים יֹדְעֵ֥י הָֽעִתִּ֑ים

R. Aibu said: What makes atonement for Israel is that when the Israelites eat and drink and make merry, they bless and praise and extol the Holy One Blessed Be He, whereas when other nations eat and drink they turn to lewdness. So here, one said, "The Median women are more beautiful," and another said, "The Persian women are more beautiful." Said that fool [Ahasuerus] to them: "The vessel which I use is neither Median nor Persian, but Chaldean. Would you like to see it?" They replied, "Yes, but she must be naked." "Very well," he said to them, "let her be naked."

12. Vashti refused to come to the king when summoned and was punished for it. Esther will come to the king unsummoned and will not be punished.

Several of the midrashim (e.g., Esther Rabbah 3.14; Abba Gorion), again seeing sexual nuances in the story, explain the predicament that led to Vashti's refusal:

She remonstrated with him, saying: "If they consider me beautiful they will want to kill you and enjoy me themselves; and if they consider me ugly, I shall bring disgrace on you."

Both the Greek stories and the midrashic explanation suggest that for Vashti to come would be tantamount to reducing herself to a concubine or dancing girl, making herself available to the other men. Vashti is in a no-win situation, and must either go against Persian mores (which banned royal women from the drinking party) or disobey the command of the king. She chose the latter in an attempt to preserve her own dignity and that of her husband—who presumably (as Abba Gorion suggests) would not have given such a command had he been sober. This calls to mind another story of a smart woman with a drunken husband: the story of Abigail, who acts on her own initiative while her husband Nabal is drunk, to avert the danger that Nabal had brought on his household (1 Sam. 25:36).

The king is exceedingly angry and his anger will not abate until some time later (cf. 2:1). He will again become angry in 7:7 when apprised that Esther and her people are in danger.

13. Herodotus 3.31 tells a story relevant to seeking legal advice about women. Like Ahasuerus, the Persian King Cambyses found himself in a predicament over a woman and needed a legal decision, although the circumstances were rather different. Cambyses fell in love with his sister and wished to marry her, although it was not a Persian custom for brothers and sisters to marry.

Because there was no precedent for this plan of his, he summoned all the royal judges, as they are called, and asked them if there was a law inviting anyone who wanted to marry his own sister to do so. These royal judges are a select band of Persians, who hold office until they die or until they are found to have committed a crime; their job is to adjudicate lawsuits for the Persians and to interpret ancestral laws and customs, and all such matters are referred to them. Anyway, their response to Cambyses' question was safe, as well as being within the letter of the law; they said that they could find no law inviting a man to marry his own

in procedure. (For it was the royal practice [to turn] to all who were versed in law and precedent. [14] His closest advisers were Carshena, Shethar, Admatha, Tarshish, Meres, Marsena, and Memucan, the seven ministers of Persia and Media who had access to the royal presence and occupied the first place in the kingdom.) [15] "What," [he asked,] "shall be done, according to law, to Queen Vashti for failing to obey the command of King Ahasuerus conveyed by the eunuchs?"

כִּי־כֵן֙ דְּבַ֣ר הַמֶּ֔לֶךְ לִפְנֵ֕י כָּל־יֹדְעֵ֖י דָּ֥ת וָדִֽין׃ [14] וְהַקָּרֹ֣ב אֵלָ֗יו כַּרְשְׁנָ֤א שֵׁתָר֙ אַדְמָ֣תָא תַרְשִׁ֔ישׁ מֶ֥רֶס מַרְסְנָ֖א מְמוּכָ֑ן שִׁבְעַ֣ת שָׂרֵ֣י ׀ פָּרַ֣ס וּמָדַ֗י רֹאֵי֙ פְּנֵ֣י הַמֶּ֔לֶךְ הַיֹּשְׁבִ֥ים רִאשֹׁנָ֖ה בַּמַּלְכֽוּת׃ [15] כְּדָת֙ מַֽה־לַעֲשׂ֔וֹת בַּמַּלְכָּ֖ה וַשְׁתִּ֑י עַ֣ל ׀ אֲשֶׁ֣ר לֹֽא־עָשְׂתָ֗ה אֶֽת־מַאֲמַר֙ הַמֶּ֣לֶךְ אֲחַשְׁוֵר֔וֹשׁ בְּיַ֖ד הַסָּרִיסִֽים׃ ס

sister, but that they found another law that the ruler of the Persians could do whatever he wanted. So by finding a regulation which could support Cambyses' desire to marry his sister, they did not let fear of Cambyses make them break the law, but they also did not destroy themselves while maintaining the law. So Cambyses married the sister he was in love with then.

Ahasuerus's legal consultants have a similar problem. They must find a legal way to deal with the king's current dilemma. In the end, it is one of the royal advisors, Memucan, who proposes a solution. The expert legal consultants remain silent.

The Greeks had an ambivalent view of Persian law, as this story in Herodotus shows. On one hand, the Persian legal system was famous, and the Greeks, who prided themselves on their own system of law, approved of peoples who were law abiding. But on the other hand, part of their view of Persia as "barbarian" included the disregard for law, so they often portrayed Persian kings as breaking the law. The Book of Esther, in which Persian law figures so often, manifests a different type of ambivalence. Legalism undergirds the plot and is part of the comic caricature of the king and the court. In chapter 1, the legal system appears ridiculous. Later, law is the vehicle for the threat to the Jews and the vehicle for their deliverance.

learned in procedure   That is, the legal experts, or perhaps better, the experts in protocol. The Hebrew, "who know the times," is an unusual expression and some scholars take it to mean astrologers. But there is little to support this view and the similar expression in 1 Chron. 12:33 argues against it.

law and precedent   Hebrew: *dat ve-din* may refer to imperial law and local law.[24] See the Commentary to 3:8. Or it may simply be one of the many dyadic expressions of which the book is so fond.

The word *dat,* "law," from the Persian *data* (also used in Aramaic) occurs nineteen times in the book, with meanings ranging from "law" to "custom" to "practice," and there is a good bit of irony connected with its use. Here the author is poking fun at a drunken and angry king so concerned that his domestic problems should be solved in a legal manner. The royal advisors, here and later, are all too eager to have new laws enacted. Concern with legality, bureaucracy, and protocol, not to mention protecting one's honor, are themes that dominate the portrayal of the Persian court and are especially evident in this chapter. Protecting the honor of the king and of Haman will play a major role in subsequent chapters as well.

14.   The list of the seven eunuchs named in verse 10 is mirrored in the list of advisors; in fact, the second list is almost the reverse of the first (Mehuman-Memucan, and so forth).[25] This increases the odds that the lists are playful devices, like the names of the seven dwarfs in "Snow White."

16 Thereupon Memucan declared in the presence of the king and the ministers: "Queen Vashti has committed an offense not only against Your Majesty but also against all the officials and against all the peoples in all the provinces of King Ahasuerus. 17 For the queen's behavior will make all wives despise their husbands, as they reflect that King Ahasuerus himself ordered Queen Vashti to be brought before him, but she would not come. 18 This very day the ladies of Persia and Media, who have heard of the queen's behavior, will cite it to all Your Majesty's officials, and there will be no end of scorn and provocation!

16 וַיֹּ֣אמֶר מומכן מְמוּכָ֗ן לִפְנֵ֤י הַמֶּ֙לֶךְ֙ וְהַשָּׂרִ֔ים לֹ֤א עַל־הַמֶּ֙לֶךְ֙ לְבַדּ֔וֹ עָוְתָ֖ה וַשְׁתִּ֣י הַמַּלְכָּ֑ה כִּ֤י עַל־כָּל־הַשָּׂרִים֙ וְעַל־כָּל־הָ֣עַמִּ֔ים אֲשֶׁ֕ר בְּכָל־מְדִינ֖וֹת הַמֶּ֥לֶךְ אֲחַשְׁוֵרֽוֹשׁ׃ 17 כִּֽי־יֵצֵ֤א דְבַר־הַמַּלְכָּה֙ עַל־כָּל־הַנָּשִׁ֔ים לְהַבְז֥וֹת בַּעְלֵיהֶ֖ן בְּעֵינֵיהֶ֑ן בְּאָמְרָ֗ם הַמֶּ֣לֶךְ אֲחַשְׁוֵר֡וֹשׁ אָמַ֞ר לְהָבִ֨יא אֶת־וַשְׁתִּ֧י הַמַּלְכָּ֛ה לְפָנָ֖יו וְלֹא־בָֽאָה׃ 18 וְֽהַיּ֨וֹם הַזֶּ֜ה תֹּאמַ֣רְנָה ׀ שָׂר֣וֹת פָּֽרַס־וּמָדַ֗י אֲשֶׁ֤ר שָֽׁמְעוּ֙ אֶת־דְּבַ֣ר הַמַּלְכָּ֔ה לְכֹ֖ל שָׂרֵ֣י הַמֶּ֑לֶךְ וּכְדַ֖י בִּזָּי֥וֹן וָקָֽצֶף׃

16. The king may be inept and unable to act, but his advisors overcompensate with too much action. They make a mountain out of a molehill; a domestic incident has become a national crisis.

The punishment of all the members of a group for the offense of one member will come up again when Haman wants to destroy Mordecai's people (Levenson).

Memucan One of the king's seven foremost advisors. It is he, and not one of the "sages learned in procedure," who suggests the solution to the king's problem. The Rabbis identified him with Haman.

17. *despise* Hebrew *b-z-h,* also in verse 18, where it is translated as "scorn." *B-z-h* is the opposite of "honor."[26] See 1 Sam. 2:30; Mal. 1:6. The theme of honor and dishonor, so crucial to the relationship between Mordecai and Haman, is already evident here.

The danger that Memucan sees in Vashti's refusal is preposterous. How will it provoke a rebellion by *all* the wives in the empire against their husbands? The burlesque of the great Persian empire, drowning in luxury, wine, courtiers, and incompetent management, reaches one of its high points here, with a touch of male sexual anxiety added for good measure. As explained above, they fear that all wives will act like Vashti when their husbands act like Ahasuerus.

18. Vashti's disobedience will begin to serve as an example "this very day" for the royal women who were on the scene. Later it will spread to all the women of the empire.

will cite it The Hebrew *to'marnah,* "they [feminine] will say," is difficult because the words that they will say are missing (that is, the verb has no object). Several solutions have been proffered. The best is to accept that the ellipsis of the direct object (what they will say) is not unusual. Ehrlich points to Gen. 43:29, where the verb *'-m-r* also occurs without an object: "Is this your little brother Benjamin of whom you spoke to me?"[27] (See Rashi; Fox, 274–75; and Bush.) Some exegetes emend the verb to *timrenah,* "they will rebel" (Bardtke,[28] Moore); some take the relative particle *'asher* as equivalent to *ki* and translate "they will say that they have heard the matter/word of the queen" (Gordis).[29]

scorn and provocation The officials' wives will scorn and provoke their husbands. Or perhaps, as Paton and Clines suggest, we should understand the terms as referring to contempt *(bizayon)* on the part of the women for their husbands and wrath *(ketzef)* on the

19 "If it please Your Majesty, let a royal edict be issued by you, and let it be written into the laws of Persia and Media, so that it cannot be abrogated, that Vashti shall never enter the presence of King Ahasuerus. And let Your Majesty bestow her royal state upon

יט אִם־עַל־הַמֶּלֶךְ טוֹב יֵצֵא דְבַר־מַלְכוּת מִלְּפָנָיו וְיִכָּתֵב בְּדָתֵי פָרַס־וּמָדַי וְלֹא יַעֲבֹר אֲשֶׁר לֹא־תָבוֹא וַשְׁתִּי לִפְנֵי הַמֶּלֶךְ אֲחַשְׁוֵרוֹשׁ וּמַלְכוּתָהּ יִתֵּן הַמֶּלֶךְ לִרְעוּתָהּ

part of the men for their wives.[30] Hakham suggests another possibility: that *bizayon* is the queen's scorn for the king, and *ketzef* is the rightful anger that the king has over the matter (in v. 12).

19. Apparently there was no law that applied to the situation so Memucan proposes making a new one. Ironically, Vashti's punishment will prevent her from ever appearing before the king in the future—the very thing she refused to do in this instance. She is being demoted and her status as a royal woman is being taken away. We know nothing else of her fate. She will play no further role in the story.

a royal edict Hebrew: *devar malkhut*, "word of kingship." As Fox observes, the *devar malkhut* will counteract the *devar ha-malkah*, literally "the matter/word of the queen," in verse 17.

cannot be abrogated This is universally understood to mean that once a law has been issued, it cannot be changed or revoked. If that is, indeed, its meaning here, the permanence of Persian laws serves two narrative purposes: it reinforces the bureaucratic maze that engulfs the court, and it sets up the main plot in which the edict to destroy the Jews cannot be annulled. The idea that a Persian law cannot be changed is found in Dan. 6:9, 13, 16 but is nowhere attested in Persian or Greek sources. Perhaps it is a literary motif shared by Daniel and Esther. As Fox mentions, it is hard to imagine that an empire could actually operate with such a constraint.

But I wonder if exegetes have placed too much weight on the phrase *lo' ya'avor*. It is not the same as the phrase in 8:5, 8: *'ein le-hashiv*, "cannot be recalled or revoked" (see the Commentary to 8:5), and I would distinguish between the two phrases. *Lo' ya'avor* is the common way in Late Biblical Hebrew and Mishnaic Hebrew of saying "to transgress, break, or contravene a law" (cf. Dan. 9:11; Job 14:5; 2 Chron. 24:20). It occurs in this sense in Esther 3:3, where Mordecai disobeys the command to bow to Haman, and in 9:27, where it refers to the observance, without fail and without exception, of Purim. In 1:19 Memucan is stressing the seriousness of the matter by saying that the king's decision should become a law that must not be broken, that is, a law to which there should be no exception.

And who was likely to break such a law? The king himself, when his anger cooled (see the Commentary to 2:1–2). Memucan is urging the king to make a firm decision that he must stick to. He accomplishes this by exaggerating the effect of Vashti's refusal and by having her punishment written into law, thereby giving it more weight than it would ordinarily have. To write such a decision into law is itself a preposterous exaggeration, for laws do not normally contain the names of specific individuals who may or may not appear at court. This is not a "real" law. And as we will see, the narrative of its publication throughout the empire is not exactly the same as in the case of Haman's edict in chapter 3 or Mordecai's in chapter 8.

Vashti Already here her title of "queen" has been removed (Fox). Before she was "Queen Vashti"; here and in 2:1 she is just "Vashti."

shall never enter the presence of King Ahasuerus Her punishment is to be deprived of her royal position and to be denied access to the royal court. Many of the midrashim interpret her punishment as execution.[31]

another who is more worthy than she. ²⁰ Then will the judgment executed by Your Majesty resound throughout your realm, vast though it is; and all wives will treat their husbands with respect, high and low alike."

²¹ The proposal was approved by the king and the ministers, and the king did as Memucan proposed. ²² Dispatches were sent to all the provinces of the king, to every province in its own script and to every

כ: וְנִשְׁמַע פִּתְגָם הַמֶּלֶךְ אֲשֶׁר־יַעֲשֶׂה בְּכָל־מַלְכוּתוֹ כִּי רַבָּה הִיא וְכָל־הַנָּשִׁים יִתְּנוּ יְקָר לְבַעְלֵיהֶן לְמִגָּדוֹל וְעַד־קָטָן: כא וַיִּיטַב הַדָּבָר בְּעֵינֵי הַמֶּלֶךְ וְהַשָּׂרִים וַיַּעַשׂ הַמֶּלֶךְ כִּדְבַר מְמוּכָן: כב וַיִּשְׁלַח סְפָרִים אֶל־כָּל־מְדִינוֹת הַמֶּלֶךְ אֶל־מְדִינָה

who is more worthy than she An echo of 1 Sam. 15:28 in which Saul is told he will lose the kingship.

20. the judgment Hebrew *pitgam* is borrowed from Persian and means "decision" or "proclamation." Compare Eccles. 8:11. It is common in Aramaic (*patgam*; several times in Daniel and Ezra). The Targum often uses this term to translate Hebrew *davar.*

Memucan is suggesting that the judgment against Vashti should not only be written into law but that, in addition, the action taken by the king should be widely publicized so that it might serve as an example to the men and as a warning to their wives. (See below, v. 22.)

vast though it is Compare Gen. 18:20. The phrase is a parenthetic interjection to emphasize the size of the empire (Fox) and the need to communicate the judgment to every corner of it.

all wives...high and low alike From the start, Memucan perceived Vashti's action as a dangerous precedent for all women (vv. 16–17), so all women must hear of the king's judgment so that they will respect their husbands.

respect Hebrew *yekar* is an important word in the book. Ahasuerus displays it in 1:4, Haman wants it and Mordecai gets it in chapter 6.

22. dispatches were sent The Persians were noted for their excellent road system, which, according to Herodotus (8.98), was a Persian invention. It served as a communications network throughout the empire; in Herodotus's view, there was no faster way to send a message.[32]

This is the first series of dispatches. See also 3:12–13 and 8:10–14, and the Commentary there. The dispatches become progressively more urgent. Here the government employs its most advanced technology for a petty purpose.

to every province in its own script and to every nation [or: people] in its own language The Persian empire was multi-ethnic and multilingual, with languages written in several different writing systems. In fact, this was one of the characteristics of the Persian empire, as we may see from an inscription of Xerxes, who says: "I am Xerxes, the great king, the king of kings, the king of [all] countries [which speak] all kinds of languages."[33]

The usual practice was for edicts and other communications to be promulgated in Aramaic, the *lingua franca* of the empire, and then to be translated into the vernacular languages upon reaching the provinces. On occasion, a communication would go out from Susa in languages other than Aramaic.[34] The famous inscription of Darius at Behistun is trilingual.

The Persian acceptance and accommodation to their multilingual empire stands in sharp contrast with the Greeks, for whom anyone who did not speak Greek was a

nation in its own language, that every man should wield authority in his home and speak the language of his own people.

וּמְדִינָה֙ כִּכְתָבָ֔הּ וְאֶל־עַ֥ם וָעָ֖ם כִּלְשׁוֹנ֑וֹ לִהְי֤וֹת כָּל־אִישׁ֙ שֹׂרֵ֣ר בְּבֵית֔וֹ וּמְדַבֵּ֖ר כִּלְשׁ֥וֹן עַמּֽוֹ׃ פ

barbarian. The Greeks themselves did not take to learning other people's languages, and so those who needed to communicate with them often had no choice but to do so in Greek.

Much is made of the multilingual edicts here, and also in 3:12 and 8:9, and this should be taken as part of the exaggerated description of the Persian bureaucracy—the machinery of state going to great lengths to send out nonsensical edicts (Fox, 23).

The construction *x va-x,* meaning "every x," sometimes with the addition of *kol,* is characteristic of Late Biblical Hebrew.[35] This construction is extraordinarily common in Esther (see, for example, 2:11; 8:11; 9:21). It tends to add to the tone of exaggeration and verbosity of the book.

Medinah and *'am,* literally "province and people" should be understood as a hendiadys representing the ethnogeographic concept that the Persian *dahyu* signifies—a geographic region that is congruent with a particular ethnic group.[36] Let us call this an "ethno-province." There is no suitable term in Hebrew for this concept. The closest term may be *goy,* but this is not appropriate because it connotes an independent kingdom, whereas the ethno-province is a subdivision of the Persian empire. The word *moledet,* often "native land," is used in 2:10 and 8:6 meaning "kindred" and is not associated with a geographic location.

Kikhtavah and *kilshonah* constitute another hendiadys, meaning "according to its written language." The entire phrase means "to every ethno-province according to its written language."

that every man should wield authority in his home A long tradition of interpretation sees this phrase and the following one as the wording of the edict that was sent throughout the empire. But, as many scholars have seen, such an edict is unenforceable, if not downright silly, even in a farce. As Fox (23) observes, this "is not exactly what Memuchan called for, which was declaration of Vashti's ouster." However, if we understand this phrase (and the following one) as *the reason for the publication* of the edict, not the edict itself, then the words make more sense. Memucan advised that Vashti be removed from her royal position and that this be written into the laws of Persia. "Then will the judgment executed by Your Majesty resound throughout your realm...and all wives will treat their husbands with respect" (v. 20). The edict is that Vashti is to be removed; the effect of publicizing this edict will be that all wives will respect their husbands. In other words, public knowledge of the existence of the edict against Vashti will serve as a warning to all women who would act as Vashti acted. Verse 22 is telling us that Memucan's advice was heeded—that dispatches were sent to every province in every language *so that* every man should wield authority in his home. The grammar supports this interpretation. Compare 3:14; 8:13; and even perhaps 9:21. In every case, after the report of the sending of a message throughout the empire, there occurs a phrase with the infinitive *lihyot* followed by a participle. This is *never* the content of the message; it is always the reason that the message is being publicized: "*so that* they might be ready for that day" (3:14); "*so that* the Jews might be ready for that day" (8:13); "*so that* they will observe the fourteenth day of the month of Adar" (9:21).

speak the language of his own people This is a difficult phrase, and seemingly not quite relevant to the issue at hand. It seems to be somehow related to each man being master in his own home, but the connection is not easy to make. The Greek versions omit it. Some modern commentators render the meaning more freely or emend the text, since they would like the meaning of "whatever suits him" (Moore, 11–12; cf. Fox, 275).

Gerleman (who also does not take this and the preceding phrase as the text of the edict, but analyzes them differently from the way I do) suggests that "the language of his own people" refers back to the multilingual nature of the communication, and means that it was to be proclaimed to each head of household in his own language.[37]

There is a long tradition of understanding this phrase as meaning that a husband could compel his foreign wife (that is, a wife whose native language was different from his) to speak the husband's language (so Rashi). Fox cites, with good reason, the concern with the preservation of Hebrew as the Jewish vernacular among intermarried Jews, expressed in Neh. 13:24, where we find the similar phrase, *kilshon 'am va-'am*, "in the language of every people" (see also Levenson). But the loss of language through intermarriage is hardly the point in Esther, and, in fact, Esther seems ignorant of or indifferent to matters in Judah (Yehud), while intermarriage among the returning Judeans was the focus of Nehemiah's concern. The closest parallel seems to be Esther 8:9: "to every province in its own script and to every people in its own language, and to the Jews in their own script and language." In 8:9 the language of the Jews is singled out for special mention because it is the Jews, above all, who need to understand the message. In our verse it is the (married) men of the empire who need to understand the message. So perhaps Gerleman has come closest to the sense of our phrase, which may mean that the dispatches were sent in vernacular languages so that every husband could readily understand the message and report the contents to his wife.[38]

CHAPTER 2

Sex and Spies

Chapter 2 continues the events of chapter 1 and brings Esther and Mordecai into the story. Both will serve the king in their own ways. Later, both will serve their own people.

The first part of the chapter draws us into the royal harem, with its overtones of sexual allure. Plans for finding the king a new wife emphasize the attractiveness of the many candidates, especially their sexual appeal to the king. The picture of court luxury drawn in chapter 1 is given a new dimension in chapter 2. The kingdom is full of young beauties, *all* of whom will be brought to the harem and given cosmetic treatments for an extended time. The lavishness of the royal harem, with its many women indulging in lengthy cosmetic treatments, is no less exaggerated than the luxuriousness of the palace and its parties. The excess of wine in chapter 1 is matched by the excess of women in chapter 2.

The second part of the chapter brings us intrigue, in the form of a plot against the king, foiled by Mordecai with the help of Esther. It is a foreshadowing of the larger intrigue perpetrated by Haman and again foiled by Mordecai with the help of Esther. There is also a certain diabolical irony in the contrast between Mordecai's informing on Bigthan and Teresh and Haman's informing on the Jews in chapter 3.

The motifs of this chapter, and they are the major motifs of the book as a whole, are also common in literature outside the Bible during the Persian period and beyond. Ancient historians charged Alexander the Great with adopting Persian customs, among them collecting a large number of concubines (360, according to Plutarch, *Artaxerxes* 27.2; 365, regally dressed and adorned and attended by herds of eunuchs, according to Quintus Curtius, *History of Alexander* 3.3.24 and 6.6.8). As Diodorus of Sicily, 17.77.5, put it:

> He added concubines to his retinue in the manner of Darius, in number not less than the days of the year and outstanding in beauty as selected from all the women of Asia. Each night these paraded about the couch of the king so that he might select the one with whom he would lie that night.

2 Some time afterward, when the anger of King Ahasuerus subsided, he thought of Vashti and what she had done and what had been decreed against her.

ב אַחַר֙ הַדְּבָרִ֣ים הָאֵ֔לֶּה כְּשֹׁ֕ךְ חֲמַ֖ת הַמֶּ֣לֶךְ אֲחַשְׁוֵר֑וֹשׁ זָכַ֣ר אֶת־וַשְׁתִּ֗י וְאֵ֛ת אֲשֶׁר־עָשָׂ֖תָה וְאֵ֥ת אֲשֶׁר־נִגְזַ֖ר עָלֶֽיהָ׃

Harem intrigues, while found in a number of sources, are especially associated with Ctesias's *Persika*. (Ctesias was a Greek physician and author who lived in the late fifth century B.C.E. and served at the Persian court under Artaxerxes II. The *Persika* survives only in passages quoted by later authors.)

Ctesias and other Greek authors also tell tales about strong royal Persian women, and Esther, to a lesser extent, may represent an imitation of such women. Of course, the Bible itself knows of strong women, such as Deborah and Jael, Abigail and Bathsheba, so the character of Esther is completely at home in the Bible and we do not need to see her as a foreign import. In some ways, the role given to Esther anticipates later literature in which female characters figure prominently. This includes Jewish works such as Susanna, Judith, Joseph, and Asenath and also the Greek romances. In the words of L. Wills:

> Women characters...are invested with the main weight of the emotional tribulations, perils, and decisions of the story. The emotional sympathies of the audience are with the woman, even if it is the male protagonist who performs most of the main actions.[1]

Much of what Wills says pertains to Esther, for it is she who stars in the emotionally tense scenes—when she approaches the king uninvited and when she makes her accusation against Haman. In chapter 2, Esther prepares for her heroic role. She emerges, first to Hegai, then to others in the harem, and then to the king, as an extraordinarily charming woman, and through the eyes of these characters, the reader comes to appreciate her fine qualities.

The king and the reader also see Mordecai's vigilance through his cameo appearance at the end of the chapter. This little spy story foreshadows many things to come.

1. Some time afterward The Hebrew *'aḥar ha-devarim ha-'eleh*, which occurs also in 3:1, is an archaizing phrase found in Genesis and Kings. The time that has passed is unspecified. Levenson points out that, according to the date in 2:16, Esther is not taken to Ahasuerus until four years after Vashti's removal—a long time for a king to be without a queen. Esther has had a year of cosmetic treatments so presumably three years have passed between Vashti's disappearance and Esther's entrance into the harem. Her arrival seems to follow shortly after the decree to gather the virgins. Fox, on the other hand, suggests that this scene is set not long after Vashti was deposed because "Xerxes does not seem like the sort of person to persist in his anger for very long."

he thought of Ahasuerus now realizes the full import of what has occurred. During the Vashti event itself he was agitated, if not inebriated, and now his agitation has abated. Judging by the servants' apparent eagerness to find a replacement for Vashti, we may conclude that Ahasuerus misses his wife and perhaps regrets the action that has been taken against her. His advisors rush in to prevent any possibility that the king will change his mind, for this would contravene the law written in 1:19–21. The scene is a masterful characterization of the servants and the king. Through this view of Ahasuerus's inner life, we see that he has only the vaguest inkling, unarticulated, of what he needs. The servants, this time unbidden, suggest another exaggerated plan, on the same scale as their last plan. Vashti's behavior threatened to cause a rebellion by *all* the women in the kingdom; and now, *all* the young virgins should be summoned.

2 The king's servants who attended him said, "Let beautiful young virgins be sought out for Your Majesty. 3 Let Your Majesty appoint officers in every province of your realm to assemble all the beautiful young virgins at the fortress Shushan, in the harem under the supervision of Hege, the king's eunuch, guardian of the women. Let them be provided with their cosmetics. 4 And let the maiden who pleases Your Majesty be queen instead of Vashti." The proposal pleased the king, and he acted upon it.

2 וַיֹּאמְרוּ נַעֲרֵי־הַמֶּלֶךְ מְשָׁרְתָיו יְבַקְשׁוּ לַמֶּלֶךְ נְעָרוֹת בְּתוּלוֹת טוֹבוֹת מַרְאֶה: 3 וְיַפְקֵד הַמֶּלֶךְ פְּקִידִים בְּכָל־מְדִינוֹת מַלְכוּתוֹ וְיִקְבְּצוּ אֶת־כָּל־נַעֲרָה־בְתוּלָה טוֹבַת מַרְאֶה אֶל־שׁוּשַׁן הַבִּירָה אֶל־בֵּית הַנָּשִׁים אֶל־יַד הֵגֶא סְרִיס הַמֶּלֶךְ שֹׁמֵר הַנָּשִׁים וְנָתוֹן תַּמְרוּקֵיהֶן: 4 וְהַנַּעֲרָה אֲשֶׁר תִּיטַב בְּעֵינֵי הַמֶּלֶךְ תִּמְלֹךְ תַּחַת וַשְׁתִּי וַיִּיטַב הַדָּבָר בְּעֵינֵי הַמֶּלֶךְ וַיַּעַשׂ כֵּן: ס

Midrash Abba Gorion constructs an amusing dialogue around this verse:

> When he recovered from his wine he sought her. They said to him, "You had her killed." He said to them, "Why?" They said to him, "When you said that she should appear before you naked and she didn't come." He said to them, "I didn't act correctly. Who advised me to have her killed?" They said to him, "The seven ministers of Persia and Media [1:14]." He immediately killed them and that is why they are not mentioned again.

2. The servants, this time the king's personal servants, hasten to suggest the remedy, in an extended speech, as Memucan did in chapter 1. In this case, though, there is no notice that the king has even asked for advice. The king is completely silent in this chapter; he is given no speaking part. As before, the servants' speech is long and spares no detail.

3. The name Hegai is here written with an *alef* at the end, yielding a contracted form *ê*. The more usual uncontracted form, *ay*, is written with a *yod*. Ctesias refers to a Greek officer of Xerxes named Hegias of Ephesus, whom one scholar equates with our Hegai.[2]

4. ***And let the maiden who pleases Your Majesty be queen instead of Vashti*** This does not sound like the way a real king would choose a queen. If we believe Herodotus 3.84, the Persian king chose his queen from one of the seven noble families of Persia. The selection of Esther in this manner is either a Cinderella motif, or, more likely, it is a search not for a primary wife for the king, but for a desirable concubine. The wording recalls the way a bed companion for King David was found in 1 Kings 1:2–3. Other details also suggest that Esther's status is murky. On the one hand, she is crowned queen but there is no mention of marriage to the king. She has no automatic access to the king, but, like other women in the harem, she must wait for an invitation. On the other hand, she could dine with the king and a male guest; and dining with Esther was considered a mark of high status.

The Hebrew wording of "the young woman who will be good in your eyes" echoes 1:19: *le-reʿutah ha-tovah mimennah*. Suddenly 1:19 becomes a double entendre: what the servants may have been suggesting before is not just a more worthy wife, but also a more attractive one, perhaps one who would be proud to display her beauty publicly if called upon to do so.

5 In the fortress Shushan lived a Jew by the name of Mordecai, son of Jair son of Shimei son of Kish,

5 אִישׁ יְהוּדִי הָיָה בְּשׁוּשַׁן הַבִּירָה וּשְׁמוֹ מָרְדֳּכַי בֶּן יָאִיר בֶּן־שִׁמְעִי בֶּן־קִישׁ אִישׁ

5-7. The hero is introduced, followed by the heroine. Mordecai is given top billing, and is presented as an independent character, while Esther is presented in relation to Mordecai, as his relative and dependent. All we know about Esther at this point is that she is Mordecai's cousin. We do not learn her father's name until 2:15. The information given about Mordecai suggests to the reader that he is a clearly identified and prominent Jew of the Babylonian exile, with an obliquely expressed link to King Saul.

5. In a book that is as nonhistorical as Esther, there is little point in looking for historical or biological information in Mordecai's genealogy. In fact, even in the more historical books of the Bible, genealogies are often designed to give the reader information about the status or social location of the character, rather than a scientifically accurate family tree.

The beginning of the introduction of Mordecai is syntactically similar to the introduction of Job, giving us the sense that we are in a folktale mode. The difference is that while Job's outstanding characteristic is his moral perfection, Mordecai's outstanding characteristic is his Jewishness.

Jew Not from the tribe of Judah, for he is from the tribe of Benjamin. Originally derived from "Judah," the name of the kingdom, it refers to all of Judah's population no matter what their tribe of origin. It is an ethnic epithet, and is used in reference to Mordecai many times (5:13; 6:10; 8:7; 9:29, 31; 10:3). (Compare "the Moabitess" used in reference to Ruth.) By placing this designation before Mordecai's proper name, emphasis is given to this aspect of his identification, which becomes crucial as the story unfolds. In the Babylonian sources, foreigners are sometimes mentioned by their ethnic identity, but this is not common. The ethnic designation "Judean" is not found in Babylonian records from the Chaldean or Achaemenian periods except when referring to King Jehoiachin.[3]

Mordecai A personal name known from Babylonian documents of the Persian period. The Babylonian form is Marduka, a form linguistically close to the Hebrew. In the past, some scholars speculatively connected Mordecai with the chief god of Babylon, Marduk (and saw in Esther a reference to the Babylonian goddess Ishtar). But Marduka, although it derives from the name of the god Marduk, appears to have been a common name, and there is no reason to press a direct connection with deities. Jews of Babylonia often took Babylonian names, just as Jews elsewhere took names common to their locations. Mordecai would be, then, a Babylonian Jew living in Susa. (Compare Ezra 2:2 and Neh. 7:7 where a man named Mordecai was one of the first exiles to return with Zerubbabel.) We may conclude that Mordecai was a common name of the Persian period for both Jews and non-Jews.

Jair This name occurs elsewhere in the Bible, as a son of Manasseh (Num. 32:41), a judge (Judg. 10:3–5), and as the patronymic of a priest of David (2 Sam. 20:26); it is not a Benjaminite name. The so-called Aramaic Proto-Esther texts from Qumran may contain the name Ya'ir (it is partially reconstructed in 4QprEsth[b] ar) and the phrase "a Jew from the chiefs of Benjam[in]" (in 4QprEsth[d] ar).

Shimei Rabbinic interpretation makes explicit that this is Shimei the son of Gera, the member of Saul's clan who supported him against David (2 Sam. 16:5–8).

Kish Biblical genealogies do not always list all the progenitors, but may list only those worthy of attention. The names in Mordecai's genealogy are best not taken as three

24

a Benjaminite, [6] who had been exiled from Jerusalem in the group that was carried into exile along with King Jeconiah of Judah, which had been driven into

6 אֲשֶׁר הָגְלָה֙ מִירוּשָׁלַ֔יִם עִם־
הַגֹּלָה֙ אֲשֶׁר הָגְלְתָ֔ה עִם יְכָנְיָ֖ה מֶֽלֶךְ־
יְהוּדָ֑ה אֲשֶׁר הֶגְלָ֔ה נְבוּכַדְנֶאצַּ֖ר מֶ֥לֶךְ

successive generations, but as figures marking points in a Benjaminite genealogical list going back to Kish, the father of Saul (although this is not expressed). By linking Mordecai obliquely with Saul, through the tribe of Benjamin and the name of Kish, the story prepares us for the linking of Haman with Agag (3:1), the arch enemy of Saul. In this way, Mordecai and Haman become latter-day embodiments of an old ethnic feud, which has its origin in the battle between King Saul and Agag, the Amalekite king (1 Samuel 15). This is only one facet of a subtle intertextual play between the Book of Esther and 1 Samuel 15 (see the Commentary to 9:10).

a Benjaminite In the postexilic period the tribal area of Benjamin remained closely associated with Judah, as it had been during the divided monarchy. In Ezra, "Judah and Benjamin" signify those returnees from Babylonia who have a legitimate claim to Judah; they constitute the authentic Jewish community (see Ezra 1:5; 4:1). This connotation may also adhere to Mordecai's genealogy. By virtue of Mordecai's being a *yehudi* and a Benjaminite he is a symbol of the authentic exilic Jew.

6. If the person who had been exiled along with King Jeconiah (Jehoiachin) in 597 B.C.E. (cf. 2 Kings 24:6–17) is Mordecai, he would be impossibly old—about 115 years old—at the time of Xerxes. Traditional Jewish exegetes eliminated this problem by interpreting the antecedent of *'asher hoglah,* "who had been exiled," as referring not to Mordecai but to Kish. But this interpretation, while syntactically possible, is less probable; and it also diminishes the connection between the Kish mentioned here and Kish, the father of King Saul (who was certainly not exiled with Jeconiah). Some modern commentators have seen the genealogy as a chronological error, although it might be possible to take it as one more exaggeration in a book full of exaggerations. But I prefer to take this as a reference to the exile of Mordecai himself, and to understand it as a literary device that bestows a pedigree on its bearer. The same literary device occurs in reference to Daniel (2:25) and to Tobit (in the apocryphal book by that name), who was exiled by Shalmaneser when the northern kingdom of Israel was conquered. Daniel and Tobit are, like Mordecai, heroes in Diaspora stories, and the notice of their having been exiled from Jerusalem (or Israel) gives them added status and authenticity in the Diaspora. Their own personal histories embody the history of the nation.

Bickerman suggests that the mention of Jeconiah's exile may indicate that Mordecai was a member of the upper class exiled with him (2 Kings 24:14–16).[4] Josephus makes this explicit, calling Mordecai "one of the principal persons among the Jews" (although he, like the Greek texts, omits the specific reference to the exile of Jeconiah). Daniel, too, was "of royal descent and of the nobility" (1:3). Our verse, then, is not to be taken as a chronological detail, but is intended to glorify Mordecai.

The root *g-l-h* is repeated four times, emphasizing the exile. Levenson offers an attractive interpretation, comparing the power and luxury of the Persian court with the powerlessness of and looming danger to the exiled Jews. I would add that for the Diaspora Jewish audience for whom this book was presumably written, the emphasis on the fact that the main characters were also Diaspora Jews would make it easy for them to identify with them. Moreover, the book advocates the position, however indirectly, that God's power extends beyond the Land of Israel and that divine providence will save the Jews of the Diaspora.

exile by King Nebuchadnezzar of Babylon. ⁷He was foster father to Hadassah—that is, Esther—his uncle's daughter, for she had neither father nor mother. The maiden was shapely and beautiful; and when her father and mother died, Mordecai adopted her as his own daughter.

⁸When the king's order and edict was proclaimed, and when many girls were assembled in the fortress Shushan under the supervision of Hegai, Esther too was taken into the king's palace under the supervision of Hegai, guardian of the women. ⁹The girl pleased

בָּבֶל: ⁷ וַיְהִי אֹמֵן אֶת־הֲדַסָּה הִיא אֶסְתֵּר בַּת־דֹּדוֹ כִּי אֵין לָהּ אָב וָאֵם וְהַנַּעֲרָה יְפַת־תֹּאַר וְטוֹבַת מַרְאֶה וּבְמוֹת אָבִיהָ וְאִמָּהּ לְקָחָהּ מָרְדֳּכַי לוֹ לְבַת: ⁸ וַיְהִי בְּהִשָּׁמַע דְּבַר־הַמֶּלֶךְ וְדָתוֹ וּבְהִקָּבֵץ נְעָרוֹת רַבּוֹת אֶל־שׁוּשַׁן הַבִּירָה אֶל־יַד הֵגָי וַתִּלָּקַח אֶסְתֵּר אֶל־בֵּית הַמֶּלֶךְ אֶל־יַד הֵגַי שֹׁמֵר הַנָּשִׁים: ⁹ וַתִּיטַב הַנַּעֲרָה בְעֵינָיו וַתִּשָּׂא חֶסֶד לְפָנָיו וַיְבַהֵל אֶת־תַּמְרוּקֶיהָ

7 Hadassah, Esther's Hebrew name, means "myrtle"; Esther is either a Babylonian name, derived from the name of the goddess Ishtar, or a Persian name from the word *stâra,* meaning "star." Jews in the Diaspora often bore both a Jewish and a vernacular name, as, for example, did Daniel and his friends and Judah Maccabee and his brothers. It is possible that Mordecai had a Jewish name also, but that it is not recorded. (The name Hadassah is not included in the Greek versions.)

Mordecai was the foster father of the orphaned Esther. Whether or not this was a formal legal arrangement, about which there is little information in the Bible, is less important than the fact that Mordecai was Esther's guardian and protector, a father figure but not her real father.

The phrase "the maiden was shapely and beautiful" is oddly placed between two facts pertaining to Esther's family status: that Esther was orphaned and taken under Mordecai's guardianship. While this is part of her description, and is the kind of information often given when a female character is introduced, we might have expected to find it in connection with Esther's entrance into the harem.

daughter The Septuagint reads "as a wife" instead of "as a daughter." B. Megillah 13a contains a *baraita* saying "Do not read 'as a daughter' (*le-vat*) but 'as a home [or, wife]' (*le-vayit*)." While the rabbinic phrase "do not read x but read y" is a form of midrashic exegesis, some modern scholars conclude that the Septuagint actually had the reading *le-vayit* instead of *le-vat.* Fox speculates that this line of interpretation eliminates the otherwise improper presence of an unmarried woman in Mordecai's house. Levenson suggests that it is because these Jewish sources were loath to see a Jewess married to a Gentile. This loathing is made more explicit in a number of rabbinic and medieval comments. For example, B. Sanhedrin 74b says that "Esther was like the ground"—that is, she was entirely passive when the king made his advances toward her. The Zohar (*Ra'ya mehemma. Ki Tetzei* 3:276a) says that God sent down a female spirit disguised as Esther to take her place with the king.[5]

9. Esther pleases everyone with whom she comes in contact, especially Hegai, who takes special care that she begins her beauty treatments immediately and is given the best service. There are echoes of Joseph and Daniel, who also served at foreign courts and rose quickly in the esteem of others (Gen. 39:4, 21; Dan. 1:9). While is it usually Mordecai who is compared to Joseph and Daniel, Esther, too, shares in the theme of the successful courtier. She does so, however, in distinctly feminine terms: it is her beauty that leads to her success.

him and won his favor, and he hastened to furnish her with her cosmetics and her rations, as well as with the seven maids who were her due from the king's palace; and he treated her and her maids with special kindness in the harem. 10 Esther did not reveal her people or her kindred, for Mordecai had told her not to reveal it. 11 Every single day Mordecai would walk about in front of the court of the harem, to learn how Esther was faring and what was happening to her.

12 When each girl's turn came to go to King Ahasuerus at the end of the twelve months' treatment prescribed for women (for that was the period spent on beautifying them: six months with oil of myrrh and six months with perfumes and women's

וְאֶת־מְנוֹתֶהָ לָתֶת לָהּ וְאֵת שֶׁבַע הַנְּעָרוֹת הָרְאֻיוֹת לָתֶת־לָהּ מִבֵּית הַמֶּלֶךְ וַיְשַׁנֶּהָ וְאֶת־נַעֲרוֹתֶיהָ לְטוֹב בֵּית הַנָּשִׁים: 10 לֹא־הִגִּידָה אֶסְתֵּר אֶת־עַמָּהּ וְאֶת־מוֹלַדְתָּהּ כִּי מָרְדֳּכַי צִוָּה עָלֶיהָ אֲשֶׁר לֹא־תַגִּיד: 11 וּבְכָל־יוֹם וָיוֹם מָרְדֳּכַי מִתְהַלֵּךְ לִפְנֵי חֲצַר בֵּית־הַנָּשִׁים לָדַעַת אֶת־שְׁלוֹם אֶסְתֵּר וּמַה־יֵּעָשֶׂה בָּהּ: 12 וּבְהַגִּיעַ תֹּר נַעֲרָה וְנַעֲרָה לָבוֹא ׀ אֶל־הַמֶּלֶךְ אֲחַשְׁוֵרוֹשׁ מִקֵּץ הֱיוֹת לָהּ כְּדָת הַנָּשִׁים שְׁנֵים עָשָׂר חֹדֶשׁ כִּי כֵּן יִמְלְאוּ יְמֵי מְרוּקֵיהֶן שִׁשָּׁה חֳדָשִׁים בְּשֶׁמֶן הַמֹּר

her rations   While Daniel (chapter 1) took pains to observe the rules of *kashrut*, as did Judith (12:2), no mention of any dietary observance is mentioned here. The absence of Jewish ritual observance in this book marks Esther as being different from other biblical and apocryphal books. The Rabbis were eager to fill this gap and assure us that Esther did not partake of nonkosher food.

Levenson sees in this word a foreshadowing of the *manot,* the food gifts, in 9:19 and 22 that are part of the celebration of Purim.

10.   It stretches credibility to imagine that Esther could keep her ethnic identity a secret, but it is vital to the plot and really no more unrealistic than many other aspects of this fictive story. Hidden identity also figures in some of the Greek stories about Persia from this period (for example, the story of Smerdis in Herodotus 3.67ff.).

her people or her kindred   Hebrew 'am and *moledet* (also in 2:20 and 8:6) are closely related in meaning and used in parallelistic constructions. The use of both terms together puts more emphasis on the ethnic dimension. For another example of *moledet* in the sense of "kin" rather than the more common "native land" see Gen. 43:7.

12–14.   This extended and detailed description emphasizes yet again the women's extensive preparation and the procedure for their first meeting with the king. It provides the standard against which to contrast Esther, whose natural beauty requires little to enhance it. The contrast is encouraged by the use of similar language at the beginning of verses 12 and 15.

12. to go to   This expression has sexual overtones. Compare 2 Sam. 11:4; Ruth 4:13.

The cosmetic treatments, like the parties in chapter 1, go on for exaggerated lengths of time.[6]

oil of myrrh   Myrrh is used often in Song of Songs and is associated with love-making. (See also Prov. 7:17.) Anointing the body with oil, after bathing and before dressing, is mentioned in the women's preparations in Ezek. 16:9, Ruth 3:3, and Jth. 10:3. Unlike those references, however, our chapter never mentions bathing or dressing. The emphasis here seems to be more on the quantities of fine products that the palace supplied rather than on the women's personal preparations.

cosmetics, [13] and it was after that that the girl would go to the king), whatever she asked for would be given her to take with her from the harem to the king's palace. [14] She would go in the evening and leave in the morning for a second harem in charge of Shaashgaz, the king's eunuch, guardian of the concubines. She would not go again to the king unless the king wanted her, when she would be summoned by name. [15] When the turn came for Esther daughter of Abihail—the uncle of Mordecai, who had adopted her as his own daughter—to go to the king, she did not ask for anything but what Hegai, the king's eunuch, guardian of the women, advised. Yet Esther won the admiration of all who saw her.

וְשִׁשָּׁה חֳדָשִׁים בַּבְּשָׂמִים וּבְתַמְרוּקֵי הַנָּשִׁים: 13 וּבָזֶה הַנַּעֲרָה בָּאָה אֶל־הַמֶּלֶךְ אֵת כָּל־אֲשֶׁר תֹּאמַר יִנָּתֵן לָהּ לָבוֹא עִמָּהּ מִבֵּית הַנָּשִׁים עַד־בֵּית הַמֶּלֶךְ: 14 בָּעֶרֶב ׀ הִיא בָאָה וּבַבֹּקֶר הִיא שָׁבָה אֶל־בֵּית הַנָּשִׁים שֵׁנִי אֶל־יַד שַׁעַשְׁגַז סְרִיס הַמֶּלֶךְ שֹׁמֵר הַפִּילַגְשִׁים לֹא־תָבוֹא עוֹד אֶל־הַמֶּלֶךְ כִּי אִם־חָפֵץ בָּהּ הַמֶּלֶךְ וְנִקְרְאָה בְשֵׁם: 15 וּבְהַגִּיעַ תֹּר־אֶסְתֵּר בַּת־אֲבִיחַיִל דֹּד מָרְדֳּכַי אֲשֶׁר לָקַח־לוֹ לְבַת לָבוֹא אֶל־הַמֶּלֶךְ לֹא בִקְשָׁה דָּבָר כִּי אִם אֶת־אֲשֶׁר יֹאמַר הֵגַי סְרִיס־הַמֶּלֶךְ שֹׁמֵר הַנָּשִׁים וַתְּהִי אֶסְתֵּר נֹשֵׂאת חֵן בְּעֵינֵי כָּל־רֹאֶיהָ:

14. The word *sheni* is a crux. It may mean that there is a second harem, supervised by Shaashgaz, for concubines, to which unsuccessful candidates are taken after their night with the king. Alternatively, the verse may mean that the women return again to the same harem, after their night with the king, this time to be looked after by Shaashgaz. It is clear that none of the women returns home. They become concubines if they are not chosen as queen.

summoned by name The virgins who have been gathered into the harem first visit the king by turn (see v. 15), and then will not come again to the king until specifically requested. Fox (35) puts it well by saying that "a woman was, so to speak, simply a number, until she received an identity of sorts by titillating the jaded monarch's fancy."

15. Esther's father's name is mentioned for the first time here, along with a restatement of her relationship to Mordecai. It is a rather formal phrase, coming as it does in the middle of the story long after the character has been introduced. I take it as Esther's formal introduction when she is presented to the king. It follows directly after "summoned by name" and illustrates what it means to be summoned by name.

Esther does not ask for anything except what Hegai has advised. Here, as later at a more important juncture in chapters 5 and 7, Esther's request is modest compared to what she might have asked for ("up to half the kingdom"—cf. Levenson). Esther seeks no special treatment and her natural beauty requires no extraordinary enhancement. Fox suggests that this is part of the motif of the refusal of heathen luxuries (as in Dan. 1:8 and Tob. 1:10–11), but I prefer to see this as a more universal motif of natural beauty over artifice and modesty over greed. (A rejection of heathen luxuries is not characteristic of this book.)

the admiration of all who saw her The narrator has characterized Esther very positively through Hegai's favorable view of her, and now he emphasizes this characterization through the view of an anonymous "everyone," as if even the other women find Esther charming. This paves the way for the king's even more positive reaction.

¹⁶ Esther was taken to King Ahasuerus, in his royal palace, in the tenth month, which is the month of Tebeth, in the seventh year of his reign. ¹⁷ The king loved Esther more than all the other women, and she won his grace and favor more than all the virgins.

16 וַתִּלָּקַ֨ח אֶסְתֵּ֜ר אֶל־הַמֶּ֤לֶךְ אֲחַשְׁוֵרוֹשׁ֙ אֶל־בֵּ֣ית מַלְכוּת֔וֹ בַּחֹ֥דֶשׁ הָעֲשִׂירִ֖י הוּא־חֹ֣דֶשׁ טֵבֵ֑ת בִּשְׁנַת־שֶׁ֖בַע לְמַלְכוּתֽוֹ׃ 17 וַיֶּאֱהַ֨ב הַמֶּ֤לֶךְ אֶת־אֶסְתֵּר֙ מִכָּל־הַנָּשִׁ֔ים

16. in his royal palace The term *bet malkhut* does not occur earlier in the chapter in reference to the other women, and it is not strictly necessary here. But it is the site of Vashti's party in 1:9, and its presence here hints that Esther is about to take Vashti's place. Esther also appears in the *bet malkhut* in 5:1. I see no reason to understand it as the king's private quarters here (as many commentators do), when it is clearly a public reception area in the other verses in which it is found. It is not hard to imagine Esther being introduced formally by name in a formal reception hall. The mild hint of voyeurism in this chapter is overshadowed by the emphasis on the carefully regulated process according to which the women are prepared, as if to remind us that all of this is official state business in a kingdom where, as we saw in chapter 1, sexuality is controlled by bureaucracy.

the tenth month, which is the month of Tebeth Throughout most of the Bible, the months are indicated by ordinal numbers ("the first month," etc.), according to the practice in ancient Israel. In the books of Zechariah, Ezra, Nehemiah, and Esther, however, a double system is used, which gives both the ordinal number and the month name. The names of the months originated in Babylonia and were adopted by the Persians. They were later adopted into the Jewish calendar.

17. The king's reaction to Esther is expressed in even stronger language than the reaction of all the others who admire her. Ahasuerus is immediately captivated by Esther. He instantly crowns her queen, although there is no mention of marrying her. We are not told where Esther goes afterward.

In the Masoretic Text, Esther is first taken to the *bet malkhut,* and the king loves her; then she is crowned, and then the king makes a party in her honor. Josephus fills in some gaps and alters the sequence; according to his account the king falls in love with Esther and marries her. Then he gives a marriage feast, at which time Esther comes to the royal palace and is crowned.

loved As Fox notices, the king's reaction to Esther is expressed in slightly different terms from other people's reaction: he loves her. The root *'-h-b* has a broad range of meanings, from a deep emotional bond to a passing fancy, and it is difficult to know which nuance it carries in our case. Does Ahasuerus love Esther the way Jacob loves Rachel, or the way Amnon loves Tamar? Does the love precede a sexual act or follow it? Or does *'-h-b* merely mean "prefer," as in Deut. 21:15–17? The term is ambiguous, but to be in character with a harem story we would expect some sexual nuance.

This may stand out more if we take apart the parallelism: "The king loved Esther more than all the women // and she won his *hen va-hesed* more than all the virgins." The terms *hen va-hesed* have appeared before in this chapter, *hen* in verse 9 indicating the grace that Hegai perceives, and *hesed* in verse 15 for the effect Esther has on all who see her. The occurrence of both terms together suggests that the king is doubly impressed with Esther's charm. He reacts even more strongly to Esther than everyone else in the harem does, but he does so in their terms, the way women and eunuchs see her. Theirs is a nonsexual admiration. But of course Ahasuerus admires her in another way, too, as a man admires a woman, and that is expressed in the first part of the parallelism. The sense is that the king finds Esther both more sexually attractive and more generally charming than anyone else.

women... virgins This pair of words also occurs in a parallelism in Lam. 5:11, but with a different effect. Ahasuerus loves Esther more than all the women, presumably those

So he set a royal diadem on her head and made her queen instead of Vashti. ¹⁸ The king gave a great banquet for all his officials and courtiers, "the banquet of Esther." He proclaimed a remission of taxes for the provinces and distributed gifts as befits a king.

¹⁹ When the virgins were assembled a second time, Mordecai sat in the palace gate. ²⁰ But Esther still did not reveal her kindred or her people, as Mordecai had instructed her; for Esther obeyed Mordecai's bidding, as she had done when she was under his tutelage.

וַתִּשָּׂא־חֵן וָחֶסֶד לְפָנָיו מִכָּל־הַבְּתוּלֹת וַיָּשֶׂם כֶּתֶר־מַלְכוּת בְּרֹאשָׁהּ וַיַּמְלִיכֶהָ תַּחַת וַשְׁתִּי: ¹⁸ וַיַּעַשׂ הַמֶּלֶךְ מִשְׁתֶּה גָדוֹל לְכָל־שָׂרָיו וַעֲבָדָיו אֵת מִשְׁתֵּה אֶסְתֵּר וַהֲנָחָה לַמְּדִינוֹת עָשָׂה וַיִּתֵּן מַשְׂאֵת כְּיַד הַמֶּלֶךְ: ¹⁹ וּבְהִקָּבֵץ בְּתוּלוֹת שֵׁנִית וּמָרְדֳּכַי יֹשֵׁב בְּשַׁעַר־הַמֶּלֶךְ: ²⁰ אֵין אֶסְתֵּר מַגֶּדֶת מוֹלַדְתָּהּ וְאֶת־עַמָּהּ כַּאֲשֶׁר צִוָּה עָלֶיהָ מָרְדֳּכָי וְאֶת־מַאֲמַר מָרְדֳּכַי אֶסְתֵּר עֹשָׂה כַּאֲשֶׁר הָיְתָה בְאָמְנָה אִתּוֹ: ס

who have already come to him; and finds her more charming than all the virgins, all those yet to come. The parallelism lends additional formality and exaggeration to the tone, and makes very clear the king's feelings toward Esther. The verse thus lays the groundwork for Ahasuerus's positive reception of Esther when she comes uninvited in chapter 5.

a royal diadem   Is it the same diadem that Vashti was bidden to appear with in 1:11? The term is indefinite in both places.

18.   Another party, in a book full of parties. Esther's coronation party suggests that perhaps the parties in chapter 1 are in honor of Vashti's coronation. Esther's coronation provides the occasion for the king to show his largesse by granting some relief from taxes and by bestowing gifts—quite a difference from the display of wealth in chapter 1.

In about 519 B.C.E., Darius regulated the system of levying taxes on the satrapies, based on the measurement of land and the crops cultivated on it. The taxes were paid in silver. Before that, there were less well-regulated forms of taxation. The gifts in this instance may have been land grants to favored relatives or officials, as was the practice in the Persian empire. Or, if we take the term *mas'et* more literally, they were portable gifts, also usual in Persia.

19.   This verse is difficult, and may be a scribal error. Its function seems to be to sum up some of the points in the preceding narration that will figure in what follows.

When the virgins were assembled a second time   The notice of a second gathering of virgins has puzzled commentators. It is omitted in the Greek versions. While some interpretations attempt to account for the verse as it is (see Levenson, 63), none is convincing.

The notice that Mordecai is stationed at the palace gate fits better in verse 21, where it is repeated. Some commentators delete it from verse 19.

20.   This verse does not present new information; it emphasizes the information given in 2:10. The syntax (a clause beginning with the subject and then a stative, or participial construction) expresses synchronicity.[7] It means "All the while, Esther did not reveal her kindred..." "kindred" and "people" are given in reverse order from v. 10). All throughout the events narrated, and even after having been made queen, Esther still does not reveal her Jewishness. Moreover, she remains obedient to Mordecai just as she was

²¹ At that time, when Mordecai was sitting in the palace gate, Bigthan and Teresh, two of the king's eunuchs who guarded the threshold, became angry, and plotted to do away with King Ahasuerus.

בַּיָּמִים הָהֵם וּמָרְדֳּכַי יֹשֵׁב בְּשַׁעַר־ 21
הַמֶּלֶךְ קָצַף בִּגְתָן וָתֶרֶשׁ שְׁנֵי־סָרִיסֵי
הַמֶּלֶךְ מִשֹּׁמְרֵי הַסַּף וַיְבַקְשׁוּ לִשְׁלֹחַ יָד

before she entered the palace and came under the king's authority. Her obedience to Mordecai, however, does not prevent her from taking some initiative later. We will see both these traits in chapter 4.

21–23. The short episode of Bigthan and Teresh is a masterful piece of foreshadowing. It demonstrates Mordecai's loyalty to the king by means of the informant motif, common in court legends and a major motif on which the plot of Esther turns; it initiates the communication system between Mordecai and Esther that will be called upon later; it introduces impalement as a punishment; and it leaves Mordecai's good deed recorded but unrewarded.[8]

The episode is recounted succinctly, with no motives ascribed to the culprits, which gave rise to a range of speculations to fill the gap, including jealousy of Mordecai, jealousy of Esther, and anger at the king for his treatment of Vashti.[9] The Septuagint recounts a variation of this episode in Addition A, which precedes the story in the Masoretic Text and appears to contain a different version of the story. According to Addition A, Mordecai was rewarded immediately with a position at court, which may explain how he came to be sitting at the king's gate. Haman, says Addition A, determined to kill Mordecai and his people because of the two eunuchs. The implication is that Haman was involved in the plot against the king, and that perhaps he had plans to take the throne himself (an idea that will emerge in chapters 6 and 7). The Septuagint's version of the episode, then, provides an alternate explanation for Haman's hatred of Mordecai and possibly also an alternative explanation for Mordecai's refusal to bow to Haman (whom he knew was disloyal to the king).[10]

21. *Mordecai was sitting in the palace gate* Hebrew: *sha'ar ha-melekh,* "the king's gate." More than reporting Mordecai's physical location, this verse states his official position in the royal court.[11] The palace gate, usually an impressive architectural structure, contained auxiliary buildings housing administrative offices and supplies and Mordecai may have had an office or room in one of these buildings.[12] What exactly is Mordecai's position? It seems likely, given the context, that Mordecai is a member of the king's secret police. These were official informers, referred to as "the eyes of the king" or "the ears of the king," and they are mentioned by Greek authors and in Aramaic papyri (the term used is *gaušaka*). They were independent of the satraps and other local authorities and reported directly to the king about any seditious speech or act.[13]

Mordecai's physical location is noted in verse 11: he walks around in front of the harem court in order to be close to Esther, and presumably he can do this by virtue of his official position. Also by virtue of his position, he can convey to Esther information about Bigthan and Teresh. His official position, and his own astuteness, permit him not only to be the eyes and ears of the king, but also to know about matters affecting the Jews.

It is not strange to have foreigners in high positions at the Persian court, at least in legends. The Bible knows of Daniel and his friends, and the Greek authors often mention Greeks serving at court or as advisors to Persian kings.

22 Mordecai learned of it and told it to Queen Esther, and Esther reported it to the king in Mordecai's name. 23 The matter was investigated and found to be so, and the two were impaled on stakes. This was recorded in the book of annals at the instance of the king.

22 וַיִּוָּדַע הַדָּבָר לְמָרְדֳּכַי וַיַּגֵּד לְאֶסְתֵּר הַמַּלְכָּה וַתֹּאמֶר אֶסְתֵּר לַמֶּלֶךְ בְּשֵׁם מָרְדֳּכָי: 23 וַיְבֻקַּשׁ הַדָּבָר וַיִּמָּצֵא וַיִּתָּלוּ שְׁנֵיהֶם עַל־עֵץ וַיִּכָּתֵב בְּסֵפֶר דִּבְרֵי הַיָּמִים לִפְנֵי הַמֶּלֶךְ: פ

22. It is Mordecai's job to ferret out plots against the king, and that is exactly what he does.

Esther reported it to the king Why doesn't Mordecai report it himself? This action establishes Esther as a reliable source of information for the king, something that will become important later in the story when Esther reveals Haman's plot.

in Mordecai's name It is vital for the events of chapter 6 that Mordecai receive credit for saving the king's life.

23. In the ancient world, crimes against the king and his family were punishable by death. Sometimes an entire family was put to death for the crime of one member.[14]

impaled on stakes A foreshadowing of the stake that Haman will erect for Mordecai, and on which Haman himself will be impaled. Impalement was not the method of execution, but the disgracing of the person, through the public display of his body after death or execution. (See Gen. 40:19; Deut. 21:22; Josh. 8:29; 10:26.) This practice has a long history in the ancient Near East. The hanging of enemy corpses, or their heads, on poles around the city is documented in the Assyrian annals and depicted on monuments. Compare the impalement of Saul's headless body in 1 Sam. 31:10.[15]

Herodotus also recounts instances of impalement by Persians, another foreign practice that was distasteful to the Greeks. In 3.125 we hear of the murder of Polycrates followed by his impalement. In 7.238, Xerxes has the head of the dead Leonides cut off and impaled (cf. also 9.79). On the meaning of this action Herodotus interjects: "This, to my mind, is the most convincing piece of evidence . . . that during his lifetime Leonides had been more of an irritation to King Xerxes than anyone else in the world." Clearly, for Herodotus, impalement was an especially strong form of disgrace in Persian society. We should expect to find the same attitude in Esther.

Herodotus uses the verb *anastauroun* for the impalement of a corpse, and *anaskolopizein* for the impalement of a living person. (The examples above feature the former.) Later, the two verbs became synonymous, which inevitably caused some confusion between impalement and crucifixion (a Greco-Roman form of execution).[16]

CHAPTER 3

Honor and Enmity

The main plot of the story begins here. It is constructed around the common folktale motif of a conflict between courtiers, but in our story the personal conflict between Haman and Mordecai escalates to a national conflict involving all of Mordecai's people. Haman's plot against the Jews is motivated by his hatred of Mordecai, which is the result of Mordecai's refusal to honor Haman, which, in turn, derives from the ancient enmity between Israel and Amalek. With Haman's decree to kill the Jews, a note of danger and urgency is introduced into the previously frivolous tone of the book. But despite the danger, the story

3 Some time afterward, King Ahasuerus promoted Haman son of Hammedatha the Agagite; he ad-

ג אַחַר ׀ הַדְּבָרִים הָאֵלֶּה גִּדַּל הַמֶּלֶךְ אֲחַשְׁוֵרוֹשׁ אֶת־הָמָן בֶּן־הַמְּדָתָא הָאֲגָגִי

remains comical in many aspects and the threat to kill the Jews is no more real than anything else in the story.

We have already met Mordecai in the preceding chapter and now Haman is introduced, rather abruptly, into the story. He is an egocentric buffoon, concerned with his image and consumed by his emotions. His reaction to Mordecai's refusal to bow, like the king's reaction to Vashti's refusal to come, is inflated far beyond what is reasonable. As the story progresses we will see Haman's mood swing between one extreme and the other, as at one moment he seems assured of honor while at the next moment he sinks into disgrace. Honor and enmity will continue to hold center stage for most of the book. The question of who will honor whom is crucial to the advancement of the plot of the story, as it was in chapter 1, for this is a story in which honor and its trappings are paramount.

The issue of Jewish distinctiveness looms large in Haman's accusation. This is an important issue in the Bible itself and throughout all of Jewish history, and it must certainly have been of concern to the Diaspora Jewish community in the Persian period. Of what is Haman accusing the Jews? As will be explained in greater detail in the Commentary to 3:8, his accusation combines an incipient anti-Jewish depiction of the Jews along with the allegation that the Jews were disloyal to the Persian empire. The last point is the most important for our story, for Mordecai's loyalty to the king has already been demonstrated and must later be rewarded; and, ironically, Haman himself will later (in chapter 7) be accused of disloyalty to the king.

Haman's accusation is, of course, false; it is nothing but the ranting of an egomaniac who has not received the honor he thinks he is due. There is no evidence to suggest that there was widespread anti-Jewish feeling or a threat to Jewish survival in the Persian period. Yet the accusation that the Jews were distinctive, and that their distinctiveness was somehow dangerous, must have rung true enough to have been used by the author of the book. We seem to have in Haman's words an early form of the type of anti-Semitism that would come to fuller bloom in the Hellenistic period and afterward.

1. Some time afterward Like chapter 2, chapter 3 opens with the passing of an unspecified period of time. By the time the decree against the Jews is issued in 3:12, it is the twelfth year of Ahasuerus's reign, five years after Esther has been chosen to be queen.

promoted Haman Haman's career reaches its high point at the start. It will be all downhill for him after chapter 3, although he will have some moments of illusory glory.

As Herodotus notes (3.154), "among the Persians a high value is placed on services to the king, and those who perform them are greatly honoured." But what was Haman's service? The juxtaposition of the seemingly unwarranted promotion of Haman with the failure to reward Mordecai makes the reader ponder whether Haman has received the recognition that should have been Mordecai's. Later, of course, Mordecai will receive the honor that Haman thinks should be his. The text, in its usual repetitious style, expresses the promotion in three different phrases—"promoted Haman, advanced him, seated him higher"—thereby adding to the grandiosity of Haman's elevation to power.

Haman Haman's name and patronymic have been identified as Persian or Elamite, although the etymology is uncertain. Haman himself, however, is clearly not a Persian or an Elamite, but an Agagite. The name Hammedatha may be the same name found in Aramaic, Elamite, and Babylonian documents.[1]

the Agagite This is not an ethnic designation that would make any real sense in the Persian empire. By so identifying Haman, the Masoretic Text of Esther makes a clear

vanced him and seated him higher than any of his fellow officials. [2] All the king's courtiers in the palace gate knelt and bowed low to Haman, for such was the

וַיְנַשְּׂאֵהוּ וַיָּשֶׂם אֶת־כִּסְאוֹ מֵעַל כָּל־הַשָּׂרִים אֲשֶׁר אִתּוֹ: [2] וְכָל־עַבְדֵי הַמֶּלֶךְ אֲשֶׁר־בְּשַׁעַר הַמֶּלֶךְ כֹּרְעִים וּמִשְׁתַּחֲוִים

connection between Haman and the Amalekite king, Agag, mentioned in 1 Sam. 15:8, thereby confirming the connection between Mordecai and King Saul hinted at in Esther 2:5 and establishing the continuation of an ancient enmity between the two characters. Haman's name and epithets are found in slightly different arrangements throughout the story, with essentially the same effect of emphasizing his Agagite connection and his status as enemy of the Jews. Compare 3:10; 8:1, 3, 5; 9:10, 24. The effect is to reinforce that an Agagite is, by definition, a Jewish enemy.[2]

The Amalekite connection is reinforced in the synagogue lectionary cycle according to which, on the Sabbath preceding Purim, the passage in Deut. 25:17–19 ("Remember what Amalek did to you . . . . you shall blot out the memory of Amalek") and the haftarah from 1 Samuel 15 (containing the story of Saul and Agag) are read. On Purim, the Torah reading is Exod. 17:8–16, the battle between Israel and Amalek. While Esther does not contain the term "Amalek," the Targums and Josephus introduce it. The very mention of Agag is enough to raise all the biblical associations with Amalek (Exod. 17:8–16; Num. 24:7; Deut. 25:17–19. Cf. 1 Chron. 4:42–43 and Fox, 42). The Amalekite connection with Saul has a sequel in 2 Samuel 1 where an Amalekite claims credit for killing Saul and is executed by David for this claim.

The Greek versions do not call Haman "the Agagite" but rather "the Bougaean" (Septuagint and Alpha-text) or "the Macedonian" (in Addition A 17 of the Alpha-text); so the Masoretic Text's ancient ethnic enmity is absent, having been replaced by ethnic identifications that were pejorative in the Greek period.[3]

Both Targums reflect the Masoretic Text's Agagite origin for Haman, and go even further by extending Haman's genealogy back to Esau, echoing Gen. 36:12. They thereby extend the rivalry between Mordecai and Haman even further back in history to Esau and Jacob.

seated him higher than any of his fellow officials   We are told by Xenophon (*Cyropaedia* 8.4.5) that Cyrus

> gave public recognition to those who stood first in his esteem, beginning even with the places they took when sitting or standing in his company. He did not, however, assign the appointed place permanently, but he made it a rule that by noble deeds any one might advance to a more honored seat, and that if any one should conduct himself badly he should go back to one less honored.

If this is the case in Esther, too, then Haman's place of honor is not permanently secure and we may "sympathize" with his constant need to garner every sign of honor. Indeed, Haman was ultimately removed from his place of honor and it was given to Mordecai.

2. *knelt and bowed low*   Mordecai does not accord Haman the honor that is officially due him. The story hinges on Mordecai's refusal to bow to Haman, for this is ostensibly what prompted Haman to plan to annihilate the Jews. Mordecai's refusal endangers the entire Jewish people, yet the reason for it is not stated. This silence has provoked much speculation, for, indeed, we cannot understand the story unless we understand what motivated Mordecai.[4]

Once again, a similar motif in the Greek writings provides a key to interpretation. Bickerman already noted the motif of bowing down, or, as the Greeks termed it,

king's order concerning him; but Mordecai would not   לְהָמָן כִּי־כֵן צִוָּה־לוֹ הַמֶּלֶךְ וּמָרְדֳּכַי לֹא

proskynesis, in connection with this passage, and concluded that "For Mordecai to pay this respect to Haman would be to 'lose face' and acknowledge the new rank of his rival."[5] Let us examine this motif more closely.

For the Greeks in the Persian period, *proskynesis,* the gesture of deference usually understood as bowing down before the Persian monarch, became one of the motifs associated with the despotism of Persia that the Greeks found inimical to their own culture.[6] The passage most relevant to our discussion is Herodotus 7.136, for it shows another instance of strong resistance to bowing down. This case involved Spartan emissaries to Persia:

> The first thing that happened, once they gained an audience with the king, was that Xerxes' guards ordered them, and tried to force them, to fall down and prostrate themselves before the king. Their response to this was to declare that even if the guards were to hurl them headlong down on to the ground they would never do any such thing, not only because it was not the Greek way to prostrate oneself before another human being, but also because that was not what they had come for.

The Persian scholar P. Briant raises some questions about the exact meaning of *proskynesis,* and notes that on the Persian monuments the gesture of obeisance is not prostration but a slight inclination of the body and a hand-kiss.[7] Perhaps the Greeks, drawing on the long ancient Near Eastern tradition of prostration before monarchs, misrepresented the Persian gesture in order to make it more offensive to their own culture. In any case, the Greeks found it abhorrent to honor the king through *proskynesis,* reserving this gesture for honoring the gods. (They falsely ascribed to the Persians the belief that their king was divine.)

The Book of Esther again, as in chapter 1, partakes of the Greek motif and sensibilities but gives them a Jewish twist. Instead of a Greek refusing on Greek ethnic grounds to perform *proskynesis,* we have a Jew refusing on Jewish ethnic grounds to bow before Haman. But for this to be credible to a Jewish audience in the Persian period, a more definitive reason for Mordecai's refusal must be added, for there is a long biblical tradition of Jews (or Israelites) bowing to human beings (Gen. 23:7; 43:28; Exod. 18:7; 1 Kings 1:23) and it is never regarded as wrong. Moreover, although the Greeks may have thought that bowing to a monarch was "undemocratic," there is no reason that the Jews should have shared this attitude. The more definitive Jewish reason is supplied by the ancient ethnic enmity between the Israelites and the Amalekites. Mordecai's Jewishness stands opposed to Haman's Agagite descent. A Greek cultural value, which disdained bowing to Persians, is transmuted into a historic Jewish enmity, which prevented a Jew from bowing to an Amalekite.

Since the Greek versions of Esther do not link Haman with Agag or the Amalekites (he is a Bougaean or a Macedonian), they do not contain the Israelite-Amalekite enmity. Without this ancient enmity, Mordecai's refusal begins to look arrogant, as if his personal feelings toward Haman have endangered the entire Jewish people. The Greek versions address this problem in Addition C, Mordecai's prayer in which he denies any arrogance and explains that he was motivated solely by his objection to bowing to anyone except God:

> It was not in insolence or pride or for any love of glory that I did this, and refused to bow down to this proud Haman; for I would have been willing to kiss the soles of his feet to save Israel! But I did this so that I might not set human glory above

kneel or bow low. ³ Then the king's courtiers who were in the palace gate said to Mordecai, "Why do you disobey the king's order?" ⁴ When they spoke to him day after day and he would not listen to them, they told Haman, in order to see whether Mordecai's resolve would prevail; for he had explained to them

יִכְרַ֖ע וְלֹ֣א יִֽשְׁתַּחֲוֶֽה: ³ וַיֹּ֨אמְרוּ֙ עַבְדֵ֣י הַמֶּ֔לֶךְ אֲשֶׁר־בְּשַׁ֖עַר הַמֶּ֑לֶךְ לְמָרְדֳּכָ֑י מַדּ֗וּעַ אַתָּה֙ עוֹבֵ֔ר אֵ֖ת מִצְוַ֥ת הַמֶּֽלֶךְ: ⁴ וַיְהִ֗י באמרם [כְּאָמְרָ֤ם] אֵלָיו֙ י֣וֹם וָי֔וֹם וְלֹ֥א שָׁמַ֖ע אֲלֵיהֶ֑ם וַיַּגִּ֣ידוּ לְהָמָ֗ן לִרְאוֹת֙ הֲיַֽעַמְדוּ֙ דִּבְרֵ֣י מָרְדֳּכַ֔י כִּֽי־הִגִּ֥יד לָהֶ֖ם אֲשֶׁר־ה֥וּא

the glory of God, and I will not bow down to anyone but you, who are my Lord; and I will not do these things in pride.

Josephus, informed by the Masoretic Text, the Septuagint, and the Jewish interpretation of his time, says that "the foreigners and Persians worshipped him...but Mordecai was so wise, and so observant of his own country's laws, that he would not worship the man."⁸ In these words Josephus echoes Addition C, suggesting that there was a religious reason for Mordecai's refusal to bow to a human being. But a few verses later he cites the enmity between Jews and Amalekites (see v. 6).

Rabbinic interpretation preserves and develops the religious objection. Targum Rishon makes the bowing to Haman objectionable on the grounds of religion by claiming that Haman had an image of a god on his chest and that Mordecai would not bow down to the image or to Haman. Targum Sheni does not mention an image, but, even more like the Greek authors, finds it totally improper that Mordecai should bow to a human being, for he bows only to God.

This idea of a religious objection found in the Greek versions and in rabbinic interpretation makes good sense in the Hellenistic and Roman periods, when religious distinctions between Jews and other peoples became more important. It is, however, completely absent from the Masoretic Text, as is all reference to religious practice.⁹

3. Why do you disobey the king's order? The courtiers' question echoes the narrator's notice in verse 2 that the king had ordered people to bow to Haman. Mordecai is therefore disobeying a royal command. This is the same Mordecai whose loyalty to the king has just been demonstrated a few verses earlier.¹⁰ It is ironic, therefore, that such a loyal man will be endangered (and all his people, too) by his refusal to obey a royal command. Mordecai's refusal to obey is put in slightly stronger language than Vashti's; she "did not do the command [*ma'amar*] of the king" (1:15) while he disobeyed (*'br*) the order (*mitzvah*) of the king. Neither refusal is explained and both provoke exaggerated responses from the offended party. Levenson (68) puts it nicely: "In both cases, a mysterious refusal...occasions a catastrophic rage in the one refused, as well as a crisis of state and an absurd imperial decree."

4. When they spoke to him day after day Notice the similarity between this verse and Gen. 39:10: "when she spoke to Joseph day after day and he did not heed her." There are other similarities between the Joseph story and Esther, since they share the motif of a Jewish courtier in a foreign court. Here we find Mordecai steadfastly refusing to perform an act that he considered offensive, even after being repeatedly urged to perform it, as did Joseph in the face of the urging of Potiphar's wife. The results, too, are similar, in that both Joseph and Mordecai suffer greatly for their refusal.

The question that the courtiers asked in verse 3 is repeated day after day. It is not a request for information, but rather a way to urge him to conform to the command. It is a rhetorical question.

that he was a Jew. ⁵ When Haman saw that Mordecai would not kneel or bow low to him, Haman was filled with rage. ⁶ But he disdained to lay hands on Mordecai alone; having been told who Mordecai's people were, Haman plotted to do away with all the Jews, Mordecai's people, throughout the kingdom of Ahasuerus.

יְהוּדִי׃ ⁵ וַיַּ֣רְא הָמָ֔ן כִּי־אֵ֣ין מָרְדֳּכַ֔י כֹּרֵ֥עַ
וּמִֽשְׁתַּחֲוֶ֖ה ל֑וֹ וַיִּמָּלֵ֥א הָמָ֖ן חֵמָֽה׃ ⁶ וַיִּ֣בֶז
בְּעֵינָ֗יו לִשְׁלֹ֤חַ יָד֙ בְּמָרְדֳּכַ֣י לְבַדּ֔וֹ כִּֽי־הִגִּ֥ידוּ
ל֖וֹ אֶת־עַ֣ם מָרְדֳּכָ֑י וַיְבַקֵּ֣שׁ הָמָ֗ן לְהַשְׁמִ֤יד
אֶת־כָּל־הַיְּהוּדִ֛ים אֲשֶׁ֥ר בְּכָל־מַלְכ֖וּת
אֲחַשְׁוֵר֖וֹשׁ עַ֥ם מָרְדֳּכָֽי׃

that he was a Jew This phrase and its placement at the end of the verse emphasize that it was Mordecai's Jewishness that prevented him from bowing to Haman. The servants wanted to see if Haman would accept Mordecai's explanation for not bowing to him—*haya'amdu divrei mordekhai*, "if Mordecai's words would stand." Haman, of course, did not accept it as an excuse and it motivates his determination to kill all the Jews, "the people of Mordecai," not just Mordecai alone (see v. 6).

The placement of the phrase "for he had explained to them" at the end of the verse has raised some interpretive problems, but see Jon. 1:10 for the similar placement of a similar phrase. It refers to past action and is correctly translated into English by a pluperfect. In our verse, the placement at the end of the verse emphasizes the reason for Mordecai's refusal.

5. *When Haman saw that Mordecai would not kneel or bow low to him* An interesting play on the perspectives of the characters is conveyed in these verses. The narrator told us in verse 2 that the courtiers "were kneeling and bowing" because the "king had commanded it." When Mordecai does not bow, it is, from the point of view of the courtiers, an act of disobedience, as we see from their question, "Why do you disobey the king's order?" In other words, all the courtiers except Mordecai are obeying the order, and they wish to understand the reason that he has exempted himself from the rule. Haman's point of view is different. What he sees is not that Mordecai is disobeying a royal command, but that Mordecai is not kneeling and bowing—that is, Mordecai is not honoring Haman.[11] Haman is most particular about his own honor, and any diminution of it is enough to enrage him. He will, however, use the idea of disobeying imperial law as a pretext to have the Jews killed.

6. *he disdained* The same word, *b-z-h,* "disdain, despise, scorn," is what Memucan worries that all the women will do in 1:17 (Levenson). This is part of the theme of honor and shame that informs the relationship between Haman and Mordecai.

to lay hands on Levenson notes that two phrases in this verse, *lishloah yad,* "to lay hands on," and *b-q-sh,* "seek, plot," also occur in 2:21, describing the action of Bigthan and Teresh. The connection between the two episodes is more explicit in rabbinic exegesis where Haman is said to have been involved in the plot of the two villains.

to do away with all the Jews, Mordecai's people Haman's arrogance and extremism stand out here, but there is a certain perverse logic in his extending his hatred to all the Jews. If Mordecai's refusal is based on ethnic grounds, then no Jew will bow down to Haman. The only way Haman can guarantee universal obeisance, which for a personality like his would be of paramount importance, is to get rid of all the Jews.

Josephus adds that Haman was "naturally an enemy to the Jews, because the nation of the Amalekites, of which he was, had been destroyed by them."

There is a parallel between the decree against all women because of the disrespect shown by one (Vashti) and the decree against all Jews because of the disrespect shown by

⁷ In the first month, that is, the month of Nisan, in the twelfth year of King Ahasuerus, *pur*—which means "the lot"—was cast before Haman concerning every day and every month, [until it fell on] the twelfth month, that is, the month of Adar. ⁸ Haman then said to King Ahasuerus, "There is a certain

7 בַּחֹ֣דֶשׁ הָרִאשׁ֗וֹן הוּא־חֹ֣דֶשׁ נִיסָן֮ בִּשְׁנַת֮ שְׁתֵּ֣ים עֶשְׂרֵה֒ לַמֶּ֖לֶךְ אֲחַשְׁוֵר֑וֹשׁ הִפִּ֣יל פּוּר֩ ה֨וּא הַגּוֹרָ֜ל לִפְנֵ֣י הָמָ֗ן מִיּ֤וֹם ׀ לְי֨וֹם וּמֵחֹ֛דֶשׁ לְחֹ֥דֶשׁ שְׁנֵים־עָשָׂ֖ר הוּא־חֹ֥דֶשׁ אֲדָֽר׃ ס 8 וַיֹּ֤אמֶר הָמָן֙ לַמֶּ֣לֶךְ אֲחַשְׁוֵר֔וֹשׁ

Mordecai. Is Haman fashioning himself after Ahasuerus? In chapter 6 it will become clear that Haman wanted to be king.

7. pur The word *pur* comes from Akkadian, and the practice of casting lots is known from ancient Mesopotamia.[12] It was done by means of a small stone die. According to our story, the name of the festival, Purim, derives from *pur.* The term *pur* occurs here and several times in chapter 9, but is not found in the Bible outside of Esther. It is here glossed by the more common term for lot, *goral.*

The Greek authors also mention the casting of lots by the Persians (Herodotus 3.128 and Xenophon, *Cyropaedia* 1.6.45; 4.5.55). Xenophon (*Cyropaedia* 1.6.46) sees lots as a form of chance, not divine direction: "So we see that mere human wisdom does not know how to choose what is best any more than if any one were to cast lots and do as the lot fell." Proverbs 16:33 reflects a similar sentiment that the human casting of lots is, in itself, inefficacious, and that it is God who determines outcomes: "Lots are cast into the lap; the decision depends on the Lord." As the English saying goes, "Man proposes and God disposes." Perhaps, then, we should view Haman's casting of lots similarly, as an inefficacious act that produced a random date. In keeping with the book's reversals, that date will turn out to be a day of Jewish deliverance instead of Jewish destruction. Indeed, the dictum of Prov. 16:33 comes true.

Which day and month did the lot indicate as being propitious? The verse is difficult. On the surface it says that the lot was cast in regard to each day and each month, presumably beginning with Nisan (the first month in the year and the time when the gods decreed the fates; and also the current month at the time the lots were cast) and continuing until Adar, the last month of the year. The propitious date, however, is not mentioned; only the mechanism for arriving at the date is specified.

Many commentators understand the verse to mean that the month of Adar was selected as propitious, but even so, the day of the month is not given. Only in verse 13 do we learn that the destruction is scheduled for 13 Adar, exactly eleven months from the time the decree was written. Because the date is omitted from verse 7, many commentators conclude that it has dropped out by error and they restore it based on the Greek versions of Esther. The Septuagint and Old Latin read "the fourteenth" and the Alpha-text has "the thirteenth." Elsewhere the date is 13 Adar, although an alternate tradition of 14 Adar may lurk in 9:17–19 where both the thirteenth and the fourteenth are days of fighting in Susa (Levenson, 70). The Masoretic Text and the Septuagint place the casting of lots here, before Haman received permission from the king; the Alpha-text places it later in the chapter, after the king has agreed to Haman's proposal.

8. Haman's accusation against the Jews contains three parts: that the Jews are scattered and dispersed; that the Jews have different customs; and that the Jews do not observe imperial law. Fox points out the rhetorical strategy behind this structure: Haman starts with the truth (that the Jews are scattered and dispersed); goes on to a half-truth (that the Jews have different laws and customs); and ends with a lie (that the Jews do not observe imperial law).

people, scattered and dispersed among the other peoples in all the provinces of your realm, whose laws are different from those of any other people and

יֶשְׁנוֹ עַם־אֶחָד מְפֻזָּר וּמְפֹרָד בֵּין הָעַמִּים בְּכֹל מְדִינוֹת מַלְכוּתֶךָ וְדָתֵיהֶם שֹׁנוֹת

But how should we understand this accusation in its historical context? Although it is clear that Haman's accusation is pure fabrication, it rings so true in terms of later anti-Semitic claims that we are forced to consider if it has a basis in history—that is, to what extent Haman's claim had currency in the Persian period (the time that most scholars date the book). It is difficult to find evidence for anti-Semitism (or, more correctly, anti-Judaism) before the Hellenistic period, for our written sources are meager. Peter Schäfer has traced anti-Jewish feeling back to Egypt and points to the destruction of the Jewish temple at Elephantine in 410 B.C.E. and to the Greek writings of two Egyptians, Hecataeus of Abdera in about 300 B.C.E. and Manetho in the third century B.C.E..[13] Both of these authors gave an account (not extant but preserved in later authors' works) of the Egyptian version of the biblical Exodus story. Hecataeus, who is not elsewhere anti-Jewish, describes the Jews of having a way of life different from all the other nations. Manetho accuses the Jews of having laws completely opposed to Egyptian custom. This is not so different from Haman's accusation that the Jews have different laws or customs. So we may have in Esther an early and milder form, already in the late Persian period, of what was later to grow into the classic anti-Semitic argument that the Jews are xenophobic and misanthropic. As Schäfer notes, the Septuagint goes beyond the Masoretic Text of Esther in developing the anti-Semitic theme.[14] Reading back into the Esther story the anti-Semitism of its own time, Addition B 5 containing Artaxerxes' letter reads:

> We understand that this people, and it alone, stands constantly in opposition to every nation, perversely following a strange manner of life and laws, and is ill-disposed to our government, doing all the harm they can so that our kingdom may not attain stability.

scattered and dispersed   Indeed, there were Jews throughout the Persian empire, as there were many other peoples. The concept of dispersion may have struck a nerve with the postexilic Diaspora community, for it underlines their lack of cohesion and vulnerability. The Jewish victory and celebration of Purim later in the story provide an antidote, as it were, through the picture of a united Jewry.

It is not clear why the Persian king would see the dispersion of the Jews as undesirable in and of itself, as there were many communities with mixed ethnic populations. Perhaps the reason has to do with the absence of a Jewish province. As Levenson points out, the book gives no notice to the Temple or to the return to Zion.[15] In fact, there is a resounding silence about the re-establishment of a Jewish jurisdiction in Judah. Perhaps Haman is insinuating that the Jews do not constitute their own province, and hence they were not obligated to pay a separate "Jewish" tribute, for tribute was assigned according to satrapies or provinces. This line of argument was more likely to convince the king that they were dispensable.

whose laws are different   *Dat* can mean "custom" or "practice" and that is probably what is meant. Although the Masoretic Text avoids any mention of religious practice, rabbinic exegesis supplied the details of the distinctively Jewish religious practices, such as eating kosher food, observing the festivals, and the like. Targum Sheni, which is especially expansive, gives a long list of Jewish observances as seen through the eyes of non-Jews. It is a humorous, pseudo-self-deprecating piece—a fine catalogue of Jewish practices with insight about how they could be perceived as inconveniencing non-Jews.[16] The rabbinic emphasis on religion per se is anachronistic. During the Persian

who do not obey the king's laws; and it is not in Your מִכָּל־עָ֗ם וְאֶת־דָּתֵ֤י הַמֶּ֙לֶךְ֙ אֵינָ֣ם עֹשִׂ֔ים

period, religion was just one aspect of communal identity (others being ethnicity and language); religion did not become an important distinctive marker until Greco-Roman times, especially in the Christian era.[17]

While the emphasis on the distinctiveness of Jewish practice sounds like an incipient anti-Jewish argument, it seems unlikely that distinctive practices would have been widely viewed as negative during the Persian period; the empire contained diverse peoples with distinctive customs and the attitude of the Persian government was tolerant toward them. Haman's accusation should be understood as the exaggeration that it is.

who do not obey the king's laws On a superficial level, this could refer to the fact that Mordecai refused to obey the royal command to bow to Haman. But the accusation is couched in different, and broader, terms. Verse 3 spoke of *mitzvat ha-melekh,* and here it is a question of *dat ha-melekh,* "imperial law."

Imperial law extended over the entire Persian empire. The provinces were permitted to retain their local laws as long as they were not in conflict with imperial law. In fact, they were urged to codify their local laws and to follow them. Imperial law was not a separate law code or juridical system superimposed on the provinces; it was essentially the bringing together of all the various law codes and customs under Persian sovereignty.[18] It was a political rather than juridical system whereby everyone gave allegiance to the king. What Haman is really saying, then, is that the Jews do not to acknowledge the sovereignty of the king; and this constitutes treason.

How did people show their lack of allegiance to the king? Aeschylus summarizes the Greek view succinctly in *The Persians,* 585–88:

> Not now for long will they that dwell throughout the length and breadth of Asia abide under the laws of the Persians, nor will they pay further tribute at the compulsion of their lord, nor will they prostrate themselves to the earth and do him reverence.

These same three items—abiding by Persian law, paying tribute, and doing obeisance—seem to be at issue in our chapter, although they are not so neatly laid out. Mordecai's refusal to do obeisance motivates Haman; Haman may be implying that the Jews do not pay tribute; and he states explicitly that they do not obey imperial law.

One or more of these three items figure in other references, also with the sense of treason. In Ezra 4:12–16 it is claimed that the Jews returning to Judah will not pay tribute or taxes and that this will constitute sedition against the Persian king. In an inscription from Persepolis, the Persian king Xerxes invokes tribute and imperial law as the signs of his suzerainty: "These are the countries . . . over which I hold sway . . . which are bringing their tribute to me . . . and they abide by my laws."[19] The author of Esther has put into Haman's mouth exactly the elements that constitute treason against the Persian king.

it is not in Your Majesty's interest Hebrew *shoveh,* literally "worth," is taken by Targum Rishon and other Jewish exegetes to mean "profit," that is, there is no profit for the king in letting the Jews live. See my interpretation of the following phrase.

to tolerate them Since they are a threat to the king's sovereignty, it is not in the king's interest to leave them alone or to let them continue to live in the empire (cf. Jer. 27:11). So most commentaries understand the phrase. Fox points to the graphically similar root *n-w-ḥ* in Esther 9:17, 18, 22 meaning "rest, respite, relief" and intimates that the irony is that the Jews ultimately achieve what Haman wants to deprive them of here.

Majesty's interest to tolerate them. ⁹ If it please Your Majesty, let an edict be drawn for their destruction, and I will pay ten thousand talents of silver to the stewards for deposit in the royal treasury." ¹⁰ Thereupon the king removed his signet ring from his hand and gave it to Haman son of Hammedatha

וְלַמֶּ֖לֶךְ אֵין־שֹׁוֶ֣ה לְהַנִּיחָֽם׃ ⁹ אִם־עַל־הַמֶּ֣לֶךְ טֹ֔וב יִכָּתֵ֖ב לְאַבְּדָ֑ם וַעֲשֶׂ֨רֶת אֲלָפִ֤ים כִּכַּר־כֶּ֙סֶף֙ אֶשְׁקֹ֗ול עַל־יְדֵי֙ עֹשֵׂ֣י הַמְּלָאכָ֔ה לְהָבִ֖יא אֶל־גִּנְזֵ֥י הַמֶּֽלֶךְ׃ ¹⁰ וַיָּ֧סַר הַמֶּ֛לֶךְ אֶת־טַבַּעְתֹּ֖ו מֵעַ֣ל יָדֹ֑ו וַֽיִּתְּנָ֔הּ לְהָמָ֖ן בֶּן־

But there is another possible interpretation. In Esther 2:18 the same word appears in the form of a noun, *hanaḥah,* most probably meaning "a remission of taxes." If, as I am arguing, Haman's accusation is largely based on the fact that the Jews do not provide their share of tribute or taxes (this being the major form of insubordination to the monarchy), then Haman may be saying here, perhaps with a touch of irony: "It is not worth giving them a release from taxes." That is, it is not in the king's interest to let the Jews get away with not paying tribute. Lest the king think that there is a way to compel the Jews to pay, Haman quickly offers him a large sum of money to make up for the financial loss, for Haman is not really interested in collecting taxes but in getting rid of the Jews.

9. Haman offers an inducement to the king in the form of revenue for the royal treasury, as if the logic of his position were not sufficient to convince the king. Or, in keeping with the practices of the time, he is offering extravagant compensation for the loss of future tribute that the Jews would have had to pay if they were to be left alive and under the king's control. Haman does not want it to look as though he is making a profit from the Jews, either from the tribute he will collect from them or from the booty he will take when they are killed (see v. 13).

ten thousand talents of silver Estimated to be 333 tons or 302 metric tons of silver—an enormous sum, almost equivalent to the total sum of the annual tribute of the entire Persian empire (see Moore and Bush). This is clearly an exaggerated amount, in keeping with the other exaggerated numbers in the book. Is this how much the Jews were worth to the king? Probably not, but it is how much it was worth to Haman to have them killed. Josephus raises the sum to forty thousand talents. He makes explicit that the silver was intended to compensate the king for the loss of tribute that the Jews would have paid if they were to remain alive.

to the stewards Literally: "into the charge of the *'osei ha-mela'khah.*" The term is a formal title, used among other high-ranking titles in 9:3. Compare 2 Kings 12:12, 15, 16; 22:5, 9; Neh. 2:16; 2 Chron. 34:10, 17. Outside of Esther, these stewards were the overseers of the Temple workmen and were given the money that was to be paid out to the workmen. These Persian stewards may have served a similar function of receiving state revenues and overseeing payment for work on government projects. This may reinforce the idea that Haman's offer of silver was to compensate for the loss of revenue from the Jews.

treasury Hebrew *ginzei* derives from Persian *ganza.* The Persian word for treasurer is *ganzabara,* which came into Hebrew as *gizbar.*

10. signet ring Gold and iron finger rings with seals from the Persian period have been found in Babylonia. The signet ring will give Haman the authority to seal the edict against the Jews in the king's name.

son of Hammedatha the Agagite, the foe of the Jews The full name and both its appellatives are given at the moment that the decree is about to be approved. This is not for the purpose of explaining who Haman is, for that was already done, but for emphasizing to the audience, with a verbal drum roll, that the archvillain is most menacing at this moment. The epithet "foe of the Jews" underlines Haman's primary role in the story.

the Agagite, the foe of the Jews. ¹¹ And the king said, "The money and the people are yours to do with as you see fit."

¹² On the thirteenth day of the first month, the king's scribes were summoned and a decree was issued, as Haman directed, to the king's satraps, to the governors of every province, and to the officials of every people, to every province in its own script and to every people in its own language. The orders were issued in the name of King Ahasuerus and sealed with the king's signet. ¹³ Accordingly, written instructions were dispatched by couriers to all the king's provinces to destroy, massacre, and exterminate all the Jews, young and old, children and women, on a single day,

הַמְּדָ֫תָא הָאֲגָגִ֖י צֹרֵ֥ר הַיְּהוּדִֽים: ¹¹ וַיֹּ֨אמֶר הַמֶּ֜לֶךְ לְהָמָ֗ן הַכֶּ֨סֶף֙ נָת֣וּן לָ֔ךְ וְהָעָ֕ם לַעֲשׂ֥וֹת בּ֖וֹ כַּטּ֥וֹב בְּעֵינֶֽיךָ: ¹² וַיִּקָּרְאוּ֩ סֹפְרֵ֨י הַמֶּ֜לֶךְ בַּחֹ֣דֶשׁ הָרִאשׁ֗וֹן בִּשְׁלוֹשָׁ֨ה עָשָׂ֣ר יוֹם֮ בּוֹ֒ וַיִּכָּתֵ֣ב כְּכָל־אֲשֶׁר־ צִוָּ֣ה הָמָ֡ן אֶ֣ל אֲחַשְׁדַּרְפְּנֵֽי־הַמֶּ֣לֶךְ וְאֶל־ הַֽפַּחוֹת֩ אֲשֶׁ֨ר ׀ עַל־מְדִינָ֤ה וּמְדִינָה֙ וְאֶל־ שָׂ֣רֵי עַ֣ם וָעָ֔ם מְדִינָ֤ה וּמְדִינָה֙ כִּכְתָבָ֔הּ וְעַ֥ם וָעָ֖ם כִּלְשׁוֹנ֑וֹ בְּשֵׁ֨ם הַמֶּ֤לֶךְ אֲחַשְׁוֵרֹשׁ֙ נִכְתָּ֔ב וְנֶחְתָּ֖ם בְּטַבַּ֥עַת הַמֶּֽלֶךְ: ¹³ וְנִשְׁל֨וֹחַ סְפָרִ֜ים בְּיַ֣ד הָרָצִים֮ אֶל־כָּל־מְדִינ֣וֹת הַמֶּלֶךְ֒ לְהַשְׁמִ֡יד לַהֲרֹ֣ג וּלְאַבֵּ֣ד אֶת־כָּל־

11. **The money and the people are yours** The nature of the financial transaction is obscure. A number of commentators see in Ahasuerus's rejection of the money a formulaic business exchange, like Abraham's exchange with Ephron over the cave of Machpelah (Gen. 23), whereby the king is actually accepting the payment. I think not. The king declines Haman's offer of payment and permits him to do as he likes with the people. It would seem that, according to Haman, the Jews were not currently providing any income to the king, so Ahasuerus would lose nothing by forgoing Haman's payment. I understand the king to be giving Haman authority over the Jews and permission to keep any tribute he collected from them. Compare Herodotus 3.160, which describes Darius's reward to Zopyrus, the incredibly loyal follower who, at great physical cost, enabled the Persians to put down the revolt of Babylonia. Among other things, Darius "gave him Babylon to be his own domain, free of taxes, for as long as he should live." But there is no good reason that Ahasuerus should be so generous to Haman. In fact, the king's generosity, like everything else he does, is exaggerated. This same exaggerated generosity will later let him offer Esther up to half his kingdom. Ahasuerus gives the impression that he cannot be bothered with such matters as Haman has described, and is all too happy to have Haman take care of any problems on his own. This is not a king with a good head for business or for politics. We again see a weak king who is easily manipulated by his advisors.

12. **On the thirteenth day of the first month** The name of the month is not mentioned here, as it often is in the story. It is the month of Nisan. The date of the writing and promulgation of the decree is 13 Nisan, just a day before Passover.

satraps…governors…officials The hierarchy described is satrap (who governed a satrapy and who was generally a Persian), governor (who governed a province within a satrapy; he was likely to be a Persian but could be from another ethnic group), and local officials. The term satrap also occurs in 8:9; 9:3; Ezra 8:36; and a number of times in Daniel 3 and 6.

its own script…its own language See 1:22.

13. The language emphasizes by its repetition the intensity, totality, and speed of the destruction. The edict was sent out eleven months before it was to take effect. This would provide plenty of advance notice. Herodotus 5.52–53 estimated that it would take three months for a message to travel to all parts of the empire.

on the thirteenth day of the twelfth month—that is, the month of Adar—and to plunder their possessions. [14] The text of the document was to the effect that a law should be proclaimed in every single province; it was to be publicly displayed to all the peoples, so that they might be ready for that day.

[15] The couriers went out posthaste on the royal mission, and the decree was proclaimed in the fortress Shushan. The king and Haman sat down to feast, but the city of Shushan was dumbfounded.

הַיְּהוּדִים מִנַּעַר וְעַד־זָקֵן טַף וְנָשִׁים בְּיוֹם אֶחָד בִּשְׁלוֹשָׁה עָשָׂר לְחֹדֶשׁ שְׁנֵים־עָשָׂר הוּא־חֹדֶשׁ אֲדָר וּשְׁלָלָם לָבוֹז: 14 פַּתְשֶׁגֶן הַכְּתָב לְהִנָּתֵן דָּת בְּכָל־מְדִינָה וּמְדִינָה גָּלוּי לְכָל־הָעַמִּים לִהְיוֹת עֲתִדִים לַיּוֹם הַזֶּה:

15 הָרָצִים יָצְאוּ דְחוּפִים בִּדְבַר הַמֶּלֶךְ וְהַדָּת נִתְּנָה בְּשׁוּשַׁן הַבִּירָה וְהַמֶּלֶךְ וְהָמָן יָשְׁבוּ לִשְׁתּוֹת וְהָעִיר שׁוּשָׁן נָבוֹכָה: פ

to plunder their possessions The potential profit from plunder would presumably motivate the non-Jews to kill the Jews. Compare 8:11 and see the Commentary to 9:15.

15. The couriers went out posthaste Compare 8:14 and see the Commentary to chapter 8 on the communication of messages.

sat down to feast The actions of the king and Haman could not contrast more with the reactions of the populace of Susa. The king and Haman resume their normal activity, drinking, as if nothing out of the ordinary had happened. This also contrasts with the fasting and mourning of the Jews at the beginning of chapter 4.

Uriel Simon notes that "obstinately ignoring the suffering of others is expressed by demonstrative feasting" and he mentions the actions of Ahasuerus and Haman along with those of Joseph's brothers after they have thrown Joseph into the pit (Gen. 37:24–25) and Jehu after his horses had trampled Jezebel (2 Kings 9:33–34).[20]

Paton suggests that "to drink" in our verse and in 7:1 means "to have a banquet" (from *mishteh,* "banquet"), and subsequent commentators have stressed that this includes both food and drink.[21] But in a *mishteh* in Esther the emphasis is on drink. A better translation is "to party." The point of our verse is not to indicate that solid food was eaten, but that Haman and Ahasuerus resumed the usual Persian practice of drinking and carousing. "Drinking" is one of the pervasive motifs in the book. The root *sh-t-h* occurs over a dozen times, while the root *'-k-l* occurs just once, in 4:16, when the Jews of Shushan are asked to fast, not to eat or drink. Drinking—that is, partying,—with its overtones of boisterousness and bawdiness, forms a striking contrast with the severity of the decree. We are also reminded of Herodotus's statement (1.134) that the Persians make or reconsider important decisions when they are drunk.

the city of Shushan was dumbfounded "The city" refers to the lower city where the population resided, in contrast to the acropolis *(birah),* which was the seat of the government. Assuming that "the city" includes a large number of non-Jews, why should the entire city be dumbfounded? Was the general population so sympathetic to the plight of the Jews, as some recent exegetes have suggested? I would not take this expression as a sociological statement, but rather as a literary indicator signaling how shocking the decree was. From a literary point of view, the reaction of the city represents the normal reaction (in contrast to Haman and Ahasuerus) and signals the opinion of the narrator, which the reader is encouraged to adopt, that Haman's decree is totally beyond the norm. The city of Shushan serves as a kind of chorus, as it were, reinforcing the decree and its effect. The counterpart is in 8:15, following the publication of the new decree permitting the Jews to save themselves: "the city of Shushan rang with joyous cries."

This phrase also marks the low point in the plot: the destruction of the Jews seems inescapable. But immediately following (4:1), plans to reverse the decree are begun.

CHAPTER 4

Mourning and Planning

This is a somber chapter. Gone are the bright lights of the palace, the luxurious food and finery, the extravagant cosmetics of the harem, the settings of power and prestige. The beautiful people living the good life fade into the distance. This is a scene of mourning garb and fasting, a reversal of the previous drinking and frivolity; and the elements of this scene will, in turn, be reversed yet again later in the story.

Chapter 4 takes place not in the royal court or king's gate or harem (all locations reserved for the privileged) but in the city square, a public plaza open to all. Although Esther remains in the harem, it is no longer a place of indulgence, but a place of constriction, which cuts Esther off both from what is happening to her people and from access to the king. Before, Mordecai would pass by the harem regularly to check on Esther's well-being (2:11). Now, because his insistence on wearing mourning garb prevents him from taking his accustomed position at court, he must make contact with Esther through an intermediary. And the purpose of his contact is not to ascertain the well-being of Esther but to ensure the well-being of the Jews.

God is most present and most absent in this chapter. Religious practice and the mention of God's name come closest to the surface here, and are most obviously suppressed. It is hard to read about fasting, mourning, and crying out without seeing God as the addressee to whom all these actions are directed. It is hard to plead for salvation from anyone but God. It is hard to imagine that salvation could come "from another place" without seeing this as a veiled reference to God. That the comic nature of the book has prevented the mention of God is most evident now, when the book is least comic. In this sad scene, the author is hard pressed to write God out of the story.

As before, the Greek sources provide a background for a number of the motifs in this chapter. Herodotus 3.117–119 contains the motifs of access to the king (a motif that appears several times in Herodotus) and intercession by a woman on behalf of family members (this motif, too, is found throughout Greek sources). Though Herodotus's story is rather different from Esther in plot and in tone, it is interesting for the way in which it joins together the same motifs that we find in our chapter. It also contains the motif of family solidarity, albeit in a much more gruesome manner.

We learn from Herodotus in 3.117 that people in need would come to Persia and cry and howl before the door of the king's palace. In 3.118 we hear the story of Intaphrenes, one of the seven rebels against the Magus. These rebels, of which Darius had been one, were heroes in the eyes of Darius and his court, and had the special privilege of free access to Darius after he became king.

> He [Intaphrenes] wanted to enter the palace to do some business with the king; and indeed the rule stated that the conspirators could go in to see the king unannounced, unless he happened to be having sex with a woman. So Intaphrenes thought it his right not to be announced, but because he was one of the seven to go right in as he wanted. But the gatekeeper and the message-bearer would not let him in, on the grounds that the king was having sex with a woman. Intaphrenes thought they were lying, however. He drew his akinakes, cut off their ears and noses, and threaded them on his horse's bridle. Then he tied the bridle around their necks and sent them away.

As a result, Intaphrenes and his sons and all his household were imprisoned and sentenced to death, for the king thought they were plotting against him.

4 When Mordecai learned all that had happened, Mordecai tore his clothes and put on sackcloth and ashes. He went through the city, crying out loudly and bitterly, [2] until he came in front of the palace gate; for one could not enter the palace gate wearing sackcloth.—[3] Also, in every province that the king's command and decree reached, there was great

ד וּמָרְדֳּכַי יָדַע אֶת־כָּל־אֲשֶׁר נַעֲשָׂה
וַיִּקְרַע מָרְדֳּכַי אֶת־בְּגָדָיו וַיִּלְבַּשׁ שַׂק וָאֵפֶר
וַיֵּצֵא בְּתוֹךְ הָעִיר וַיִּזְעַק זְעָקָה גְדֹלָה
וּמָרָה: 2 וַיָּבוֹא עַד לִפְנֵי שַׁעַר־הַמֶּלֶךְ כִּי
אֵין לָבוֹא אֶל־שַׁעַר הַמֶּלֶךְ בִּלְבוּשׁ שָׂק:
3 וּבְכָל־מְדִינָה וּמְדִינָה מְקוֹם אֲשֶׁר דְּבַר־

Intaphrenes' wife took to coming to the doors of the palace and breaking down in tears and grief. This behaviour of hers eventually moved Darius to pity, and he sent a messenger out to her. "Woman," he said, "King Darius permits you to choose one member of your imprisoned family to save."

She thought about it and replied, "If, thanks to the king, I have to choose the life of one person, out of all of them I choose my brother."

When Darius heard what her reply had been, he was surprised and sent another message to her as follows: "Woman, the king would like to know what your reason was for abandoning your husband and children and deciding to save your brother's life, when he is not as near to you as your children or as dear to you as your husband."

"My lord," she replied, "God willing I may get another husband and more children, if I lose the ones I have at the moment. But my parents are dead, so there's no way I can get another brother. That was why I said what I said."

1. When Mordecai learned   Mordecai heard the decree at the same time as the city of Shushan. Unlike the dumbfounded city, Mordecai springs into action, taking definite steps to publicly demonstrate his feelings.

Mordecai tore his clothes   Mordecai's actions are typical signs of mourning, and contrast vividly with the actions of the king and Haman in 3:15. Compare their respective actions to those of the king of Nineveh in Jon. 3:6–7, who took off his robe, put on sackcloth, sat in ashes, and made a proclamation. This mourning is not for a past loss but for a future threat. It is actually a kind of public protest.

crying out loudly and bitterly   Mordecai is not crying to God, but is shouting aloud to the city. He does not fast, although the Jews throughout the empire do, and so does Esther at the end of the chapter.

3. great mourning   The typical signs of mourning are present—fasting, sackcloth and ashes, weeping—but there is no praying or calling on God for his help, for God is not mentioned in the book. Fasting and sackcloth are probably not to be seen as specifically Jewish religious practices, but as universal expressions of mourning in the ancient Near East. In Jonah, the people of Nineveh also fast and wear sackcloth.

While for the modern reader grief and joy are considered internal emotional experiences, in ancient Israel they are represented through specific types of public behavior.[1]

They are performative; they are registered through ritual or symbolic actions rather than through feelings. Our verse is a clear example. Compare the expression of joy in 8:15–17; 9:17–19, 22.

The Greek versions remedy the religious omission in the Masoretic Text by supplying a prayer that Mordecai uttered to God. In these versions Esther, too, prayed and dressed in mourning, removing her lavish attire and expensive cosmetics and covering her head with ashes and dung.

mourning among the Jews, with fasting, weeping, and wailing, and everybody lay in sackcloth and ashes.—⁴When Esther's maidens and eunuchs came and informed her, the queen was greatly agitated. She sent clothing for Mordecai to wear, so that he might take off his sackcloth; but he refused. ⁵Thereupon Esther summoned Hathach, one of the eunuchs whom the king had appointed to serve her, and sent him to Mordecai to learn the why and wherefore of it all. ⁶Hathach went out to Mordecai in the city

הַמֶּלֶךְ וְדָתוֹ מַגִּיעַ אֵבֶל גָּדוֹל לַיְּהוּדִים וְצוֹם וּבְכִי וּמִסְפֵּד שַׂק וָאֵפֶר יֻצַּע לָרַבִּים: ⁴וַתָּבוֹאינָה נַעֲרוֹת אֶסְתֵּר וְסָרִיסֶיהָ וַיַּגִּידוּ לָהּ וַתִּתְחַלְחַל הַמַּלְכָּה מְאֹד וַתִּשְׁלַח בְּגָדִים לְהַלְבִּישׁ אֶת־מָרְדֳּכַי וּלְהָסִיר שַׂקּוֹ מֵעָלָיו וְלֹא קִבֵּל: ⁵וַתִּקְרָא אֶסְתֵּר לַהֲתָךְ מִסָּרִיסֵי הַמֶּלֶךְ אֲשֶׁר הֶעֱמִיד לְפָנֶיהָ וַתְּצַוֵּהוּ עַל־מָרְדֳּכָי לָדַעַת מַה־זֶּה וְעַל־מַה־זֶּה: ⁶וַיֵּצֵא הֲתָךְ אֶל־

Compare another case of public mourning to ward off a threat of calamity: Jth 4:9–12.

> And every man of Israel cried out to God with great fervor, and they humbled themselves with much fasting. They and their wives and their children and their cattle and every resident alien and hired laborer and purchased slaves—they all put sackcloth around their waists. And all the Israelite men, women, and children living at Jerusalem prostrated themselves before the temple and put ashes on their heads and spread out their sackcloth before the Lord. They even draped the altar with sackcloth and cried out in unison, praying fervently to the God of Israel.…

4. Esther, secluded in the harem, did not see what was happening in the city, but was informed by her servant women and eunuchs. She learns only belatedly about the decree against the Jews and the Jewish reaction to it.

informed her Of Mordecai's attire and actions and the widespread Jewish mourning. It is only later, when her servant Hathach speaks with Mordecai and conveys the information to Esther, that Esther learns the reason for all this—the decree against the Jews.

agitated From the root ḥ-y-l, "to writhe." The form here, with the reduplication of ḥlḥl, is unusual. The more common form of the hitpa'el is hitḥolel, as in Job 15:20 and Jer. 23:19. It means "to writhe in fear," suggesting a physiological reaction. The knowledge that Mordecai and all the other Jews are mourning puts dread into Esther's heart, for it is a sign that something terrible has happened.

she sent clothing If Esther were to learn directly from Mordecai what had happened, he would have to enter the palace precinct. Since he could not do so dressed in sackcloth, she sends him appropriate clothing. Mordecai refuses to remove his sackcloth for he has not finished making his point.

5. Esther, having failed to achieve contact with Mordecai directly, must now find an indirect means. Esther cannot leave the harem and Mordecai cannot enter it, so, if they are to communicate, it must be through an intermediary who has access to both places. That person is Hathach, one of the eunuchs.

the why and wherefore of it all A nice phrase to express the bewilderment that Esther must have felt: "What's going on? What's this all about?"

6. Hathach had to meet Mordecai in the city square in front of the king's gate because Mordecai could not enter it (his usual place) because he was still wearing his mourning attire. This will be the same place where later Haman will honor Mordecai (see 6:9, 11).

square in front of the palace gate; 7 and Mordecai told him all that had happened to him, and all about the money that Haman had offered to pay into the royal treasury for the destruction of the Jews. 8 He also gave him the written text of the law that had been proclaimed in Shushan for their destruction. [He bade him] show it to Esther and inform her, and charge her to go to the king and to appeal to him and to plead with him for her people. 9 When Hathach came and delivered Mordecai's message to Esther, 10 Esther told Hathach to take back to Mordecai the following reply: 11 "All the king's courtiers and the people of the king's provinces know that if any person, man or woman, enters the king's presence in

מָרְדֳּכַי אֶל־רְחוֹב הָעִיר אֲשֶׁר לִפְנֵי שַׁעַר־
הַמֶּלֶךְ: 7 וַיַּגֶּד־לוֹ מָרְדֳּכַי אֵת כָּל־אֲשֶׁר
קָרָהוּ וְאֵת ׀ פָּרָשַׁת הַכֶּסֶף אֲשֶׁר אָמַר
הָמָן לִשְׁקוֹל עַל־גִּנְזֵי הַמֶּלֶךְ בַּיְּהוּדִיִּים
בַּיְּהוּדִים לְאַבְּדָם: 8 וְאֶת־פַּתְשֶׁגֶן כְּתָב־
הַדָּת אֲשֶׁר־נִתַּן בְּשׁוּשָׁן לְהַשְׁמִידָם נָתַן
לוֹ לְהַרְאוֹת אֶת־אֶסְתֵּר וּלְהַגִּיד לָהּ
וּלְצַוּוֹת עָלֶיהָ לָבוֹא אֶל־הַמֶּלֶךְ לְהִתְחַנֶּן־
לוֹ וּלְבַקֵּשׁ מִלְּפָנָיו עַל־עַמָּהּ: 9 וַיָּבוֹא
הֲתָךְ וַיַּגֵּד לְאֶסְתֵּר אֵת דִּבְרֵי מָרְדֳּכָי:
10 וַתֹּאמֶר אֶסְתֵּר לַהֲתָךְ וַתְּצַוֵּהוּ אֶל־
מָרְדֳּכָי: 11 כָּל־עַבְדֵי הַמֶּלֶךְ וְעַם־מְדִינוֹת

7. *all that had happened to him*   All of Mordecai's adventures leading up to the present situation, including, presumably, that Mordecai refused to bow to Haman. I do not think that Mordecai is blaming himself for the current predicament; he is just presenting the background.

about the money that Haman had offered   Was this public knowledge, or did Mordecai know it because he was well-placed to know everything that happened at court? The story seems to emphasize the financial aspect of Haman's deal here, in 3:9 and in 7:4. Whenever it is mentioned, it adds to the maliciousness of Haman's plan.

8. *the written text*   The book is fond of referring to documents, although, unlike the Greek versions of Esther and biblical books like Ezra, it does not often quote the full text of the document. The written text would be even stronger proof than Mordecai's words of the seriousness of the threat to the Jews, since this threat of destruction was in an official document. Esther would be able to see it firsthand.

This is not the first time that Esther has served as a link between Mordecai and the king. In 2:22 she informed the king that Mordecai had discovered a plot against the king's life.

10.   Until this point, the words of Esther and Mordecai have been summarized, not quoted directly, and the presence of the messenger, Hathach, and his function of reporting have been strongly felt. From here on we will be privy to the direct discourse of Mordecai and Esther, with the concurrent diminution of the role of the messenger (Levenson). This serves to build the drama and escalate the tension. It is here that we have a foreshadowing of what is to follow in the plot. It is not only a question of whether Esther will carry out Mordecai's instructions, but how she will carry them out. It is here, too, that the character of Esther begins to change from passive to active.

11.   Esther's response to Mordecai opens with the words "All the king's courtiers . . . know," implying that Mordecai should also have known. Was Esther scolding or criticizing Mordecai, as some commentators suppose, or refusing to do his bidding? I think not, for I see in their conversation a more subtle series of moves. Esther is introducing a new piece of information. She is hinting at the strategy she will use to carry out Mordecai's instructions and at the same time indicating the risk it entails.

the inner court without having been summoned, there is but one law for him—that he be put to death. Only if the king extends the golden scepter to him may he live. Now I have not been summoned to visit the king for the last thirty days."

¹² When Mordecai was told what Esther had said,

הַמֶּ֡לֶךְ יוֹדְעִ֞ים אֲשֶׁ֣ר כָּל־אִ֣ישׁ וְאִשָּׁ֣ה אֲשֶׁ֣ר
יָבֽוֹא־אֶל־הַמֶּ֣לֶךְ אֶל־הֶחָצֵ֣ר הַפְּנִימִ֗ית
אֲשֶׁ֣ר לֹֽא־יִקָּרֵא֮ אַחַ֣ת דָּת֣וֹ לְהָמִ֣ית לְבַ֗ד
מֵאֲשֶׁ֣ר יֽוֹשִׁיט־ל֣וֹ הַמֶּ֣לֶךְ אֶת־שַׁרְבִ֣יט
הַזָּהָ֣ב וְחָיָ֑ה וַאֲנִ֗י לֹ֤א נִקְרֵ֨אתִי֙ לָב֣וֹא
אֶל־הַמֶּ֔לֶךְ זֶ֖ה שְׁלוֹשִׁ֥ים יֽוֹם׃
¹² וַיַּגִּ֣ידוּ לְמׇרְדֳּכָ֔י אֵ֖ת דִּבְרֵ֥י אֶסְתֵּֽר׃ פ

man or woman   Even a woman of whom the king may be enamored. The wording emphasizes that Esther has no special privilege in this regard, even as Mordecai stresses in verse 13 that Esther has no special privilege when it comes to the decree against the Jews.

enters the king's presence in the inner court   Mordecai said nothing, as far as we have been told, about going to the inner court. He merely instructed Esther to go to the king, without specifying how or where. Surely there were other ways to petition the king. Esther had initiated a communication with him in 2:22; Haman will go uninvited to the outer court in 6:4 to seek the king's approval to impale Mordecai. Would not Esther be called regularly to the king's bed, and what better time to entreat him? But Esther specifies being called to the inner court. In light of the Greek motifs about the difficulty and danger in obtaining an audience with the king, I suggest that what Esther is doing is outlining a daring plan whereby she can carry out Mordecai's bidding.

extends the golden scepter   Earlier in his version of the story, Josephus had recounted that

> the king had made a law that none of his own people should approach him unless they were called, when he sat upon his throne; and men, with axes in their hands, stood round about his throne, in order to punish such as approached to him without being called. However, the king sat with a golden sceptre in his hand, which he held out when he had a mind to save anyone of those that approached to him without being called; and he who touched it was free from danger.

for the last thirty days   A long time. Is Esther implying that she is not often called and therefore does not expect an invitation in the near future, or that, since she has not been invited recently, she should bide her time a bit longer until the next invitation comes? In either case, Mordecai urges quick action.

To sum up, Esther is not refusing the task that Mordecai set before her; she is proposing a plan whereby it can be accomplished, and at the same time warning of the risk inherent in it. She risks losing her own life, which is not only a problem for her but, more to the point of the dialogue, means that she would then be unable to plead for the Jews. Does Mordecai understand what she is saying, or is there a touch of comic misunderstanding here, too?

12. was told   The Hebrew uses a third-person plural active verb, "they told," which functions like a passive. It must have been Hathach who told Mordecai. Levenson observes that from this point on, Hathach disappears. Instead of having him repeat information we now have messages being delivered in a more impersonal way (vv. 13, 14). The effect is to make the communication between Esther and Mordecai more direct and hence more dramatic.

13 Mordecai had this message delivered to Esther: "Do not imagine that you, of all the Jews, will escape with your life by being in the king's palace. 14 On the contrary, if you keep silent in this crisis, relief and deliverance will come to the Jews from another quarter, while you and your father's house will perish. And who knows, perhaps you have attained to royal position for just such a crisis."15 Then Esther sent back this answer to Mordecai: 16 "Go, assemble all the Jews who live in Shushan, and fast in my behalf; do not eat or drink for three days, night or day. I and my

13 וַיֹּאמֶר מָרְדֳּכַי לְהָשִׁיב אֶל־אֶסְתֵּר אַל־
תְּדַמִּי בְנַפְשֵׁךְ לְהִמָּלֵט בֵּית־הַמֶּלֶךְ מִכָּל־
הַיְּהוּדִים: 14 כִּי אִם־הַחֲרֵשׁ תַּחֲרִישִׁי
בָּעֵת הַזֹּאת רֶוַח וְהַצָּלָה יַעֲמוֹד לַיְּהוּדִים
מִמָּקוֹם אַחֵר וְאַתְּ וּבֵית־אָבִיךְ תֹּאבֵדוּ
וּמִי יוֹדֵעַ אִם־לְעֵת כָּזֹאת הִגַּעַתְּ
לַמַּלְכוּת: 15 וַתֹּאמֶר אֶסְתֵּר לְהָשִׁיב אֶל־
מָרְדֳּכָי: 16 לֵךְ כְּנוֹס אֶת־כָּל־הַיְּהוּדִים
הַנִּמְצְאִים בְּשׁוּשָׁן וְצוּמוּ עָלַי וְאַל־
תֹּאכְלוּ וְאַל־תִּשְׁתּוּ שְׁלֹשֶׁת יָמִים לַיְלָה

13–14. Mordecai's response makes it seem that he took her words as a refusal to go to the king. I think, though, that his response is calculated to convince her that her plan is a good one and that the risk she outlined is worth taking. The danger, he argues, is greater to Esther if she refuses to go. If she goes to the king, she has a chance to be spared and to save the Jews; if she refuses to go to the king, she will certainly die, even if the other Jews are saved.

13. *of all the Jews* Separate from the rest of the Jews. Being in the palace, Esther is physically separated from the other Jews, but the decree applies to her, too, and her royal position will not afford her special protection.

14. *you and your father's house will perish* The Masoretic Text does not state the source of Esther's punishment. Josephus says that she will be destroyed by those she now despised.

Mordecai's words appear deficient in logic, for who was left of Esther's father's house except perhaps Mordecai? However, it is not a question of logic, but of rhetoric. Mordecai wants to personalize the danger to Esther. Another example of this type of personalization of a prediction of doom is seen in the confrontation between Amos and Amaziah. When Amaziah rejected Amos's prophecy of the destruction of Israel, Amos reiterated his prediction by describing in detail how Amaziah himself and his own family would come to a bad end as a result of the exile (Amos 7:17). The rhetorical effect is to bring home the danger to oneself and one's closest kin in an immediate way. (Compare the protecting of members of one's father's house above others in the choice that Intaphrenes' wife made.)

perhaps you have attained to royal position for just such a crisis You did not attain your royal position in order to be saved apart from all the Jews (v. 13); you attained it in order to save the Jews. A wonderful expression, further reinforcing that the many coincidences of the story are moving toward a happy ending. Just as Mordecai refers to her *malkhut*, "royal position," here, so Esther will put on *malkhut* in 5:1 when she carries out her plan. She will not go to the king as a seductress, but as a dignified woman of high royal stature.

16. Esther requests that all the Jews of Susa join her and her maidens in a fast. The chapter's ending is similar to its beginning, but there is no mention of sackcloth or wailing or mourning.

do not eat or drink for three days A long time for a fast, if we take this literally. It is better to take it as a formulaic expression marking a short time. The post-talmudic Fast of Esther lasts from sunrise until sundown on 13 Adar.

maidens will observe the same fast. Then I shall go to the king, though it is contrary to the law; and if I am to perish, I shall perish!" [17] So Mordecai went about [the city] and did just as Esther had commanded him.

וְי֣וֹם גַּם־אֲנִ֧י וְנַעֲרֹתַ֛י אָצ֖וּם כֵּ֑ן וּבְכֵ֞ן אָב֣וֹא אֶל־הַמֶּ֗לֶךְ אֲשֶׁ֤ר לֹֽא־כַדָּת֙ וְכַאֲשֶׁ֣ר אָבַ֔דְתִּי אָבָֽדְתִּי: [17] וַֽיַּעֲבֹ֖ר מָרְדֳּכָ֑י וַיַּ֙עַשׂ֙ כְּכֹ֛ל אֲשֶׁר־צִוְּתָ֥ה עָלָ֖יו אֶסְתֵּֽר: ס

though it is contrary to the law   Esther returns to her original argument, but, with some reluctance, acknowledges that Mordecai's argument is stronger. Esther is ready to go against *dat* in a land that is entirely ruled by *dat*.

if I am to perish, I shall perish   Esther echoes Mordecai's term "perish" in verse 14, but applies it to the opposite case. Mordecai said she will perish if she doesn't go to the king; Esther is resigned to the possibility of perishing if she does go to the king. The grammatical construction, here and in Gen. 43:14 where the same syntax occurs, betokens a fatalistic acceptance of a choice of action to which there is really no alternative.

17.   Here Esther gives the orders and Mordecai follows them—a reversal from 2:20 where Esther followed Mordecai's orders.

CHAPTER 5

Party Favors

Parties set the scene at the story's beginning and parties are the backdrop of the denouement. Spliced between Esther's banquets in chapters 5 and 7 is the continuation of the contest between Haman and Mordecai over the matter of honor. The banquets have a role in this contest also, for the invitations to Haman put him off his guard by according him the very high honor of dining privately with the king and queen. A second purpose served by the banquets is to delay the queen's declaration of the "favor" she wants from the king. She goes to him to plead for her people at the beginning of chapter 5, but the actual request to save them is not made until chapter 7. Meanwhile, the delightful anticipation builds.

In chapter 5, Esther shows her courage and her cleverness even more than before. At the risk of her life, she goes unsummoned to the king. As suggested earlier, in chapter 4 Esther devised the strategy she would use to gain access to the king. In chapter 5 she goes further, engineering the circumstances under which she will make her plea and accuse her adversary. None of this was mentioned in Mordecai's instructions. It was Esther alone who planned the parties and invited the guests. It was she who arranged exactly the right setting to expose the wickedness of Haman, much to the surprise of both the king and Haman. Mordecai is barely mentioned in chapters 5–7, and when he is, his silent presence is there as a foil to Haman.

The motifs employed in chapters 5 and 7—a strong and clever royal woman, the king's willingness to grant extravagant requests, and a banquet scene for securing retaliation against one's enemy—are not the creation of the author of Esther, but are among those literary motifs current during the Persian period. In a plot very different from the Esther story, Herodotus 9.109–111 combines all these motifs.

Herodotus recounts that Xerxes' wife Amestris had made for her husband a brightly colored shawl, with which he was quite pleased, and he wore it when he went to Artaynte. (Artaynte was the daughter of Xerxes' brother Masistes and the wife of Xerxes' son Darius, and Xerxes had fallen in love with her himself.) As Herodotus puts it:

5 On the third day, Esther put on royal apparel and stood in the inner court of the king's palace, facing

ה וַיְהִי | בַּיּוֹם הַשְּׁלִישִׁי וַתִּלְבַּשׁ אֶסְתֵּר מַלְכוּת וַתַּעֲמֹד בַּחֲצַר בֵּית־הַמֶּלֶךְ

She [Artaynte] gave him pleasure too—so much so that he told her he would give her anything she wanted in return for the favours she had granted him; whatever she asked for, he assured her, she would get... so she asked Xerxes, "Will you really give me anything I want?" Not suspecting for a moment what she was going to ask for, he promised her that he would and gave his word—and now that she had his word, she boldly asked for the shawl. Xerxes did everything he could to dissuade her, because he really did not want to give it to her, for one reason and one reason alone: he was afraid that Amestris [his wife] would have her suspicions confirmed and find out what he was up to. He offered Artaynte cities, unlimited gold, and sole command of an army (a typically Persian gift), but she refused everything. Eventually, then, he gave her the shawl, which she liked so much that she used to wear it and show it off.

Of course that confirmed for Amestris her husband's unfaithfulness. Amestris did not wish to take revenge on Artaynte, however, but rather on her mother, whom she (mistakenly) blamed for the situation. Amestris waited for Xerxes to give his royal birthday banquet, for on this occasion "no request could be refused." At the banquet, Amestris asked for Artaynte's mother to be given to her. Amestris then mutilated her and sent her home. The story ends with the murder of Masistes, the husband of the unfortunate woman and the father of Artaynte. (For other banquets at which guests are punished in grotesque ways see Herodotus 1.118–119; 2.100; 2.107.)

The plot of Herodotus's tale is altogether different from Esther; it reads like a Greek tragedy as opposed to the comedy of Esther, and is much bloodier and suffused with illicit and semi-incestuous relationships. Nevertheless, we can see that similar motifs were used in both stories. Esther's role combines the roles of Artaynte, a woman who pleased the king and could receive anything she asked for and whose house was doomed, and of Amestris, the queen who used the occasion of a banquet to make a request of the king and to get revenge on her enemy.

1. On the third day After the three days of fasting referred to in 4:16. "Three days" is the biblical way of indicating the passage of a short period of time.

put on royal apparel Hebrew: "she dressed in royalty." She is dressed in her best for this important occasion, and, more to the point, she is dressed in her official garb as queen. See the Commentary to *malkhut* at 1:9. If Esther had been wearing sackcloth during her fast, as some commentators suggest, she could not come before the king so dressed. (Just as in 4:2 Mordecai could not come to the king's gate in sackcloth.) But it is not necessary to make this assumption. The point is that she dressed for a formal audience with the king.

The Masoretic Text is terse almost to a fault here, but Targum Sheni captures the sense of royalty in its expanded description:

> She then adorned herself with the jewelry that queens adorn themselves—*she put on a royal garment,* embroidered with the fine gold of Ophir, a fine silk dress encrusted with precious stones, and pearls which were brought from the land of Africa; then she placed a fine gold crown upon her head and put shoes on her feet (made of) pure refined gold.

The Targum's description of African gold and gems is faintly reminiscent of the gifts brought by the Queen of Sheba (1 Kings 10:2, 10–11), another queen who came for a formal audience with the king. It strengthens the impression that Esther dressed herself for a royal

the king's palace, while the king was sitting on his royal throne in the throne room facing the entrance of

הַפְּנִימִית נֹכַח בֵּית הַמֶּלֶךְ וְהַמֶּלֶךְ יוֹשֵׁב עַל־כִּסֵּא מַלְכוּתוֹ בְּבֵית הַמַּלְכוּת נֹכַח

business meeting, not for a seduction scene (as in chapter 2). Although they may share the element of putting on jewelry with the "dress for success" motif of royal appearances, preparations for seduction have a slightly different convention, focusing on the preparations of the body—washing, anointing, dressing (cf. Ruth 3:3). A good illustration is in Jth. 10:3–4, when Judith prepares to go to Holofernes:

> She removed the sackcloth she had been wearing, took off her widow's garments, bathed her body with water, and anointed herself with precious ointment. She combed her hair, put on a tiara, and dressed herself in the festive attire that she used to wear while her husband Manasseh was living. She put sandals on her feet, and put on her anklets, bracelets, rings, earrings, and all her other jewelry. Thus she made herself very beautiful, to entice the eyes of all the men who might see her.

The same motif of washing, anointing, dressing, and putting on jewelry in preparation for a sexual encounter is found in a Sumerian song of Inanna and Dumuzi.[1] The themes of royal station and seduction are intertwined in the metaphorical description in Ezek. 16:9–15.

The full expression is, according to a number of commentators, *levush malkhut,* "royal apparel," as in Esther 6:8 and 8:15, with the word *levush,* "apparel," to be understood. This is possible, but it is not strictly necessary. Compare the similar construction in Ps. 93:1: *ge'ut lavesh,* "robed in grandeur." Compare also the following pairs of phrases, which show that the word for "clothing of" may either be expressed or not.

> Ps. 132:16: "I will clothe its priests *in victory.*"
> Isa. 61:10: "He has clothed me in *garments of victory.*"
> Prov. 31:22: "*Linen* and purple is her dress."
> Gen. 41:42: He dressed him *in garments of linen.*"

In light of these verses we may take *malkhut* as an abstract, "royalty," as it is in Esther 4:14: "who knows, perhaps you have attained *malkhut* for just such a crisis." Esther is clothed in royalty as befits one who is of royal position (Fox). Or as Levenson puts it, "we see Esther the beauty queen giving way to Esther the true queen."

inner court   The area where it was forbidden to come unsummoned (4:11).

sitting on his royal throne   The same phrase as in 1:2, but here he is physically present on his throne.

The positioning of the characters is explicitly described: they are able to observe each other before Esther actually enters the room in which the king is sitting. Esther sees the king sitting on the throne, and the king sees her standing in the inner court.

Esther must have been exceedingly nervous, but no description of her emotional state is given. This omission is remedied in the Greek versions, which read like later Greek novels and modern romance novels. Esther's attire and beauty are described in detail and her "heart is frozen with fear." Upon seeing the king in his awesome splendor, fierce-looking as he was, Esther became pale and faint, and collapsed. Her weakness elicited the sympathy of the king, who sprang up and took her in his arms. Josephus and Esther Rabbah contain similar accounts.

in the throne room   Hebrew *bet ha-malkhut* occurs also in 1:9, where Vashti held the women's party, and in 2:16, where Esther was taken to meet Ahasuerus. See the Commentary to 1:9.

the palace. ² As soon as the king saw Queen Esther standing in the court, she won his favor. The king extended to Esther the golden scepter which he had in his hand, and Esther approached and touched the tip of the scepter. ³ "What troubles you, Queen Esther?" the king asked her. "And what is your request? Even to half the kingdom, it shall be granted you." ⁴ "If it please Your Majesty," Esther replied, "let Your Majesty and Haman come today to the feast that

פֶּתַח הַבָּיִת: ² וַיְהִי כִרְאוֹת הַמֶּלֶךְ אֶת־אֶסְתֵּר הַמַּלְכָּה עֹמֶדֶת בֶּחָצֵר נָשְׂאָה חֵן בְּעֵינָיו וַיּוֹשֶׁט הַמֶּלֶךְ לְאֶסְתֵּר אֶת־שַׁרְבִיט הַזָּהָב אֲשֶׁר בְּיָדוֹ וַתִּקְרַב אֶסְתֵּר וַתִּגַּע בְּרֹאשׁ הַשַּׁרְבִיט: ס ³ וַיֹּאמֶר לָהּ הַמֶּלֶךְ מַה־לָּךְ אֶסְתֵּר הַמַּלְכָּה וּמַה־בַּקָּשָׁתֵךְ עַד־חֲצִי הַמַּלְכוּת וְיִנָּתֵן לָךְ: ⁴ וַתֹּאמֶר אֶסְתֵּר אִם־עַל־הַמֶּלֶךְ טוֹב יָבוֹא הַמֶּלֶךְ וְהָמָן הַיּוֹם אֶל־הַמִּשְׁתֶּה אֲשֶׁר־עָשִׂיתִי לוֹ:

2. The king stretches out his scepter to Esther before she enters the throne room. She may now approach him, knowing there will be no penalty for coming uninvited into the presence of the king (cf. 4:11).

Queen Esther The formal title is used when the king's perspective is being indicated, and when he addresses her in verse 3. Otherwise, the narrator refers to her as "Esther."

won his favor Once again, as in chapter 2, Esther immediately wins favor. This may be part of the motif in which a woman makes a request from a king, as found also in Herodotus's tale when Xerxes is pleased with Artaynte.

3. What troubles you Esther's agitation is obvious to the king. As Fox notes, the phrase *mah l-* always suggests that the person (or thing) to whom this question is addressed is perturbed. Compare Gen. 21:17, "What troubles you, Hagar?", and Ps. 114:5, "What alarmed you, O sea, that you fled." Indeed, Esther must have been greatly troubled if she risked coming uninvited to the king.

even to half the kingdom The Persian king often gave gifts, including land grants, to those he favored. Compare the offer made by Xerxes to Artaynte of cities, gold, and an army. Or, it may be better to take this as a biblical idiom for a large gift, like "half your wealth" in 1 Kings 13:7.

4. Esther's language is very formal and proper. She addresses the king in the third person. It would appear that Esther is about to make a large request but she deflects the king's magnanimous offer and instead issues an invitation to a banquet.

that I have prepared for him The party is already prepared, so how can he refuse? Compare 5:8 where the wording is "which I will prepare for them." In verse 4 only Ahasuerus is present, so the party is "for him," whereas in verse 8 both he and Haman are present, so the party is "for them." Esther modified her use of pronouns to fit the situation. Compare Gen. 39:14 and 17, where the wife of Potiphar shifts from "to dally with us" when speaking to the servants to "to dally with me" when speaking to her husband.²

In chapter 1 we read of the king's extravagant parties with their extensive lists of guests, an institution in the Persian empire for the exchange of royal gifts. The parties in chapters 5 and 7 are of a different nature. They are intimate meals reserved for those of very high status, as reflected in the statement of Plutarch, *Artaxerxes* 5:

> No one shared the table of a Persian king except his mother or his wedded wife, the wife sitting below him, the mother above him; but Artaxerxes invited to the same table with him his brothers Ostanes and Oxathres, although they were his juniors.

I have prepared for him." 5 The king commanded, "Tell Haman to hurry and do Esther's bidding." So the king and Haman came to the feast that Esther had prepared.

6 At the wine feast, the king asked Esther, "What is your wish? It shall be granted you. And what is your request? Even to half the kingdom, it shall be fulfilled." 7 "My wish," replied Esther, "my request— 8 if Your Majesty will do me the favor, if it please Your Majesty to grant my wish and accede to my request— let Your Majesty and Haman come to the feast which I will prepare for them; and tomorrow I will do Your Majesty's bidding."

9 That day Haman went out happy and light-hearted. But when Haman saw Mordecai in the palace gate, and Mordecai did not rise or even stir on his account, Haman was filled with rage at him. 10 Nevertheless, Haman controlled himself and went

5 וַיֹּאמֶר הַמֶּלֶךְ מַהֲרוּ אֶת־הָמָן לַעֲשׂוֹת אֶת־דְּבַר אֶסְתֵּר וַיָּבֹא הַמֶּלֶךְ וְהָמָן אֶל־הַמִּשְׁתֶּה אֲשֶׁר־עָשְׂתָה אֶסְתֵּר:
6 וַיֹּאמֶר הַמֶּלֶךְ לְאֶסְתֵּר בְּמִשְׁתֵּה הַיַּיִן מַה־שְּׁאֵלָתֵךְ וְיִנָּתֵן לָךְ וּמַה־בַּקָּשָׁתֵךְ עַד־חֲצִי הַמַּלְכוּת וְתֵעָשׂ: *7 וַתַּעַן אֶסְתֵּר וַתֹּאמַר שְׁאֵלָתִי וּבַקָּשָׁתִי: 8 אִם־מָצָאתִי חֵן בְּעֵינֵי הַמֶּלֶךְ וְאִם־עַל־הַמֶּלֶךְ טוֹב לָתֵת אֶת־שְׁאֵלָתִי וְלַעֲשׂוֹת אֶת־בַּקָּשָׁתִי יָבוֹא הַמֶּלֶךְ וְהָמָן אֶל־הַמִּשְׁתֶּה אֲשֶׁר אֶעֱשֶׂה לָהֶם וּמָחָר אֶעֱשֶׂה כִּדְבַר הַמֶּלֶךְ:
9 וַיֵּצֵא הָמָן בַּיּוֹם הַהוּא שָׂמֵחַ וְטוֹב לֵב וְכִרְאוֹת הָמָן אֶת־מָרְדֳּכַי בְּשַׁעַר הַמֶּלֶךְ וְלֹא־קָם וְלֹא־זָע מִמֶּנּוּ וַיִּמָּלֵא הָמָן עַל־מָרְדֳּכַי חֵמָה: 10 וַיִּתְאַפַּק הָמָן וַיָּבוֹא

v. 7. חצי הספר בפסוקים

6. The king offers Esther a second opportunity to make her request. The words are similar to verse 3 but fuller and more formally arranged in a parallelism.

it shall be granted The verb is in the masculine, not in the expected feminine to accord with "your wish." It is most likely an impersonal passive; such constructions are often in the masculine (also in 5:3 and 9:12).[3] The feminine in 7:2 has no apparent explanation.

7. Esther is about to state her request in response to the king's offer, but she interrupts herself with another invitation, thereby postponing her request and raising the level of tension in the story.

8. See the Commentary to verse 4. Some commentators see in the word "them"—that is, the inclusion of Haman, an attempt by Esther to make Ahasuerus jealous by equating him and Haman. I prefer to see it, as I explained above, as a clever move on Esther's part to disarm Haman and make him think he was the center of attention. This plays to Haman's personal weakness and also to Esther's plan. It was crucial, after all, that Haman attend the next party, where he would indeed be the center of attention; the party to come was, then, as much for Haman as for the king.

tomorrow I will do Your majesty's bidding Esther has not yet made her request, as she was bidden by the king, but has stalled by issuing another party invitation. She promises to make her request tomorrow. Much will happen in the contest over honor between Mordecai and Haman before the next party.

9. Haman's mood changes rapidly as he moves from being honored as a royal dinner guest to being dishonored by Mordecai's refusal to bow to him.

did not rise or even stir Not only had Mordecai earlier (3:2) refused to bow to Haman, here he makes no motion at all to even acknowledge him. As in 3:5, this fills Haman with fury.

home. He sent for his friends and his wife Zeresh, [11] and Haman told them about his great wealth and his many sons, and all about how the king had promoted him and advanced him above the officials and the king's courtiers. [12]"What is more," said Haman, "Queen Esther gave a feast, and besides the king she did not have anyone but me. And tomorrow too I am invited by her along with the king. [13] Yet all this means nothing to me every time I see that Jew Mordecai sitting in the palace gate." [14]Then his wife Zeresh and all his friends said to him, "Let a stake be put up, fifty cubits high, and in the morning ask the king to have Mordecai impaled on it. Then you

אֶל־בֵּיתֽוֹ וַיִּשְׁלַ֣ח וַיָּבֵ֔א אֶת־אֹהֲבָ֖יו וְאֶת־
זֶ֥רֶשׁ אִשְׁתּֽוֹ: 11 וַיְסַפֵּ֨ר לָהֶ֥ם הָמָ֛ן אֶת־כְּב֥וֹד
עָשְׁר֖וֹ וְרֹ֣ב בָּנָ֑יו וְאֵת֩ כָּל־אֲשֶׁ֨ר גִּדְּל֤וֹ הַמֶּ֙לֶךְ֙
וְאֵ֣ת אֲשֶׁ֣ר נִשְּׂא֔וֹ עַל־הַשָּׂרִ֖ים וְעַבְדֵ֥י
הַמֶּֽלֶךְ: 12 וַיֹּ֙אמֶר֙ הָמָ֔ן אַ֣ף לֹא־הֵבִ֩יאָה֩
אֶסְתֵּ֨ר הַמַּלְכָּ֧ה עִם־הַמֶּ֛לֶךְ אֶל־הַמִּשְׁתֶּ֥ה
אֲשֶׁר־עָשָׂ֖תָה כִּ֣י אִם־אוֹתִ֑י וְגַם־לְמָחָ֛ר
אֲנִ֥י קָרֽוּא־לָ֖הּ עִם־הַמֶּֽלֶךְ: 13 וְכָל־זֶ֕ה
אֵינֶ֥נּוּ שֹׁוֶ֖ה לִ֑י בְּכָל־עֵ֗ת אֲשֶׁ֨ר אֲנִ֤י רֹאֶה֙
אֶת־מָרְדֳּכַ֣י הַיְּהוּדִ֔י יוֹשֵׁ֖ב בְּשַׁ֥עַר הַמֶּֽלֶךְ:
14 וַתֹּ֣אמֶר לֹ֣ו זֶ֣רֶשׁ אִשְׁתּוֹ֮ וְכָל־אֹהֲבָיו֒
יַֽעֲשׂוּ־עֵץ֮ גָּבֹ֣הַּ חֲמִשִּׁ֣ים אַמָּה֒ וּבַבֹּ֣קֶר ׀
אֱמֹ֣ר לַמֶּ֗לֶךְ וְיִתְל֤וּ אֶֽת־מָרְדֳּכַי֙ עָלָ֔יו וּבֹֽא־

11. *his great wealth and his many sons*   Like Ahasuerus in chapter 1, Haman brags about his wealth to his friends. As in Job 1:2–3, great wealth and many children are a sign of success. Haman will lose both. His estate will be given to Esther in 8:1, and his sons will be killed in 9:6ff.

12.   Having recounted his former marks of status and honor, Haman now tells of his most recent honor, the invitations to him alone to party with the king and queen. Little does he know what awaits him at the next party.

13. *sitting in the palace gate*   The very presence of Mordecai is enough to upset Haman. But more than this, Mordecai is *sitting*. He did not rise or stir (v. 9), let alone bow. But Haman cannot bring himself to express the full measure of Mordecai's disrespect for him even to his closest friends, so he uses the ambiguous "sitting," which may designate Mordecai's position at court (2:21) as well as his physical pose. The narrator has already given the reader a more accurate and vivid description in verse 9.

14. *his wife Zeresh and all his friends*   The order is reversed from verse 10, giving the impression that Zeresh now takes the lead. She along with the friends play a small though important role. They guide Haman in his quest to bring shame on Mordecai, and in the next chapter they realize that Haman's attempt to destroy Mordecai will not succeed. The Greek writers also give wives important roles in advising their husbands.

fifty cubits high   (Cf. 7:9). Fifty cubits is equivalent to about twenty meters (seventy-five feet), which would make the stake as tall as a seven-story building. Imagine such a structure standing in Haman's backyard! It would have towered over everything in the city, if, indeed, it could stand erect. We know of the practice of impaling corpses on stakes, or on city walls, but such a high stake would be totally impractical. How would one raise the corpse so high? Who could recognize it from the street? Moreover, in the context of the Bible the height of fifty cubits is clearly an exaggeration. No structure that the Bible describes is fifty cubits high. Even Solomon's Temple is only thirty cubits high. Archaeologists estimate that the palaces of ancient capitals like Susa were perhaps forty to fifty feet high. The description of Haman's stake makes a mockery of the man who would construct such a stake, and a further mockery of him when he is hung on the very stake he built for his enemy.

can go gaily with the king to the feast." The proposal pleased Haman, and he had the stake put up.

עִם־הַמֶּלֶךְ אֶל־הַמִּשְׁתֶּה שָׂמֵחַ וַיִּיטַב הַדָּבָר לִפְנֵי הָמָן וַיַּעַשׂ הָעֵץ׃ פ

impaled on it   See the Commentary to 2:23. Impalement is the ultimate form of disgrace. Zeresh's proposal of the stake is meant to dishonor Mordecai after he is dead in such a way that Haman will have the last word in the contest over honor and dishonor. Once the king has approved the plan for impalement, Haman will be able to enjoy himself again.

CHAPTER 6

Honor Gained and Honor Lost

If there was any doubt about the comic nature of the Book of Esther, it is completely dispelled in this chapter, one of the funniest anywhere is the Bible. The plot is constructed on coincidence, misunderstanding, and reversal.

It just so happens that the king was having a sleepless night and to pass the time he requested that his chronicles be read to him. When the passage mentioning Mordecai's good deed is read, the king realizes that his benefactor has not been rewarded. The problem of how to honor Mordecai will, like all problems the king confronts, be put to an advisor. Now it just so happens that the most convenient advisor is none other than Haman, who has come to see the king on a different matter, which turns out to be the same matter in reverse: how to disgrace Mordecai. But since neither character knows what is in the mind of the other, there is a comic misunderstanding of enormous proportion.

The plot takes good advantage of the characterization of Ahasuerus and Haman. Ahasuerus is always generous in giving gifts and honors. He has already elevated Haman and has promised Esther whatever she wants, so it is not strange that he should wish to be generous in his honor to Mordecai, and Haman will unwittingly help him to be very generous. Equally in character is Ahasuerus's need to obtain advice, as he did before punishing Vashti and before selecting a new queen. And he always heeds the advice he receives, whether or not it is requested. He has already approved Haman's plan to kill the Jews, and Haman has every reason to expect that he will approve his latest plan to impale Mordecai on a stake, which is the ultimate disgrace. Little does Haman know as the king accepts his advice yet again, that it will backfire so greatly.

The most outstanding characteristic of Haman is that he is a glutton for honor. He, and he alone, must have the highest recognition and acclaim, and this blinds him to everything else. It is Mordecai who always dampens Haman's enjoyment of his honors, and here Mordecai will be his true nemesis, for Haman will have to honor the very person he seeks to disgrace.

The motif of rewarding benefactors is nicely documented in another of Herodotus's stories, relevant to this chapter and to chapter 7. In 3.140 we hear of Syloson, one of Darius's benefactors. Before Darius had become king, while on a military campaign, Darius noticed that Syloson had a lovely red cloak and he offered to buy it from him. Syloson refused money and gave it to Darius as a gift. After Darius had become king, Syloson went up to Susa and told the royal gatekeeper that he was one of Darius's benefactors. Syloson was admitted to the palace and told the king about the cloak, explaining that he was the one who had given it to Darius. Darius, ever grateful for this favor, offered Syloson

6 That night, sleep deserted the king, and he ordered the book of records, the annals, to be brought; and it was read to the king. [2] There it was found written that Mordecai had denounced Bigthana and Teresh, two of the king's eunuchs who guarded the threshold, who had plotted to do away with King Ahasuerus. [3] "What honor or advancement has been conferred on Mordecai for this?" the king inquired. "Nothing at all has been done for him," replied the king's servants who were in attendance on him. [4] "Who is in the court?" the king asked. For Haman had just

בַּלַּ֣יְלָה הַה֔וּא נָדְדָ֖ה שְׁנַ֣ת הַמֶּ֑לֶךְ
וַיֹּ֗אמֶר לְהָבִ֞יא אֶת־סֵ֤פֶר הַזִּכְרֹנוֹת֙ דִּבְרֵ֣י
הַיָּמִ֔ים וַיִּהְי֥וּ נִקְרָאִ֖ים לִפְנֵ֥י הַמֶּֽלֶךְ׃
[2] וַיִּמָּצֵ֣א כָת֔וּב אֲשֶׁר֩ הִגִּ֨יד מָרְדֳּכַ֜י עַל־
בִּגְתָ֣נָא וָתֶ֗רֶשׁ שְׁנֵי֙ סָרִיסֵ֣י הַמֶּ֔לֶךְ מִשֹּׁמְרֵ֖י
הַסַּ֑ף אֲשֶׁ֤ר בִּקְשׁוּ֙ לִשְׁלֹ֣חַ יָ֔ד בַּמֶּ֖לֶךְ
אֲחַשְׁוֵרֽוֹשׁ׃ [3] וַיֹּ֣אמֶר הַמֶּ֔לֶךְ מַֽה־נַּעֲשָׂ֞ה
יְקָ֧ר וּגְדוּלָּ֛ה לְמָרְדֳּכַ֖י עַל־זֶ֑ה וַיֹּ֨אמְרוּ֙ נַעֲרֵ֤י
הַמֶּ֨לֶךְ֙ מְשָׁ֣רְתָ֔יו לֹא־נַעֲשָׂ֥ה עִמּ֖וֹ דָּבָֽר׃
[4] וַיֹּ֣אמֶר הַמֶּ֔לֶךְ מִ֣י בֶחָצֵ֑ר וְהָמָ֣ן בָּ֗א לַחֲצַ֤ר

"abundance of gold and silver, that you may never repent of the service you did Darius son of Hystaspes." "No," Syloson answered, "I ask neither gold, O king, nor silver; only win me back my fatherland of Samos . . . give me back Samos, but so that there be no bloodshed nor enslaving."

Here we see the importance that Persian kings attached to rewarding their benefactors. Syloson's reward also sounds faintly similar to the request that Esther will make in the next chapter.

1. That night   The same night that Haman erected a stake to hang Mordecai on; and the same day (see 5:9) that Esther's first party had taken place. After the passage of a number of years in the early chapters, time has slowed down, for we are now in the midst of the main action.

the book of records   Apparently the same book mentioned in 2:23 although the title of it is slightly different. Compare the archives at Babylon mentioned in Ezra 5:17.

We get the impression that, had it not been for the king's sleeplessness, Mordecai's unrewarded deed would have been completely forgotten. In other words, coincidence, or luck, is at work here. Coincidence is, in fact, at work throughout this chapter and it is what makes the chapter so effective.

2. Mordecai had denounced   As noted in 2:22, the plot of Bigthan and Teresh was reported in Mordecai's name.

3. honor or advancement   The theme of honor emerges again, this time on the side of Mordecai. Benefactors of the king, called *orosangae,* according to Herodotus 8.85, might be rewarded by a grant of land. Plutarch, *Artaxerxes* 15, tells about Mithridates, who had received clothing and gold jewelry from the king for the service he had rendered him.

The king here mentions "honor," *yekar,* and "advancement," *gedulah.* Indeed, Mordecai had received neither and Haman had received both. Later, in verse 6 when speaking to Haman, the king mentions only *yekar.* Since Haman had already received advancement (3:1), and he hears only about honor (of which he never has enough), he can easily mistake himself for the person to receive the honor (Levenson).

servants who were in attendance on him   The same servants that advised him to gather all the virgins (2:2). These seem to be his personal servants and are with him at night and at private moments.

4. Who is in the court?   Does the king hear someone come in? Or, is he simply inquiring as to who is available to give him advice, since he rarely does anything on his

entered the outer court of the royal palace, to speak to the king about having Mordecai impaled on the stake he had prepared for him. ⁵"It is Haman standing in the court," the king's servants answered him. "Let him enter," said the king. ⁶Haman entered, and the king asked him, "What should be done for a man whom the king desires to honor?" Haman said to himself, "Whom would the king desire to honor more than me?" ⁷So Haman said to the king, "For the man whom the king desires to honor, ⁸let royal garb

בֵּית־הַמֶּ֙לֶךְ֙ הַחִ֣יצוֹנָ֔ה לֵאמֹ֣ר לַמֶּ֔לֶךְ לִתְלוֹת֙ אֶֽת־מָרְדֳּכַ֔י עַל־הָעֵ֖ץ אֲשֶׁר־הֵכִ֥ין לֽוֹ: ⁵ וַיֹּ֙אמְרוּ֙ נַעֲרֵ֤י הַמֶּ֙לֶךְ֙ אֵלָ֔יו הִנֵּ֥ה הָמָ֖ן עֹמֵ֣ד בֶּחָצֵ֑ר וַיֹּ֥אמֶר הַמֶּ֖לֶךְ יָבֽוֹא: ⁶ וַיָּבוֹא֘ הָמָן֒ וַיֹּ֤אמֶר לוֹ֙ הַמֶּ֔לֶךְ מַה־לַעֲשׂ֕וֹת בָּאִ֕ישׁ אֲשֶׁ֥ר הַמֶּ֖לֶךְ חָפֵ֣ץ בִּיקָר֑וֹ וַיֹּ֤אמֶר הָמָן֙ בְּלִבּ֔וֹ לְמִ֗י יַחְפֹּ֥ץ הַמֶּ֛לֶךְ לַעֲשׂ֥וֹת יְקָ֖ר יוֹתֵ֥ר מִמֶּֽנִּי: ⁷ וַיֹּ֤אמֶר הָמָן֙ אֶל־הַמֶּ֔לֶךְ אִ֕ישׁ אֲשֶׁ֥ר הַמֶּ֖לֶךְ חָפֵ֥ץ בִּיקָרֽוֹ: ⁸ יָבִ֙יאוּ֙ לְב֣וּשׁ מַלְכ֔וּת

own initiative? He does not seek advice from his servants nor do they offer it; rather, he calls on Haman for advice.

Haman had just entered the outer court It was apparently permitted to enter the outer court without a summons from the king, but to enter the *inner* court, one needed a summons (4:11). The passage of time is not marked. It seems that Haman comes to the court that night, not the following morning as his wife suggested (5:14). He is so eager that he cannot wait until morning. He comes to obtain approval to hang Mordecai on the stake that he has already erected. He obviously thinks it is a *pro forma* request: the verb is *'-m-r,* literally, "say" or "speak" (also in 5:14), as though he is merely reporting his intention rather than asking for permission.

6. The comic misunderstanding begins. Each man has something on his mind that he needs to discuss immediately with the other one. The reader knows what is in the mind of both characters, but they know only their own thoughts, so the reader can enjoy the comedy of errors as each character misunderstands the intention of the other.

As is proper, the king speaks first, and it turns out that Haman never gets a chance to say what he came for, which was to disgrace the very person the king wishes to honor. The king does not specify which man he wishes to honor, and Haman, the egomaniac, naturally thinks he is the one. And why not? He has already been raised to a position above all the other courtiers, and has been singled out twice for a special invitation to dine with the king and queen.

7. ***For the man whom the king desires to honor*** Haman repeats the king's words, as if savoring them. The first words he utters are not a complete sentence. He, like Esther in 5:7, repeats the king's words, which encapsulate the main theme, and leaves them hanging, and then goes on to formulate the required response. Unlike Esther, Haman does not speak in the formal or flowery language of an inferior addressing a superior. He gets right to the point, as if speaking to his equal.

Haman, following the king's lead, gives no indication of the identity of the one to be honored, but the reader has heard Haman's inner thoughts and knows that Haman expects to receive the honor himself. As the king had done, Haman speaks in very general terms, without specifying the recipient of the honor, thereby prolonging the misunderstanding.

8. There are conventional ways of honoring those favored by the king, both in the Bible and in the Greek sources. Haman's suggestions partake of these, but there is ample reason, as will be explained below, to think that Haman is requesting things that go far beyond the normal gifts bestowed by the king upon his benefactors. Haman can never get enough honor.

אֲשֶׁר לָבַשׁ־בּוֹ הַמֶּלֶךְ וְסוּס אֲשֶׁר רָכַב עָלָיו   which the king has worn be brought, and a horse on

The biblical model is the honor that Joseph received from Pharaoh in Gen. 41:42–43:

> And removing his signet ring from his hand, Pharaoh put it on Joseph's hand; and he had him dressed in robes of fine linen, and put a gold chain about his neck. He had him ride in the chariot of his second-in-command, and they cried before him "Abrek!"

As Fox notes, Haman had already received the signet ring, and his other desires are more lavish than what Joseph received. Instead of fine linen robes, he wants the king's own robe; instead of riding in the viceroy's chariot, Haman wants the king's own horse; instead of the (obscure) exclamation "Abrek," Haman wants a long and clear proclamation of his honor.

An Assyrian example of royal honor is found in the description of the honor bestowed on the Egyptian king Necho by Ashurbanipal (*ANET*, 295).

> I clad him in a garment with multicolored trimmings, placed a golden chain on him (as the) insigne of his kingship, put golden rings on his hands; I wrote my name upon an iron dagger (to be worn in) the girdle, the mounting of which was golden, and gave it to him. I presented him with chariots, horses and mules as means of transportation (befitting) his position as ruler.

Here, as in the Joseph story, we are in the realm of Egyptian ceremonial honor, for a king or his deputy.

Greek sources also describe how Persian kings honored their benefactors. For example, Xenophon, *Anabasis* 2, mentions that Cyrus gave to Syennesis gifts that were regarded at court as tokens of honor (and could only be given by the king). They included a horse with a gold-mounted bridle, a gold necklace and bracelets, a gold dagger, and a Persian robe.

Later Jewish writings also draw on a combination of these conventions for honoring deserving men. 1 Esd. 3:6–7 has the wisest man being clothed in purple, drinking from gold cups, sleeping on a gold bed, having a chariot with gold bridles, a turban of fine linen, a necklace, and a seat next to King Darius. Josephus, like the story of Joseph and the passage in 1 Esdras 3, adds a gold necklace to the honors suggested by Haman.

royal garb which the king has worn   Not just clothing that would be suitable for a royal courtier, but clothing actually worn by the king. This is a very serious request, tantamount to asking for the kingship.

A person's garment is considered a part of his body, or a part of his being. Tearing one's clothes in mourning is permitted, as a kind of substitute for injuring one's body (which is prohibited in Deut. 14:1–2); cutting off half of a person's garment and shaving off half his beard is a way of humiliating him without actually causing bodily harm (2 Sam. 10:4–5); when the army commanders spread their clothes on the stairs under Jehu they are signaling their submission and loyalty to him (2 Kings 9:13); Aaron's priestly garments are donned by Eleazar, his son, as he inherits the priestly office (Num. 20:25–28); Elijah's cloak symbolizes the prophetic office as well as the person of Elijah, and Elisha's receiving this cloak means that he has replaced Elijah. David's cutting off a corner of Saul's cloak (1 Sam. 24) registers in both men's minds as the symbolic taking of the kingship.[1] So there is an extensive biblical tradition that provides a context for Haman's request for the king's robe.

There is also a Greek context of a similar nature, underlining the seriousness of wearing the king's own garment. One of the ceremonies in the initiation of a new Persian king was, according to Plutarch (*Artaxerxes* 3), the laying aside of his own personal robe and the putting on of the robe of Cyrus the Elder. In *Artaxerxes* 5 we are given to

which the king has ridden and on whose head a royal　הַמֶּלֶךְ וַאֲשֶׁר נִתַּן כֶּתֶר מַלְכוּת בְּרֹאשׁוֹ:

understand that it was forbidden for anyone to wear the king's robe. This is in the story of Teribazus.

> Again, when he was hunting once and Teribazus pointed out that the king's coat was torn, he asked him what was to be done. And when Teribazus replied, "Put on another for yourself, but give this one to me," the king did so, saying, "I give this to you, Teribazus, but I forbid you to wear it." Teribazus gave no heed to this command... and at once put on the king's coat, and decked himself with golden necklaces and women's ornaments of royal splendor. Everybody was indignant at this (for it was a forbidden thing); but the king merely laughed, and said: "I permit you to wear the trinkets as a woman, and the robe as a madman."

We see from this story that no one in his right mind would wear the king's robe and that Teribazus can get away with doing so only if he is considered mad.

We have already made reference in the introduction to chapter 5 to the king's robe in the story of Artaynte. In regard to this story, it has been noted that

> From other similar stories we know more about the king's robe. There is a taboo on wearing the royal robe by anyone else but the king.... On the level of literature the person wearing the royal robe is the king: the first act of any usurper of the throne is to put on the royal robe. It is part of the regalia with which the king is invested on his accession. What Artaynte asks for in the tale is not only a beautiful garment but the kingship with it.[2]

a horse on which the king has ridden and on whose head a royal diadem has been set The Hebrew syntax leaves some ambiguity about who is the wearer of the diadem. The best interpretation is that the diadem had been set on the head of the horse when the king had ridden on it, to indicate that it was the king himself who was on it. (Much as a presidential limousine might have a special flag flying from it.) Haman's description of the horse emphasizes that he wants to be seen mounted on the king's own horse. The diadem is not mentioned in verses 9 and 11 when the ceremony is described and carried out. This supports the idea that the placing of the crown on the horse was not part of the ceremony that Haman envisioned, but was simply a way of clarifying which horse was to be used.

Fox mentions that Assyrian reliefs show the king's horses wearing tall head ornaments. Moore refers to reliefs in Xerxes' *apadana* at Persepolis, which, according to him, show horses with crowns. Actually, though, the crowns seem to be formed from a tuft of the horse's hair tied in a band and sticking up like a crown.

Some interpreters prefer to understand "on whose head" as referring to the head of the honoree, rather than the horse. In either case, the mounted figure will be perceived as having royal status.

The significance of mounting the king's horse is similar to 1 Kings 1:32–49, where David orders that Solomon be mounted on the king's mule, led to the Gihon, anointed king, and then returned to sit on the king's throne. In both cases a figure is mounted on the king's mount and in a public place. It is as if the mule or horse served as a portable throne that could be set up outside for all to see. The nexus between the throne and the horse, both extensions of the royal personage and symbols of his royalty, can be seen in M. Sanhedrin 2:5, which forbids one to ride on the king's horse, to sit on his throne, or to use his scepter.

All of these details hint that Haman is aiming to take the place of the king (see Levenson, 97). In fact, the root *m-l-k,* "king, royal," occurs seven times in Haman's speech in verses 8–9, suggesting that the kingship is surely on Haman's mind. He has already been

diadem has been set; 9 and let the attire and the horse be put in the charge of one of the king's noble courtiers. And let the man whom the king desires to honor be attired and paraded on the horse through the city square, while they proclaim before him: This

9 וְנָתוֹן הַלְּבוּשׁ וְהַסּוּס עַל־יַד־אִישׁ מִשָּׂרֵי
הַמֶּלֶךְ הַפַּרְתְּמִים וְהִלְבִּישׁוּ אֶת־הָאִישׁ
אֲשֶׁר הַמֶּלֶךְ חָפֵץ בִּיקָרוֹ וְהִרְכִּיבֻהוּ עַל־
הַסּוּס בִּרְחוֹב הָעִיר וְקָרְאוּ לְפָנָיו כָּכָה

designated as a person to whom everyone must bow, making him a kind of surrogate king, and now he wants to masquerade as the king, wearing the king's own robe and sitting on the king's own horse. All that is missing is his taking the king's wife, and that is what it looks to Ahasuerus that he is doing in 7:8.

Several midrashim also suggest that Haman is aiming for the kingship. Pirke de-Rabbi Eliezer, for example, understands the diadem to be the king's, not the horse's, and explains its omission in verse 9 as follows:

> Haman said in his heart: He does not desire to exalt any other man except me. I will speak words so that I shall be king just as he is. He said to him: Let them bring the apparel which the king wore on the day of the coronation, and (let them bring) the horse upon which the king rode on the coronation day, and the crown which was put upon the head of the king on the day of coronation. The king was exceedingly angry because of the crown. The king said: It does not suffice this villain, but he must even desire the crown which is upon my head. Haman saw that the king was angry because of the crown; he said: "And let the apparel and the horse be delivered to the hand of one of the king's most noble princes."

9. one of the king's noble courtiers Part of the honor consists of being dressed and displayed by an attendant who is himself a man of very high rank. Little does Haman suspect that it will be a man of the highest rank—that he himself will have the "honor" of serving as Mordecai's attendant.

paraded on the horse through the city square The verb *r-k-b* means "mount" or "ride." The word *reḥov,* which in modern Hebrew means "street," refers to the wide place (*r-ḥ-b*), that is, the city square. See 4:6: "the city square in front of the king's gate." I am persuaded that we should see this scene as one in which the honoree is to be mounted on a horse in the city square, rather than to be led through the streets or the square.[3] In either case, the man will be honored very publicly.

If, indeed, the location is the city square in front of the king's gate (where Hathach conferred with Mordecai in 4:6), then this suggestion is calculated to place Haman, as he is being publicly honored, right in front of Mordecai's eyes—right in front of Mordecai's usual station at the king's gate (cf. also 2:21; 6:10).

Another Greek tale is relevant here, and again suggests that Haman's vision of the honor due him is grandiose, impinging on the office of the king.[4] Plutarch, *Themistocles* 29, tells of a Spartan named Demaratus who, like Haman, overreached when asking for a gift.

> And when Demaratus the Spartan, being bidden to ask for a gift, asked that he might ride in state through Sardis, wearing his tiara upright after the manner of the Persian kings, Mithropaustes the King's cousin said, touching the tiara of Demaratus: "This tiara of yours has no brains to cover; indeed you cannot be Zeus merely because you grasp the thunderbolt." The King also repulsed Demaratus in anger at his request.

We note here the public exhibition, riding in state through Sardis. The same type of public exhibition may be used for disgrace, as we see in the following passage from the annals of Esarhaddon (*ANET,* 290–91):

is what is done for the man whom the king desires to honor!" ¹⁰ "Quick, then!" said the king to Haman. "Get the garb and the horse, as you have said, and do this to Mordecai the Jew, who sits in the king's gate. Omit nothing of all you have proposed." ¹¹ So Haman took the garb and the horse and arrayed Mordecai and paraded him through the city square; and he proclaimed before him: This is what is done for the man whom the king desires to honor!

¹² Then Mordecai returned to the king's gate,

יֵעָשֶׂה לָאִישׁ אֲשֶׁר הַמֶּלֶךְ חָפֵץ בִּיקָרוֹ: 10 וַיֹּאמֶר הַמֶּלֶךְ לְהָמָן מַהֵר קַח אֶת־הַלְּבוּשׁ וְאֶת־הַסּוּס כַּאֲשֶׁר דִּבַּרְתָּ וַעֲשֵׂה־כֵן לְמָרְדֳּכַי הַיְּהוּדִי הַיּוֹשֵׁב בְּשַׁעַר הַמֶּלֶךְ אַל־תַּפֵּל דָּבָר מִכֹּל אֲשֶׁר דִּבַּרְתָּ: 11 וַיִּקַּח הָמָן אֶת־הַלְּבוּשׁ וְאֶת־הַסּוּס וַיַּלְבֵּשׁ אֶת־מָרְדֳּכָי וַיַּרְכִּיבֵהוּ בִּרְחוֹב הָעִיר וַיִּקְרָא לְפָנָיו כָּכָה יֵעָשֶׂה לָאִישׁ אֲשֶׁר הַמֶּלֶךְ חָפֵץ בִּיקָרוֹ: 12 וַיָּשָׁב מָרְדֳּכַי אֶל־שַׁעַר הַמֶּלֶךְ וְהָמָן

As for Sanduarri, king of Kundi and Sizu, an inveterate enemy, unwilling to recognize me as ruler...I caught him like a bird in his mountains and cut off his head. I hung the heads of Sanduarri and of Abdimilkutte around the neck of their nobles/chief officials to demonstrate to the population the power of Ashur, my lord, and paraded (thus) through the wide main street of Nineveh with singers (playing on) *sammu*-harps.

10.   As before, the king takes the advice offered to him. It is not until the second part of the verse that he makes clear upon whom the honor will be bestowed.

Mordecai the Jew, who sits in the king's gate   The descriptive words that Ahasuerus uses to identify Mordecai point to exactly those characteristics of Mordecai that antagonize Haman. Haman hates all the Jews (chapter 3), and is further disturbed every time he sees Mordecai sitting in the king's gate (5:9, 13). The king, unknowingly, is pouring salt on Haman's wounds.

Omit nothing of all you have proposed   The king likes this advice so much that he wants it carried out to the letter. Haman's words come back to haunt him.

11.   Haman personally carries out the ceremony he designed. In verse 9 the verbs for dressing and parading the honoree and proclaiming before him were in the third-person plural, signifying an impersonal; here is it clear that Haman performed all of these actions. The last time Mordecai was in the city square (4:6) he was dressed in mourning garb. What a reversal!

Some of the midrashim (Panim Aherim, for example) add to Haman's subservience to Mordecai by imagining a scene in which Haman is obliged to act as Mordecai's personal servant: to wash and dress Mordecai, since he was still covered in the sackcloth and ashes of mourning; and to lower himself so that Mordecai could step upon his neck in order to mount the horse, since Mordecai was weak from fasting.

12.   The story is silent about Mordecai's reaction to all this honor. Afterward, he simply returns to his usual station at the king's gate. Haman returns home crestfallen, and once again confides his feelings to his wife and friends.

hurried   The same root occurs in 3:15 describing the speed of the messengers.

his head covered in mourning   Haman is ashamed and dejected. He is mourning for his lost honor, as it were (Fox). For a covered head as a sign of mourning, despair, and/or humiliation see 2 Sam. 15:30, where David walks weeping, head covered, and barefoot,

while Haman hurried home, his head covered in mourning. [13] There Haman told his wife Zeresh and all his friends everything that had befallen him. His advisers and his wife Zeresh said to him, "If Mordecai, before whom you have begun to fall, is of Jewish stock, you will not overcome him; you will fall before him to your ruin."

[14] While they were still speaking with him, the

נִדְחַף אֶל־בֵּיתוֹ אָבֵל וַחֲפוּי רֹאשׁ׃

13 וַיְסַפֵּר הָמָן לְזֶרֶשׁ אִשְׁתּוֹ וּלְכָל־אֹהֲבָיו אֵת כָּל־אֲשֶׁר קָרָהוּ וַיֹּאמְרוּ לוֹ חֲכָמָיו וְזֶרֶשׁ אִשְׁתּוֹ אִם מִזֶּרַע הַיְּהוּדִים מָרְדֳּכַי אֲשֶׁר הַחִלּוֹתָ לִנְפֹּל לְפָנָיו לֹא־תוּכַל לוֹ כִּי־נָפוֹל תִּפּוֹל לְפָנָיו׃

14 עוֹדָם מְדַבְּרִים עִמּוֹ וְסָרִיסֵי הַמֶּלֶךְ

and the people do the same, in the wake of Absalom's rebellion; see also Jer. 14:3. A similar custom is attested in Greek writings, for instance, in the first-century C.E. novel, *Chaereas and Callirhoe,* we have "Chaereas was in the body of the ship weeping, his head covered up."[5] The picture of Haman mourning completes the reversal between him and Mordecai; just as Mordecai has gone from mourning to splendor, Haman has gone from splendor to mourning.

The word "mourning" is somewhat strange, and the Rabbis, who lost no opportunity to besmirch and humiliate Haman, told a wonderfully gross midrashic tale to explain it (see, for example, B. Megillah 16a). While Haman was leading Mordecai through the streets, Haman's daughter was standing on the roof of her house and saw the two men, one leading the other on a horse. Thinking that the man on the horse was her father, being led by Mordecai, she took a chamber pot and hurled it upon the head of the man leading the horse. He looked up and then she saw that it was her father, whereupon she fell from the roof and died.

This rabbinic comment is not as idiosyncratic as it may at first appear. M. Bakhtin observes that the drenching or drowning in urine in Rabelais is part of the carnivalesque nature of his work. Bakhtin then notes that the tossing of excrement is known from ancient literature.[6] A chamber pot is thrown at the head of Odysseus in Aeschylus's "The Collector of Bones" and a similar episode is found in Sophocles' "The Feast of the Achaeans." Ancient Greek vases picture Heracles lying drunk at a prostitute's door while the procuress empties a chamber pot on his head. Although the text of Esther contains none of this bodily humor, the midrashic addition to the story is completely within the spirit of the ancient expression of the carnivalesque.

13. Haman's "friends" in verse 13a become "his advisors" in 13b. They no longer offer friendly words of support but a warning that Haman does not heed. Haman's coming downfall is already foreseen by his friends and wife, and through them by the reader. Their words, like the words of Abigail in 1 Sam. 25:28–30 hinting at David's future kingship, are more for the benefit of the audience than for the character being addressed, and they foreshadow events to come. There are other instances of non-Jews uttering the foreshadowing of the destruction of Israel's enemies (Num. 22–24, especially 24:20; Dan. 3:28–33; Jth. 5:5–21). This prediction resonates with readers who know other biblical predictions about Amalek (Exod. 17:16; Num. 24:20; Deut. 25;17–19; 1 Samuel 15).

The emphasis is on Mordecai's "Jewish stock"—a ray of hope that the Jews will prevail. Once again, in a reversal of chapter 3, Mordecai's fate is the fate of his people.

14. We do not know if Haman grasped the full meaning of these words. He had no time to ponder their implication, for he was immediately whisked off to the next party, where the denouement will occur and the words of this verse will come true.

king's eunuchs arrived and hurriedly brought Haman to the banquet which Esther had prepared.

הִגִּיעוּ וַיַּבְהִלוּ לְהָבִיא אֶת־הָמָן אֶל־
הַמִּשְׁתֶּה אֲשֶׁר־עָשְׂתָה אֶסְתֵּר׃

> ***While they were still speaking with him***   A phrase that conveys that one thing is happening quickly after another, so there is no time to recover from the first incident before the second begins. See Job 1:16–18. The quick pace indicated in this verse is typical of farce.[7]

> ***hurriedly***   The term connotes excitement or agitation. Other terms for haste have been used in this chapter and before: Haman hurries to the banquet (5:5), hurries to honor Mordecai (6:10), then hurries home dejected (6:12). Fox says that Haman's hurrying evinces a lack of inner certitude and self-assurance. The haste also keeps Haman moving swiftly and inexorably to his doom.

CHAPTER 7

Another Party Favor

This chapter brings to an end the rivalry between Haman and Mordecai. Previously, Mordecai received the honor that Haman had designed for himself, and now Haman will receive the disgrace that he had designed for Mordecai: Haman will be impaled on the stake he prepared for Mordecai. The denouement of the plot also begins, as Esther takes the first major step in carrying out her mission to save the Jews. She goes about it in two stages. In chapter 7 she unmasks Haman as the villain that he is, a danger not only to the Jews but to the king, too. Her rhetoric is subtle and effective. She builds her case on the king's personal feelings for her and on the harmful, even treasonous, actions of her adversary, Haman. Haman is removed and disgraced, and the evil that he represents is gone; but this is not the end of the story, for the Jews are yet to be saved. This will form the second stage in Esther's mission, and it will occur in chapter 8.

As in chapter 6, the high point in chapter 7 is structured around a misperception. This time it is Ahasuerus who misunderstands, mistaking Haman's gesture of pleading for his life before Esther for an attempt to seduce the queen. As in chapter 1, we are again in a setting of drinking parties with sexual overtones; but this time the queen is off-limits to the invited guest.

But is the king really so obtuse? Does he really believe that Haman, who has just been denounced by Esther, would try to ravish her? I see a double level of humor in this scene. It is amusing enough to have the king, who has been caricatured as a bumbling fool earlier in the story, innocently misinterpret the scene that greets his eyes as he returns to the banquet room. But it is even funnier if his misinterpretation is intentional. And I suspect that it is. The king has found a different pretext to do away with Haman. Esther had argued that Haman's actions were calculated to wrest power away from the king and therefore constituted a form of treason (see the Commentary to v. 4). An attempt to ravish the queen is no less treasonous (see the Commentary to v. 8), and, unlike the plot against the Jews, it did not have the king's prior approval. The king's accusation against Haman achieves, in a much more direct way, the same end that Esther's was intended to have. Haman must have been doubly shocked: once by Esther's true accusation and again by Ahasuerus's false one. The irony is that now both Esther and Ahasuerus have accused Haman of gross insubordination—of wishing to supplant the king. That presumably was not his goal in arranging the annihilation of the Jews; but, as we saw in chapter 6, Haman

7 So the king and Haman came to feast with Queen Esther. [2] On the second day, the king again asked Esther at the wine feast, "What is your wish, Queen Esther? It shall be granted you. And what is your request? Even to half the kingdom, it shall be

ז וַיָּבֹא הַמֶּ֫לֶךְ וְהָמָ֖ן לִשְׁתּ֥וֹת עִם־אֶסְתֵּ֥ר הַמַּלְכָּֽה: [2] וַיֹּאמֶר֩ הַמֶּ֨לֶךְ לְאֶסְתֵּ֜ר גַּ֣ם בַּיּ֤וֹם הַשֵּׁנִי֙ בְּמִשְׁתֵּ֣ה הַיַּ֔יִן מַה־שְּׁאֵלָתֵ֛ךְ אֶסְתֵּ֥ר הַמַּלְכָּ֖ה וְתִנָּ֣תֵֽן לָ֑ךְ וּמַה־בַּקָּשָׁתֵ֖ךְ

would have liked nothing better than to become king. Haman's lust for honor has at last been laid bare, and it proves to be his undoing.

Ahasuerus looks a bit more kingly by the end of the chapter. He is still a comic figure, and is still led by the suggestions of his inferiors; but, his emotions and decisions are, at last, fitting for the occasion, even if he came to them slowly and not altogether for the right reasons. We can almost feel sorry for Haman, caught as he is by the king's misconstrual of his action. Actually, it is an appropriate touch, given the comic nature of the story, that the villain be punished for something he did not do. Moreover, since Haman's plot against the Jews had the full consent of the king, it would be awkward for the king to punish him for it. In any case, it is too late for Haman, and we cheer as he gets what he deserves. The dishonor done to him, impalement on the stake that he had erected for Mordecai, is another of the book's reversals. As the Psalmist says of the evildoer, "He has dug a pit and deepened it, and will fall into the trap he made. His mischief will recoil upon his own head; his lawlessness will come down upon his skull" (Ps. 7:16–17).

The events of chapter 7 flow naturally from what precedes them; and, as we have seen in so many cases in Esther, the motifs are completely at home in the literary world of stories about Persia. Banquet scenes with guests reclining on couches are known from literature and art of the ancient Near East and the classical world.[1] The couch is a commonplace at a Persian banquet—remember the gold and silver couches of 1:6—and is used to good comic effect in the present chapter.

As for Haman's attempt to plead with Esther for his life, this fits nicely with the motif of women as intercessors often found in the Greek sources and elsewhere in the Bible. More to the point of our chapter, the accounts of Ctesias are full of conflicts between royal ministers and the king's wife or mother.[2] The motif of treason against the king's sovereignty, which I see at work in this chapter, is both biblical and Greek, and is explained in detail in the Commentary.

1. to feast with Queen Esther Literally: "to drink," that is, to party. Compare 3:15 where the king and Haman were partying together, without anyone else, after the decree against the Jews was issued. Now, as events begin to unfold that will countermand the decree, Haman and the king are again partying, but this time Esther is with them.

Queen Esther Her title underscores her official position and the honor that derives from being invited to party with her. See also 5:12, where Haman notes that he has been invited by *Queen* Esther. The title is used frequently in this chapter and contributes to the formality, or mock formality, of the proceedings. However much Esther may have seemed like a concubine earlier in the story, after chapter 5 she is the queen and her royal status is emphasized.

2. On the second day At the second party. Esther never gave her answer so Ahasuerus puts the question to her once more.

It shall be granted to you This time, the verb "it shall be granted" is in the feminine, whereas it was in the masculine in 5:3 and 5:6 (see the Commentary to 5:6). The feminine verb corresponds to the word "my life" (which is grammatically feminine), which forms Esther's wish in the next verse (Levenson).

fulfilled." ³Queen Esther replied: "If Your Majesty will do me the favor, and if it pleases Your Majesty, let my life be granted me as my wish, and my people as my request. ⁴For we have been sold, my people and I, to be destroyed, massacred, and exterminated. Had we only been sold as bondmen and bondwomen, I

עַד־חֲצִי הַמַּלְכוּת וְתֵעָשׂ: 3 וַתַּעַן אֶסְתֵּר הַמַּלְכָּה וַתֹּאמַר אִם־מָצָאתִי חֵן בְּעֵינֶיךָ הַמֶּלֶךְ וְאִם־עַל־הַמֶּלֶךְ טוֹב תִּנָּתֶן־לִי נַפְשִׁי בִּשְׁאֵלָתִי וְעַמִּי בְּבַקָּשָׁתִי: 4 כִּי נִמְכַּרְנוּ אֲנִי וְעַמִּי לְהַשְׁמִיד לַהֲרוֹג וּלְאַבֵּד

3. The first part of Esther's answer is weighted down with formal language that slows down the action and increases the tension. Echoing the king's use of "wish" and "request" in a parallelistic construction, she asks for her life as her wish and her people as her request. Surely this was not what the king expected to hear, and he cannot fully comprehend until Esther explains further.

Despite the rather flowery introduction, Esther is clearly building her case on her personal relationship to the king: "If I have found favor in your eyes, O King." She will use a similar line of argument in 8:5. No matter what Ahasuerus thought of the Jews, he clearly loved Esther and would not want harm to befall her. Besides, as Levenson remarks, the king has already lost one queen on the advice of an advisor, and he presumably would not like to lose another one.

my life…my people   Compare also "My people and I" in the next verse. It may appear selfish for Esther to place herself ahead of her people, but she is rhetorically correct to start with the Jew nearest and dearest to the king, and then to expand to the rest of the Jews. The Jews will benefit by being Esther's people. Now Esther firmly links herself with her people but even at this crucial moment she does not name them as the Jews. Compare 3:6 where the Jews are "Mordecai's people."

4. ***We have been sold***   Once again, there is a hint of the financial transaction that Haman had attempted. Esther had learned about it from Mordecai in 4:7. Or alternatively, we may understand *m-k-r* in its sense of "handed over, betrayed" as in Judg. 2:14; 3:8; and elsewhere when God hands Israel over to its enemies. The term was not used earlier in the story in connection with Haman's financial offer; Esther introduces it here, perhaps for its negative connotations. It also forms yet another bond with the Joseph story, reminding us that Joseph was sold by his brothers (Gen. 37:28, 36; 45:4).

to be destroyed, massacred, and exterminated   The same three terms are used in Haman's edict in 3:13. The infinitives are in the active form with passive meaning.[3]

The juxtaposition of "we have been sold" with "to be destroyed" is somewhat jarring. The Masoretic Text uses "we have been sold" in two senses that are carefully distinguished: sold for destruction and sold as slaves. The Septuagint, however, combines the two into "we have been sold, I and my people, to be destroyed, plundered, and made slaves"— which completely alters Esther's rhetorical point.

Had we only been sold as bondmen and bondwomen   This ironic understatement is an important part of Esther's rhetorical strategy but it is not easy to understand. The usual explanation is that Esther is constructing the hypothetical threat of slavery—certainly a grave matter but one that appears trivial in light of the real threat of death. By saying that she would not trouble the king over enslavement, she makes clear that if she is now troubling the king, it is for a matter of utmost importance. While this is correct, the mention of enslavement is not a throw-away line. It is intended to recast Haman's plot as a treasonous act against the king.

What are the connotations of "had we only been sold as bondmen"? On one level, in ancient Near Eastern terminology being someone's "slave" can simply mean recognizing

would have kept silent; for the adversary is not worthy of the king's trouble."

וְאִלּוּ לַעֲבָדִים וְלִשְׁפָחוֹת נִמְכַּרְנוּ הֶחֱרַשְׁתִּי כִּי אֵין הַצָּר שֹׁוֶה בְּנֵזֶק הַמֶּלֶךְ: ס

the superior authority of that person. The Persian nobles were known as the *bandaka*, "slaves" of the king, meaning that they were loyal to him.[4] From a Jewish perspective, enslavement could mean to be under the sovereignty of a foreign ruler, which the Jews were as subjects to the Persian king. As Ezra 9:9 says: "For bondsmen we are, though even in our bondage God has not forsaken us, but has disposed the king of Persia favorably toward us." Part of what a Diaspora Jewish audience may have heard in this phrase is "had we just been allowed to remain loyal subjects of the Persian king." In other words, the Jews were satisfied with the status quo and would gladly reaffirm their loyalty to the Persian king. This is, as I suggested in chapter 3, precisely what Haman accused them of not doing.

If we take the reference to being sold into slavery more literally, it becomes even more puzzling. While individuals could be sold into slavery for debt, the selling of an entire people into slavery is strange. An entire people could become enslaved only if another political entity conquered them. In fact, both killing and enslaving—the two elements in Esther's speech—go along with battles of conquest. (Note the phrase in Herodotus 3.140, quoted in the Commentary to chapter 6, where Syloson says "give me back Samos, but so that there be no bloodshed nor enslaving.") To sell the Jews into slavery implies that they are being wrested away from the sovereignty of the king and given over to the sovereignty of another power. This is a treasonous offense. If this is what Haman had proposed, then he is a traitor to the king. The king, of course, had not understood Haman's proposal in that light, if he had understood it at all. And, although Haman may have wished to be king (as we saw in chapter 6), there is no hint that his plot against the Jews was intended to usurp part of the empire from the king. But in Esther's account, Haman's plan has ostensibly become a way to deprive Ahasuerus of a group of his subjects, including his queen. The false lead about slavery reframes the "selling to be destroyed" as a power grab by Haman against the king. Esther is framing Haman as a traitor. And how sweet is the irony, for, as I have interpreted 3:8, Haman had framed the Jews as traitors.

My interpretation that Esther's words are a veiled accusation of treason finds support in the Greek versions. While they confuse and combine annihilation and enslavement in the main story, Addition E, which follows 8:12 and contains the text of the new edict favoring the Jews, also turns Haman (who is a Macedonian) into a traitor. Verse 2 accuses him of undertaking to scheme against his own benefactor, and in verses 12–14 we are told that,

> unable to restrain his arrogance, he undertook to deprive us of our kingdom and our life.... He thought that by these methods he would catch us undefended and would transfer the kingdom of the Persians to the Macedonians.

While Addition E has arrived at this portrayal of Haman in a different way and for a different reason, the effect of its accusation (put into the mouth of the king) is quite similar to Esther's accusation in the Masoretic Text.

The fact that the king had earlier agreed to a plan so contrary to his interests is something that Esther omits, for it surely would not help her case for Ahasuerus to be revealed as the fool that he is. Her whole speech is designed to present her as one who, like Mordecai, has uncovered a plot against the king. She is pleading for the king to save her own life and the lives of her people because it is in his best interest to do so.

I would have kept silent   Mordecai warned her in 4:14 what would happen if she kept silent.

the adversary is not worthy of the king's trouble   The phrase is ambiguous and lends itself to different interpretations, depending on the meaning of *ha-tzar* and *nezek*.

⁵ Thereupon King Ahasuerus demanded of Queen Esther, "Who is he and where is he who dared to

⁵ וַיֹּ֙אמֶר֙ הַמֶּ֣לֶךְ אֲחַשְׁוֵר֔וֹשׁ וַיֹּ֖אמֶר לְאֶסְתֵּ֣ר הַמַּלְכָּ֑ה מִ֣י ה֥וּא זֶה֙ וְאֵֽי־זֶ֣ה ה֔וּא אֲשֶׁר־

Ha-tzar can mean either "the adversary" or "the adversity." A case could be made for either meaning, but it may be better to take it as a double-entendre with both meanings registering together. Haman is called *'ish tzar ve-'oyev* in verse 6. He is the adversary of Esther and the Jews. If the matter had not been so serious, suggests Esther, he could be dealt with at a lower level. At the same time, the adversity, that is, the possibility of Jewish enslavement, would normally not come to the attention of the king.

Nezek, which does not occur elsewhere in the Bible, here seems to mean "trouble, annoyance." Compare Akkadian *niziqtu* and *nizqu* with the same meaning. There is, however, a tradition of interpreting *nezek* in its Mishnaic Hebrew sense of "damage," referring to the financial loss that the king might suffer if the hypothetical sale of the Jews into bondage were to be rescinded. This interpretation makes possible an additional irony, for the Jews were "sold" for no money. They were to be killed for free; the king made no profit from Haman's plot. "If," says Esther, "you stood to suffer a financial loss, I would not be making this request." How fiscally conservative for someone who has just been offered half the kingdom!

The term *'ein shoveh,* "it is not worth," occurs also in 3:8, in Haman's argument to Ahasuerus to destroy the Jews. I agree with the commentators who see in this phrase an additional echo of Haman's proposal; it supports my argument that Esther is reframing Haman's proposal in terms much more damaging to the king.

However we understand the individual terms in this verse, the statement is ironic in the extreme. Esther is making light of the hypothetical bondage that, if it were true, would constitute treason against the king, and would certainly merit troubling him about.

    5. In Hebrew the beginning of the verse reads "Said the king Ahasuerus, said he to Esther the queen." The repetition of the verb "he said" with no intervening direct discourse has troubled some commentators. But a similar repetition of the verb "to say" also occurs in Ezek. 10:2; Gen. 22:7; 46:2; 2 Sam. 24:17; and Neh. 3:34 with the effect of slowing the narration and lending solemnity to it.[5] Alternatively, the repetition may, as in Gen. 22:7, represent the hesitation of the speaker.[6] Both of these explanations fit our verse. We are at the height of the denouement and Esther has just dropped a bombshell, which may have left Ahasuerus momentarily speechless. The verse starts hesitatingly, repeating the verb "he said," as if the king is having trouble formulating his words. The phrasing also gives equal weight to the speaker and the person being addressed, both of them carrying their royal titles: literally, "King Ahasuerus" and "Esther the queen." This is a dialogue between the royal couple. As far as Ahasuerus is concerned, Haman is out of the picture. But Haman, of course, hears all of this, and will be very much in the picture in a moment. While Ahasuerus's question is not addressed to him, he is vitally interested in Esther's answer.[7]

    who is he and where is he   If *'ei-zeh hu'* is rendered "where is he," it lends a certain irony because the culprit is sitting right there at the table with the king. The expression may also be rendered "which one is he." Compare Jon. 1:8; Eccles. 2:3; 11:6, and Mishnaic Hebrew (with which the Hebrew of Esther shares many features), for example, the series in M. Avot 4:1: *'eizehu ḥakham,* "who is wise," etc. Ahasuerus's utterance is, then, redundant, an indication of his amazement and his sputtering attempt to make sense of what he is hearing. His amazement will turn to anger when the name of the villain is revealed. The redundancy is also in keeping with the repetitious style of the book, and here it heightens the build-up before the pronouncement of Haman's name.

do this?" ⁶ "The adversary and enemy," replied Esther, "is this evil Haman!" And Haman cringed in terror before the king and the queen. ⁷ The king, in his fury, left the wine feast for the palace garden, while Haman remained to plead with Queen Esther for his life;

מִלָּא֥וֹ לִבּ֖וֹ לַעֲשׂ֥וֹת כֵּֽן: ⁶ וַתֹּ֣אמֶר־אֶסְתֵּ֔ר אִ֚ישׁ צַ֣ר וְאוֹיֵ֔ב הָמָ֥ן הָרָ֖ע הַזֶּ֑ה וְהָמָ֣ן נִבְעַ֔ת מִלִּפְנֵ֥י הַמֶּ֖לֶךְ וְהַמַּלְכָּֽה: ⁷ וְהַמֶּ֜לֶךְ קָ֤ם בַּחֲמָתוֹ֙ מִמִּשְׁתֵּ֣ה הַיַּ֔יִן אֶל־גִּנַּ֖ת הַבִּיתָ֑ן וְהָמָ֣ן עָמַ֗ד לְבַקֵּ֤שׁ עַל־נַפְשׁוֹ֙ מֵֽאֶסְתֵּ֔ר

who dared to do this Literally, "whose heart filled him to do this." The heart is the seat of thoughts. In 8:3 we find a reference to "the thoughts that Haman thought about the Jews"—that is, the evil he plotted against them.

6. Esther's response is not directed only to the king, for Haman is meant to hear it.

the adversary and the enemy The phrase echoes "the foe of the Jews" in 3:10. But here he is not only an enemy of the Jews, but of the queen, and hence of the king. The epithets precede the naming of Haman to further heighten the dramatic tension. *Tzar ve-'oyev* is a hendiadys (cf. Lam. 4:12) meaning: hostile enemy" or "vicious enemy."

cringed in terror When Haman heard his name, he cringed in terror. He was terrified of both the king and the queen. But he will appeal to the queen for mercy, partly because it is a convention that women, especially queens, serve as intercessors, and partly because, as the next verse tells us, Haman realized that the king was dead set against him.

7. **The king, in his fury, left** The word *kam,* rendered "left," is literally "rose." The king is appropriately enraged. We have seen him angry for lesser causes. The king is angry not only that someone would harm the queen, but that the someone is his most trusted advisor, Haman. He does not express his anger verbally; indeed, the implication is that he is so angry that he cannot contain himself and so he leaves the room.

In fact, there is no verbal reaction to Esther's accusation from either of the other characters. Instead, there are gestures, as if a pantomime is being enacted: Haman cringes, Ahasuerus rises, Haman stands, the king returns, and Haman falls. The syntax of all of these actions is not a series of *vav*-consecutive verbs as is normally used for a narrative progression of actions, but rather a series of conjunctively linked clauses with the subject of each clause preceding the verb. The effect is a chain reaction of movements by the characters. When Esther utters her accusation, Haman cringes; the king rises to leave; Haman stands to plead; and the king returns.

There has been much speculation about why the king leaves the room. Explanations range from Ahasuerus's need to calm down and collect his thoughts, to get out of the sight of the evil Haman, or to relieve himself after having drunk much wine. From a literary perspective, he must leave the room in order that he can return to see Haman falling upon Esther's couch, for this is the climax of the scene.

the palace garden The banquet was probably held in the *bitan,* the hall used for parties. The location is referred to as the *bet mishteh,* "banquet room," in verse 8. The garden was mentioned in 1:5.

Haman remained Hebrew *'amad* means "to stand, to take up a position." Haman had been reclining on his couch, as one did at ancient banquets, and now he stands so that he may approach Esther to plead for his life. The word *'-m-d* is associated with intercession in Jer. 15:1 (Hakham).

to plead . . . for his life If she doesn't change her story, he will be guilty of treason, a capital offense. Haman saw that the king was already convinced of his guilt, so his only

for he saw that the king had resolved to destroy him. ⁸ When the king returned from the palace garden to the banquet room, Haman was lying prostrate on the couch on which Esther reclined. "Does he mean," cried the king, "to ravish the queen in my own palace?" No sooner did these words leave the

הַמַּלְכָּה כִּי רָאָה כִּי־כָלְתָה אֵלָיו הָרָעָה מֵאֵת הַמֶּלֶךְ: ⁸ וְהַמֶּלֶךְ שָׁב מִגִּנַּת הַבִּיתָן אֶל־בֵּית | מִשְׁתֵּה הַיַּיִן וְהָמָן נֹפֵל עַל־הַמִּטָּה אֲשֶׁר אֶסְתֵּר עָלֶיהָ וַיֹּאמֶר הַמֶּלֶךְ הֲגַם לִכְבּוֹשׁ אֶת־הַמַּלְכָּה עִמִּי בַּבָּיִת

recourse was to Esther. In addition, the use of a woman as an intercessor is a common motif of storytelling from this period.

    8. *lying prostrate*   As the king is leaving the room, Haman begins to position himself in the pose of a supplicant, to plead with Esther for his life. But it is not clear if the king noticed. As the king re-enters the room, the sight that greets his eyes is Haman falling upon Esther's couch. The reader understands that this is the pose of a supplicant. In fact, the same verb, *n-p-l*, "to fall," is used in 8:3 when Esther entreats the king (see also 1 Sam. 25:24). But, in the funniest scene of this comic farce, Ahasuerus misinterprets Haman's pose, casting the supplicant as a seducer. That the king accuses Haman of an inappropriate sexual advance is even funnier in light of the king's own improprieties in chapter 1.

    Falling down before someone is a gesture of supplication, and should not be confused with bowing down in obeisance (for which *korea' u-mishtaḥaveh* is used). The term *n-p-l*, "to fall," was used by Haman's companions and his wife in 6:13 to predict Haman's downfall before Mordecai, and here it is coming to pass quite literally through Mordecai's counterpart, Esther.

    to ravish the queen in my own palace   The literal meaning is even stronger, "with me in the house"—that is, with me present. The comedy reaches its high point here, as it introduces a note of bawdiness (so familiar from earlier in the story) into the dramatic denouement. The scene, which appeared serious at the start, immediately becomes mock-serious.

    Seduction was certainly the last thing on Haman's mind. And it is hard to believe that even the none-too-sharp Ahasuerus could misjudge the situation so badly. So I raise the possibility that the king's misunderstanding is intentional. It gives the king a pretext to punish Haman, for Haman's real wrong, plotting to kill the Jews, had the king's full endorsement, so how could he fault Haman for something he earlier had approved? Persian kings never make mistakes.

    It is not merely a question of a sexual advance. To ravish the queen, literally "to conquer the queen," has all the political connotations always associated with an attempt to take someone else's (especially a king's) wife or concubine: it signals an attempt to supplant the husband's authority and replace it with the usurper's (see Ibn Ezra). We know it from the biblical stories of Abner and Saul's concubine (2 Sam. 3:7); Absalom and David's concubines (2 Sam. 16:21–22); Adonijah's request for Abishag (1 Kings 2:15–17); and Reuben's taking of his father's concubine (Gen. 35:22). Solomon, upon hearing Adonijah's request for David's concubine Abishag says that it might just as well be a request for the kingdom (1 Kings 2:22).

    In Greek writing about Persia, as in the Bible, a request for a king's concubine is a claim to the throne. Plutarch, *Artaxerxes* 26.2, records that Ochus, the youngest son of Artaxerxes, had secret relations with one of his father's wives in an attempt to get the throne. And Darius, the son whom Artaxerxes proclaimed the heir to his throne, offended his father by asking for his father's concubine. As Plutarch explains: "The Barbarian folk are terribly jealous in all that pertains to the pleasures of love, so that it is death for a man, not only to come up and touch one of the royal concubines, but even in journeying to go

king's lips than Haman's face was covered. ⁹Then Harbonah, one of the eunuchs in attendance on the king, said, "What is more, a stake is standing at Haman's house, fifty cubits high, which Haman made for Mordecai—the man whose words saved the king." "Impale him on it!" the king ordered. ¹⁰ So they impaled Haman on the stake which he had put up for Mordecai, and the king's fury abated.

הַדָּבָר יָצָא מִפִּי הַמֶּלֶךְ וּפְנֵי הָמָן חָפוּ: ס ⁹ וַיֹּאמֶר חַרְבוֹנָה אֶחָד מִן־הַסָּרִיסִים לִפְנֵי הַמֶּלֶךְ גַּם הִנֵּה־הָעֵץ אֲשֶׁר־עָשָׂה הָמָן לְמָרְדֳּכַי אֲשֶׁר דִּבֶּר־טוֹב עַל־הַמֶּלֶךְ עֹמֵד בְּבֵית הָמָן גָּבֹהַּ חֲמִשִּׁים אַמָּה וַיֹּאמֶר הַמֶּלֶךְ תְּלֻהוּ עָלָיו: ¹⁰ וַיִּתְלוּ אֶת־הָמָן עַל־הָעֵץ אֲשֶׁר־הֵכִין לְמָרְדֳּכָי וַחֲמַת הַמֶּלֶךְ שָׁכָכָה: פ

along past the wagons on which they are conveyed." In this context it becomes clear that Ahasuerus is accusing Haman of an act no less treasonous than the one that Esther was exposing. If Ahasuerus couldn't get Haman on his real act of treason, he would get him on a trumped-up charge of treason.

The motif of a false accusation of a sexual advance occurs in a very different context in Xenophon, *Cyropaedia* 5.2.28. The king of Assyria had one of his comrades castrated. The reason for this, according to some people, was that the king's concubine had praised the comrade's handsomeness. But the king maintained that it was because the comrade had made advances toward his concubine.

Haman's face was covered The meaning of this phrase is not clear. Many commentators take it as a gesture indicating that Haman was condemned to death, but there is little evidence to support it. Perhaps, as Ibn Ezra suggests, the covering of the face was a sign that the king was angry at someone and did not want to see his face. Haman, who until this point had ready access to the royal presence, who was to be considered one of those who "saw the face of the king" (1:14), now loses this privilege. Alternatively, some commentators read *ḥ-p-r-w,* "ashamed, downcast," as in Ps. 34:6. The sense of the phrase is clearly negative but there is no consensus on the precise meaning of the words. Nor is it obvious if there is a connection with 6:12, where Haman's head was covered.

9. Harbonah Another servant, whose name appeared in the list in 1:10, steps up to provide information. It is the king, however, who orders that Haman be impaled on his own stake. It is only now that the king learns of Haman's stake and its intended purpose, for Haman never had the chance to tell him in chapter 6.

The punishment of impalement for a sexual offense is mentioned by Herodotus (4.43). A certain Sataspes had raped a virgin and for this offense King Xerxes ordered that he be impaled. Sataspes' mother pleaded for his life and suggested that he be assigned to sail around Libya (Africa) instead. Xerxes accepted the suggestion, but when Sataspes failed to sail around Libya, Xerxes had him impaled.

the king's fury abated As in 2:1. At the beginning of the story, the king's fury led to the dismissal of his queen, and when his fury abated he needed a new queen. Now, his fury leads to the impalement of his highest official, and when his fury abates he will need a replacement for this official. This will take place at the beginning of chapter 8.

8 That very day King Ahasuerus gave the property of Haman, the enemy of the Jews, to Queen Esther. Mordecai presented himself to the king,

ח בַּיּ֣וֹם הַה֗וּא נָתַ֞ן הַמֶּ֤לֶךְ אֲחַשְׁוֵרוֹשׁ֙ לְאֶסְתֵּ֣ר הַמַּלְכָּ֔ה אֶת־בֵּ֥ית הָמָ֖ן צֹרֵ֣ר הַיְּהוּדִ֑ים וּמָרְדֳּכַ֗י בָּ֚א לִפְנֵ֣י הַמֶּ֔לֶךְ כִּי־הִגִּ֥ידָה אֶסְתֵּ֖ר מַ֥ה הוּא־לָֽהּ׃

CHAPTER **8**

A Reversal of Fortunes

Haman is gone but his edict against the Jews is still in force. Now the second stage of Esther's mission must be accomplished: to save the Jews from destruction. Since a royal edict cannot, according to our story, be revoked, it must be neutralized with another one, equally binding. It is here that Esther and Mordecai, working together publicly for the first time, show themselves to be the heroes of the story. Through their agency, a new edict is written that effectively cancels out the former one. While we hear of the Jewish and some of the non-Jewish reaction to the publication of the new edict, the discharging of its stipulations does not occur until chapter 9.

Chapter 8 is a chapter of reversals, and will replay, with significant changes, some of the motifs and actions from earlier in the story. Esther will again make a request to the king and plead for her people. Again, the king will elevate a man and bestow upon him the power to write a royal edict. Again, an edict will be sent posthaste throughout the empire, an edict with reverse stipulations in similar language to the first one, and equally irrevocable. Again, the edict will provoke a reaction in the city of Shushan; and again the Jews throughout the empire will greet it with a public response, this time with joy instead of with mourning.

As noted by modern commentators and medieval Jewish exegetes, much of the language and many of the details of chapter 8 parallel those of Haman's edict and its publication in chapter 3.[1] This is not surprising in a story so artfully structured, with its symmetries and its inversions. The large number of similarities between the two chapters provides the background against which the differences stand out. I will highlight many of these differences in the Commentary. In general, chapter 8 contains more description and detail, with the effect of making the new edict more important and more urgent than the old one, and showing Mordecai in higher esteem than Haman had been.

1. Haman has been dispatched, and publicly shamed by impalement. One last ignominy occurs here: his property, which reverts to the crown, is turned over to his nemesis. For impalement followed by the confiscation of property see Ezra 6:11: "I also issue an order that whoever alters this decree shall have a beam removed from his house, and he shall be impaled on it and his house confiscated [or: destroyed]." Herodotus 3.129 also records the seizure of a traitor's property.

That very day The king lost no time in following up on the punishment of the villain and on the rewarding of the heroes. The actual time and place of the events in these verses is vague. We do not know if the royal couple is still in the banquet room when Esther repeats her plea to Ahasuerus (v. 3).

Haman's impalement has two immediate consequences: his estate is given to Esther, and Mordecai comes into the presence of Ahasuerus. That is, Mordecai begins to take the place of Haman. This replacement of Haman becomes more explicit in verse 2.

for Esther had revealed how he was related to her. ²The king slipped off his ring, which he had taken back from Haman, and gave it to Mordecai; and Esther put Mordecai in charge of Haman's property.

³Esther spoke to the king again, falling at his feet and weeping, and beseeching him to avert the evil plotted by Haman the Agagite against the Jews. ⁴The king extended the golden scepter to Esther, and Esther arose and stood before the king. ⁵"If it please

² וַיָּ֨סַר הַמֶּ֜לֶךְ אֶת־טַבַּעְתּ֗וֹ אֲשֶׁ֤ר הֶעֱבִיר֙
מֵֽהָמָ֔ן וַֽיִּתְּנָ֖הּ לְמָרְדֳּכָ֑י וַתָּ֧שֶׂם אֶסְתֵּ֛ר
אֶֽת־מָרְדֳּכַ֖י עַל־בֵּ֥ית הָמָֽן׃ פ

³ וַתּ֣וֹסֶף אֶסְתֵּ֗ר וַתְּדַבֵּר֙ לִפְנֵ֣י הַמֶּ֔לֶךְ וַתִּפֹּ֖ל
לִפְנֵ֣י רַגְלָ֑יו וַתֵּ֣בְךְּ וַתִּתְחַנֶּן־ל֗וֹ לְהַעֲבִיר֙
אֶת־רָעַת֙ הָמָ֣ן הָֽאֲגָגִ֔י וְאֵת֙ מַֽחֲשַׁבְתּ֔וֹ
אֲשֶׁ֥ר חָשַׁ֖ב עַל־הַיְּהוּדִֽים׃ ⁴ וַיּ֤וֹשֶׁט הַמֶּ֨לֶךְ֙
לְאֶסְתֵּ֔ר אֵ֖ת שַׁרְבִ֣ט הַזָּהָ֑ב וַתָּ֣קׇם אֶסְתֵּ֔ר
וַֽתַּעֲמֹ֖ד לִפְנֵ֥י הַמֶּֽלֶךְ׃ ⁵ וַתֹּ֗אמֶר אִם־עַל־

King Ahasuerus gave the property of Haman, the enemy of the Jews, to Queen Esther   Esther, who had been promised "up to half the kingdom," now gets Haman's estate.

The emphasis here and throughout this chapter is on Haman's relationship to the Jews, and so his Agagite ancestry is mentioned in verses 3 and 5. In 7:6 he is just *'ish tzar ve-'oyev,* "the adversary and enemy"—an enemy of the state as well as of the Jews. Esther also relates herself to the Jews in chapter 8 as she pleads not for herself, but for her people.

Mordecai presented himself to the king   In a formal audience. This is the first time that Mordecai and the king have come face to face.

for Esther had revealed how he was related to her   Mordecai is given a royal audience because of his relationship to Esther, and not on his own merit (Fox). We are not told exactly when this relationship was revealed. Although Mordecai is mentioned in 7:9–10, his relationship to Esther is not alluded to.

It may be that the words "what he is to her" indicate more than a familial relationship and point to the fact that Esther wants and needs Mordecai with her. The two of them worked as a team earlier in the story, he outside the palace and she inside. Now Mordecai, too, will gain access to the palace, where he will work with Esther even more closely and more openly.

2.   The king gives Haman's ring to Mordecai. This signifies that Mordecai now has the authority that Haman once had, and with it, the power to sign royal edicts. Mordecai is replacing Haman at court.

Esther put Mordecai in charge of Haman's property   Another sign that Mordecai is replacing Haman. Mordecai now controls all of Haman's wealth.

3. Esther spoke to the king again   Esther continues to entreat the king, as she did in the previous chapter. It is not clear if this continuation takes place at the same banquet or some time later. Esther's petition is more emotional now. Here she not only speaks in formal flowery language, but falls at the king's feet, cries, and pleads.

beseeching   The verb *hithannen* was the one Mordecai used in 4:8. Esther is now fulfilling Mordecai's instructions to plead for her people.

4.   Once more Esther takes the initiative and the king indicates by extending his scepter that he will hear what she has to say. She has permission to make her request. The king apparently thought he had already fulfilled her previous request by impaling Haman.

5.   In 3:9 Haman also opens his request with polite language, but Esther's language here is more exaggerated. Compare 7:3. Esther reverses two of the components of

Your Majesty," she said, "and if I have won your favor and the proposal seems right to Your Majesty, and if I am pleasing to you—let dispatches be written countermanding those which were written by Haman son of Hammedatha the Agagite, embodying his plot to annihilate the Jews throughout the king's provinces. ⁶ For how can I bear to see the disaster which will befall my people! And how can I bear to see the destruction of my kindred!"

⁷ Then King Ahasuerus said to Queen Esther and Mordecai the Jew, "I have given Haman's property

הַמֶּלֶךְ טוֹב וְאִם־מָצָאתִי חֵן לְפָנָיו וְכָשֵׁר הַדָּבָר לִפְנֵי הַמֶּלֶךְ וְטוֹבָה אֲנִי בְּעֵינָיו יִכָּתֵב לְהָשִׁיב אֶת־הַסְּפָרִים מַחֲשֶׁבֶת הָמָן בֶּן־הַמְּדָתָא הָאֲגָגִי אֲשֶׁר כָּתַב לְאַבֵּד אֶת־הַיְּהוּדִים אֲשֶׁר בְּכָל־מְדִינוֹת הַמֶּלֶךְ: ⁶ כִּי אֵיכָכָה אוּכַל וְרָאִיתִי בָּרָעָה אֲשֶׁר־יִמְצָא אֶת־עַמִּי וְאֵיכָכָה אוּכַל וְרָאִיתִי בְּאָבְדַן מוֹלַדְתִּי: ס ⁷ וַיֹּאמֶר הַמֶּלֶךְ אֲחַשְׁוֵרֹשׁ לְאֶסְתֵּר הַמַּלְכָּה וּלְמָרְדֳּכַי הַיְּהוּדִי הִנֵּה בֵית־הָמָן

her earlier request and adds two more: "[if] the proposal seems right to Your Majesty, and if I am pleasing to you." Her argument is based on the king's personal fondness for her and also on his judgment of what is proper. This reminds us of the king's previous concern with legal propriety (in chapter 1). Esther, of course, is about to request something that is not proper—the reversal of a royal decree.[2] Esther's manipulation of the situation is again masterful.

countermanding Revoking the edict made by Haman. We learn in verse 8 that edicts written in the king's name and sealed with his seal cannot be revoked. Did Esther not know this? See also Dan. 6:9, 13, 16. The Hebrew term for revoking is *sh-w-b*; it occurs also in Judg. 11:35 in connection with Jephthah's vow: "I have uttered a vow to the Lord and I cannot retract." This is to be distinguished from the term in 1:19, *ya'avor,* which means "to break the law." (See the Commentary to 1:19.)

written by Haman . . . Esther stresses that Haman was the author of the plot, and again carefully omits any role that Ahasuerus may have played in it.

6. Her words are poetically, plaintively, expressed. She portrays herself as a potential witness to the destruction of her own people, which she finds unbearable. Hakham notes that she has no need to ask for her own life, for that has been assured.

how '*eikhakhah* is a lengthened form of '*eikh* or '*eikhah,* or perhaps a contraction of '*ei* + *kakhah.* It occurs only here and in Song of Songs 5:3 (twice). In all instances it opens a rhetorical question posed in the first person by a woman: "How could I" in the sense of "It would be impossible for me to."

The terms '*am,* "people," and *moledet,* "kindred," are closely associated here as in Esther 2:10, 20. Whereas before Esther did not reveal her people and kindred, here she identifies publicly with their plight.

the disaster which will befall The Hebrew has a feminine subject, *ra'ah,* and a masculine verb, *yimtza'.* It is perhaps influenced by Gen. 44:34 where "disaster," *ra',* is masculine and the same masculine verb occurs. Compare also Deut. 31:17.

7. *Mordecai the Jew* Fox suggests that Mordecai's epithet "the Jew" now becomes a fixed title, parallel to "the Queen" (Esther's title) and equally honorable. But is the use of "the Jew" here any different from its use elsewhere in the story (5:13; 6:10; 9:29, 31; 10:3)? "Mordecai the Jew" is similar to "Ruth the Moabitess" (Ruth 1:22; 2:2, 21; 4:5, 10) in that the ethnic designation of one character stands out in contrast to the other charac-

to Esther, and he has been impaled on the stake for scheming against the Jews. ⁸And you may further write with regard to the Jews as you see fit. [Write it] in the king's name and seal it with the king's signet, for an edict that has been written in the king's name and sealed with the king's signet may not be revoked."

נָתַ֣תִּי לְאֶסְתֵּ֗ר וְאֹתוֹ֙ תָּל֣וּ עַל־הָעֵ֔ץ עַ֛ל אֲשֶׁר־שָׁלַ֥ח יָד֖וֹ ביהודיים בַּיְּהוּדִֽים: ⁸וְ֠אַתֶּם כִּתְב֨וּ עַל־הַיְּהוּדִ֜ים כַּטּ֤וֹב בְּעֵֽינֵיכֶם֙ בְּשֵׁ֣ם הַמֶּ֔לֶךְ וְחִתְמ֖וּ בְּטַבַּ֣עַת הַמֶּ֑לֶךְ כִּֽי־כְתָ֞ב אֲשֶׁר־נִכְתָּ֣ב בְּשֵׁם־הַמֶּ֗לֶךְ וְנַחְתּ֛וֹם בְּטַבַּ֥עַת הַמֶּ֖לֶךְ אֵ֥ין לְהָשִֽׁיב:

ters. Mordecai's Jewishness is certainly an issue in our story (it is the first thing we learn about him in 2:5) just as Ruth's Moabiteness is an issue in the Book of Ruth. Such ethnic or gentilic labels are known from the onomasticon of Babylonia in the Persian period, and are not literary inventions. But the author uses them to especially good effect in instances such as 5:13 and 6:10 where the mention of Mordecai's Jewishness adds to Haman's discomfort. In this connection it may also be noted that in verse 1 Haman's epithet is "enemy of the Jews," rather than "the Agagite" (as in v. 5). This chapter is, indeed, about the triumph of the Jews over their enemy.

for scheming against the Jews This is not quite correct, for the king impaled Haman for his putative seduction attempt. But, as Fox says, if Ahasuerus wishes to present himself as the protector of the Jews, so much the better.

Ahasuerus thinks that he has done all that he could by disposing of Haman and his estate. But the problem of the decree against the Jews remains.

8. As before, Ahasuerus turns over the writing of a royally authorized edict to someone else. He addresses himself to both Esther and Mordecai because Esther is the one who pleaded for the decree and Mordecai is the one who has the king's ring, the authorization to issue the decree (Hakham).

and you The emphasis is on the pronoun, referring to Mordecai and Esther, who together are bidden to write as they like concerning the Jews. "You" is in contrast to "I" the king, who has already done his part (Fox). This emphasizes that Mordecai and Esther are the heroes; it is they who author the proclamation that will save the Jews.

may not be revoked By saying this, Ahasuerus assures them that their new edict has full legal authority.

This is the first time we are told of the irrevocability of imperial edicts (if one excludes 1:19, as I do—see the Commentary to 1:19 and 8:5). Most readers have assumed it from the beginning of the story, and it has become one of the key points in the plot. But it may not always have been part of the story, at least in an earlier, pre-Masoretic version. The Greek Alpha-text yields the following information:

(1) In 4:10, when the king grants Haman authority to write his edict, he assures him that "there is none who will reject the [king's] seal." (2) In 8:16–17 the king asks Mordecai what he wants and Mordecai responds "that you should revoke the letter of Haman." (3) In 8:33–34, Mordecai's letter (which is quite different from the letter in the Masoretic Text), no mention is made of revoking a letter.

Fox suggests that the author of the Masoretic Text had in his source a phrase like Alpha-text 4:10, which actually signified that no one would reject or repudiate a letter properly sealed with the royal seal. But the Masoretic author took the phrase to mean that a royal decree could not be revoked, thereby introducing a different theme into the story, a theme also found in Daniel 6.³

9 So the king's scribes were summoned at that time, on the twenty-third day of the third month, that is, the month of Sivan; and letters were written, at Mordecai's dictation, to the Jews and to the satraps, the governors and the officials of the one hundred and twenty-seven provinces from India to Ethiopia: to every province in its own script and to every people in its own language, and to the Jews in their own

9 וַיִּקָּרְא֣וּ סֹפְרֵֽי־הַמֶּ֣לֶךְ בָּעֵת־הַהִ֗יא בַּחֹ֨דֶשׁ הַשְּׁלִישִׁי֙ הוּא־חֹ֣דֶשׁ סִיוָ֔ן בִּשְׁלוֹשָׁ֤ה וְעֶשְׂרִים֙ בּ֔וֹ וַיִּכָּתֵ֞ב כְּֽכָל־אֲשֶׁר־צִוָּ֣ה מָרְדֳּכַ֣י אֶל־הַיְּהוּדִ֡ים וְאֶ֣ל הָאֲחַשְׁדַּרְפְּנִֽים־ וְהַפַּחוֹת֩ וְשָׂרֵ֨י הַמְּדִינ֜וֹת אֲשֶׁ֣ר ׀ מֵהֹ֣דּוּ וְעַד־כּ֗וּשׁ שֶׁ֤בַע וְעֶשְׂרִים֙ וּמֵאָ֣ה מְדִינָ֔ה מְדִינָ֤ה וּמְדִינָה֙ כִּכְתָבָ֔הּ וְעַ֥ם וָעָ֖ם כִּלְשֹׁנ֑וֹ וְאֶ֨ל־הַיְּהוּדִ֔ים כִּכְתָבָ֖ם וְכִלְשׁוֹנָֽם׃

9. the twenty-third day of the third month As many commentators note, the second decree was issued seventy days after the first decree. The number seventy is often symbolic of completion or perfection in the Bible. But the reader must infer this, for the story makes no mention of the number seventy.

On the publication of the decree see the Commentary to 1:22 and 3:12. Our verse adds the dimensions of the empire, from India to Ethiopia, 127 provinces (as in 1:1) to further impress the reader with the distance encompassed by the decree.

at Mordecai's dictation Mordecai, the enemy of Haman, now reverses the edict of Haman. Although both Esther and Mordecai are empowered by the king to write the edict (v. 8), Mordecai is the one who supervises its preparation. See also verse 10, literally "he wrote . . . he sealed"—that is, Mordecai had the edict written in the king's name and sealed with the royal seal—because he is the one in possession of the royal signet ring. It is not impossible that a woman would do these things—compare 1 Kings 21:8 where Jezebel wrote and sealed (unauthorized) letters in Ahab's name. But the reversal in power between Mordecai and Haman stands out more clearly if Mordecai alone writes the edict and rises to a high position immediately following.

to the Jews The edict is directed specifically to the Jews, in addition to the satraps, governors, and officials.

to the Jews in their own script and language The Jews are mentioned here specifically, because the message affects them in particular.

The notice here and before about messages going far and wide in different languages reflects the practical necessity of conveying official information in forms that would be legible and intelligible to the recipients. But behind the verisimilitude about operations of the empire lies the use of language as a code for ethnicity. This is old and enduring in the Bible, from the origin of diverse peoples of the world through the creation of different languages in the Tower of Babel story (Genesis 11) to the concern of Nehemiah that intermarriage leads to the loss of the Judean language (Neh. 13:23–24: "I saw that Jews had married Ashdodite, Ammonite, and Moabite women; a good number of their children spoke the language of Ashdod and the language of those various peoples, and did not know how to speak Judean"). Language signifies peoplehood. By saying that the Jews of the Persian empire retain their own language, the verse signals that the Jews have preserved their Jewishness. This is yet another way of making the point about Jewish identity that is so important in this story.

The linguistic marker continued to be significant for questions of national identity in later times; for example, among the merits that the Midrash ascribes to the Israelites in Egypt is that they did not change their language (Mekhilta. Bo. 5). Language as a sign of ethnic vitality and power has a long and interesting history throughout the world, as we

script and language. ¹⁰He had them written in the name of King Ahasuerus and sealed with the king's signet. Letters were dispatched by mounted couriers, riding steeds used in the king's service, bred of the royal stud, ¹¹to this effect: The king has permitted the Jews of every city to assemble and fight for their lives; if any people or province attacks them, they may destroy, massacre, and exterminate its armed force together with women and children, and plunder

10 וַיִּכְתֹּב בְּשֵׁם הַמֶּלֶךְ אֲחַשְׁוֵרֹשׁ וַיַּחְתֹּם
בְּטַבַּעַת הַמֶּלֶךְ וַיִּשְׁלַח סְפָרִים בְּיַד
הָרָצִים בַּסּוּסִים רֹכְבֵי הָרֶכֶשׁ
הָאֲחַשְׁתְּרָנִים בְּנֵי הָרַמָּכִים: 11 אֲשֶׁר נָתַן
הַמֶּלֶךְ לַיְּהוּדִים ׀ אֲשֶׁר בְּכָל־עִיר־וָעִיר
לְהִקָּהֵל וְלַעֲמֹד עַל־נַפְשָׁם לְהַשְׁמִיד
וְלַהֲרֹג וּלְאַבֵּד אֶת־כָּל־חֵיל עַם וּמְדִינָה
הַצָּרִים אֹתָם טַף וְנָשִׁים וּשְׁלָלָם לָבוֹז:

learn from a variety of attempts to suppress the languages of conquered peoples and to revive dying languages.

10. *steeds used in the king's service, bred of the royal stud* The technical terms in this verse are not well understood. *Rekhesh* (also in v. 14 and in 1 Kings 5:8 and Mic. 1:13), is a team of horses used in the Persian postal system. The term is found in an ostracon 6:1 from Arad.[4] *'Aḥashteran* is derived from the Persian term *khshatra* meaning "royal, governmental." *Rammakhim,* with cognates in Aramaic and Arabic, is here taken to mean quick mares. The horses were specially bred for speed.

11. *to assemble and fight for their lives* Permission is given for defensive measures, "to fight for their lives," against anyone attacking the Jews. That is, if and when Persians initiated an attack on the Jews (in accordance with the first decree) the Jews should counterattack. Would the Jews have otherwise stood by passively as they were attacked? Were they so law-abiding that they would let themselves be easily killed if such were the law? It would seem that the second decree is not so much to give the Jews permission to defend themselves as to serve as a deterrent to those who might attack them. See verse 17.

destroy, massacre, and exterminate its armed force together with women and children The original edict in 3:13 contained similar wording and so the same terms occur in its reversal.

together with women and children The women and children of those who attack the Jews. Such a stipulation is distasteful to the modern reader, but quite normal in the ancient world, where members of a family were an extension of the head of the family and could suffer because of the deeds of the head. Some commentators interpret this in the context of the *ḥerem,* the ban in war on all the enemy's family and possessions. In fact, the reports of battles and conquests from the ancient Near East attest to practices much more cruel and grotesque than these.

From a literary point of view, the mention of women and children parallels the mention of Jewish women and children in Haman's decree (3:13). This is part of the reversal of Haman's decree and so the stipulations are the same.

plunder their possessions The original edict provided for the plundering of Jewish possessions (3:13), and so this one allows the Jews to plunder the possessions of their enemies. But see 9:10, 15, 16, where it is made clear that the Jews did not take booty.

The Greek versions have an addition, Addition E, containing the text of the new edict. Among its stipulations are that the recipients are not to act on Haman's edict but are, rather, to give aid to the Jews so they may defend themselves. In addition, the celebration of Purim is enjoined upon Persians as well as Jews.

their possessions—¹²on a single day in all the provinces of King Ahasuerus, namely, on the thirteenth day of the twelfth month, that is, the month of Adar. ¹³The text of the document was to be issued as a law in every single province: it was to be publicly displayed to all the peoples, so that the Jews should be ready for that day to avenge themselves on their enemies. ¹⁴The couriers, mounted on royal steeds, went out in urgent haste at the king's command; and the decree was proclaimed in the fortress Shushan.

בְּיוֹם אֶחָד בְּכָל־מְדִינוֹת הַמֶּלֶךְ 12
אֲחַשְׁוֵרוֹשׁ בִּשְׁלוֹשָׁה עָשָׂר לְחֹדֶשׁ שְׁנֵים־
עָשָׂר הוּא־חֹדֶשׁ אֲדָר: 13 פַּתְשֶׁגֶן הַכְּתָב
לְהִנָּתֵן דָּת בְּכָל־מְדִינָה וּמְדִינָה גָּלוּי
לְכָל־הָעַמִּים וְלִהְיוֹת היהודיים הַיְּהוּדִים
עתידים עֲתִידִים לַיּוֹם הַזֶּה לְהִנָּקֵם
מֵאֹיְבֵיהֶם: 14 הָרָצִים רֹכְבֵי הָרֶכֶשׁ
הָאֲחַשְׁתְּרָנִים יָצְאוּ מְבֹהָלִים וּדְחוּפִים
בִּדְבַר הַמֶּלֶךְ וְהַדָּת נִתְּנָה בְּשׁוּשַׁן
הַבִּירָה: פ

13. *so that the Jews should be ready* In 3:14 all the peoples had to be ready to take action; here the edict is directed toward the Jews for it is they who must take action.

avenge themselves The term *n-k-m* does not signify senseless killing, but rather justified retaliation. In Fox's words, it "everywhere designates a punitive action and presupposes a prior wrong." The Jews were permitted to fight back against anyone who sought to harm them.

14. *urgent haste* The messengers must hurry even more urgently than in 3:15, for there is less time before 13 Adar, the date of the scheduled destruction. The new edict is promulgated on 23 Sivan (v. 9), leaving less than nine months to publicize it throughout the empire. This would still be enough time, if, as Herodotus 5.52–53 estimates, it takes three months for a message to reach all parts of the empire.

Rashi suggests that the haste was intended so that the second set of messengers could overtake the first, presumably so that both edicts could be delivered at the same time. (The first edict would have to be delivered, since it cannot be revoked; and the second edict makes no sense without the first.)

A literary perspective suggests that it may not be a question of the need for greater haste but rather the escalation of the literary motif of the postal system. In 3:15 the couriers, who are not further defined, go out in haste; here the couriers, who were "mounted on royal steeds," go out in *urgent* haste. As we near the climax of the story, the pace quickens and the description thickens.

Herodotus 3.128 tells a story that also involves multiple messages. When Darius became king he wished to punish Oroetes, the satrap of Phrygia, Lydia, and Ionia whose residence was in Sardis. He did not wish to send an army against Oroetes so he resorted to a more devious means. A volunteer named Bagaeus was chosen by lot.

> Now that the mission was his, Bagaeus had a number of letters written, on various matters, and sealed them with Darius' seal. Then he took these letters with him to Sardis. When he got there and came into Oroetes' presence he opened the letters and gave them one by one to the royal secretary.... Bagaeus gave the secretary the letters to read so that he could see whether the members of Oroetes' personal guard might possibly be receptive to the idea of rising up against Oroetes. It was clear that they respected the letters and still more the message they contained, so he gave another letter to the secretary. This time the content of the letter was as follows: "Men of Persia, King Darius forbids you to serve as Oroetes' personal guard."

15 Mordecai left the king's presence in royal robes of blue and white, with a magnificent crown of gold and a mantle of fine linen and purple wool. And the

15 וּמָרְדֳּכַי יָצָא ׀ מִלִּפְנֵי הַמֶּלֶךְ בִּלְבוּשׁ
מַלְכוּת תְּכֵלֶת וָחוּר וַעֲטֶרֶת זָהָב גְּדוֹלָה
וְתַכְרִיךְ בּוּץ וְאַרְגָּמָן וְהָעִיר שׁוּשָׁן צָהֲלָה

When the soldiers heard these words, they let their spears fall to the ground, and Bagaeus could see that they were obeying the letters' command so far. This encouraged him, and he gave the secretary the last of his letters, which read: "King Darius orders the Persians in Sardis to kill Oroetes." At these words the guardsmen drew their *akinakeis* and killed him on the spot.

In Herodotus, as in Esther, letters are written and sealed with the king's seal, delivered to distant parts of the empire, and, because their authority is so highly respected, they give rise to killing with no further explanation.

15. *royal robes of blue and white...* Mordecai's outfit reminds us of both Joseph and Daniel, two other Jewish courtiers who achieved high standing in foreign courts. Joseph's royal investiture is described in Gen. 41: 42: "And removing his signet ring from his hand, Pharaoh put it on Joseph's hand; and he had him dressed in robes of fine linen, and put a gold chain about his neck." Daniel is clothed in purple and has a gold chain placed around his neck, signifying that he rules as one of three in the kingdom (Dan. 5:7, 29). The colorful textiles of Mordecai's costume also recall the hangings of the party scene in 1:6. Mordecai has, indeed, become a royal personage in the court, and is dressed in the typical fashion of the Persian court.

We might have expected this description in verse 1 or 2, when Mordecai enters the king's presence, but its occurrence here serves the larger picture of reversal. After Haman's edict, Mordecai dressed in mourning garb (4:1); after Mordecai's own edict he dresses in royal splendor. Moreover, with the writing of his own edict, Mordecai becomes a permanent and highly-placed royal official, second to the king, as we learn in 10:3.

The word *takhrikh*, "mantle," is a Late Biblical Hebrew term. It later becomes limited to the mantle for the dead, or shroud.

a crown of gold The Hebrew is *'atarah*, an older term, not *keter* as in 1:11 and 6:8. Perhaps this is to tell us that, unlike Haman, Mordecai does not wish to be king.

the city of Shushan rang with joyous cries At the end of chapter 3, the city of Shushan was dumbfounded by the news of the decree against the Jews. Now, when the decree is reversed, the city of Shushan is joyous. This is both a reversal of 3:15 and an embodiment of Prov. 11:10: "When the righteous prosper the city exults; When the wicked perish there are shouts of joy."

Compare Herodotus 8.98–99, which also recounts the sending of messages via the Persian post, described in detail, and the reactions in Susa to the messages. In this case, there was first a message of victory followed by a message of defeat.

At the same time, Xerxes also dispatched a messenger to Persia with news of their defeat. There is nothing mortal that is faster than the system the Persians have devised for sending messages. Apparently, they have horses and men posted at intervals along the route, the same number in total as the overall length in days of the journey, with a fresh horse and rider for every day of travel. Whatever the conditions—it may be snowing, raining, blazing hot, or dark—they never fail to complete their assigned journey in the fastest possible time. The first man passes his instructions on to the second, the second to the third, and so on, in the same kind of relay found in Greece in the torch-race which is run during the festival

city of Shushan rang with joyous cries. ¹⁶ The Jews enjoyed light and gladness, happiness and honor. ¹⁷ And in every province and in every city, when the king's command and decree arrived, there was gladness and joy among the Jews, a feast and a holiday. And many of the people of the land professed

וְשָׂמֵחָה: ¹⁶ לַיְּהוּדִ֗ים הָֽיְתָה֙ אוֹרָ֣ה
וְשִׂמְחָ֖ה וְשָׂשֹׂ֥ן וִיקָֽר: ¹⁷ וּבְכָל־מְדִינָ֣ה
וּמְדִינָ֗ה וּבְכָל־עִ֣יר וָעִ֔יר מְקוֹם֙ אֲשֶׁ֣ר דְּבַר־
הַמֶּ֤לֶךְ וְדָתוֹ֙ מַגִּ֔יעַ שִׂמְחָ֤ה וְשָׂשׂוֹן֙
לַיְּהוּדִ֔ים מִשְׁתֶּ֖ה וְי֣וֹם ט֑וֹב וְרַבִּ֞ים מֵֽעַמֵּ֤י

of Hephaestus. The Persian word for this postal system involving horses is called *angareion*.

The first report that reached Susa, that Xerxes had taken Athens, caused the Persians who had stayed at home so much pleasure that they spread myrtle over all the roads, burnt perfumed spices, and spent their time performing sacrificial rites and feasting. However, the arrival of the second message on top of the first so overwhelmed them that they all tore their tunics and gave themselves over to unending weeping and wailing.

16. This refers to the Jews of Shushan who, even more than the rest of the city, were overjoyed at the new edict. This verse is recited in the *Havdalah* service, the service marking the conclusion of the Sabbath.

17. As the new edict reaches each province, the Jews there rejoice also, for they know that they have been saved. Their joyousness is the antithesis of their mourning recorded in 4:3; the construction of the verses is similar. As before, their response involves performative actions, a public demonstration of their feelings. See the Commentary to 4:3 and compare also 9:17–19, 22. The reversal from mourning to joy brings to mind Ps. 30:12: "You turned my lament into dancing, you undid my sackcloth and girded me with joy."

holiday *Yom tov*; also in 9:19, 22, 28, 31, 32. Esther is the only place in the Bible where *yom tov* is used, as it is in the Mishnah and later literature, in reference to a specific set festival time.[5]

people of the land *'Ammei ha-'aretz,* that is, non-Jews. The term is often used in the postexilic period in contrast or opposition to the Jews, especially those returning to Judah. Here it refers to people of the Persian empire who were not Jews.

professed to be Jews A denominative verb in the *hitpaʿel* form, with the possible meanings ranging from "they pretended to be Jews" to "they made themselves Jews" (that is, they converted to Judaism). The precise nuance of this form has engaged many commentators. The translation, "professed to be Jews," is nicely indeterminate. I favor Levenson's translation, "they identified themselves with the Jews," which I take to mean "they sided with the Jews." Apparently one had to be either for or against the Jews in this matter; there was no middle ground.

There is a body of interpretation advocating the meaning that some non-Jews converted to Judaism. Judith 14:10, where Achior converts to Judaism, is used as support. But religious conversion in the technical sense is later than I would date the Book of Esther. Moreover, religious conversion seems far-fetched in a book in which any mention of religious practice is studiously avoided. The emphasis here is not on religion, but on ethnic identification. The closest biblical parallel is Ruth's declaration of her identification with Naomi's people and God (Ruth 1:16).

Religious conversion begins in Hellenistic times, so it is not surprising that the Greek versions have understood this verse in the context of their own times and practices. The Septuagint reads: "And many of the Gentiles were circumcised and became Jews." Compare Jth. 14:10: "So he [Achior] was circumcised, and joined the house of Israel."

to be Jews, for the fear of the Jews had fallen upon them.

הָאָרֶץ מְתְיַהֲדִים כִּי־נָפַל פַּחַד־הַיְּהוּדִים
עֲלֵיהֶם:

Circumcision was (and still is), for a male, the *sine qua non* for conversion to Judaism and was seen as the main symbol of being Jewish.

fear of the Jews This fear is not a feeling of spiritual awe, but fear of a calamity, a military defeat.[6] It is the usual sense of "fear fell upon"—see also Exod. 15:16; 1 Sam. 11:7; Ps. 105:38; Job 13:11. The non-Jews feared the Jews—that is, feared to attack them in accordance with Haman's edict, for they knew that the Jews would fight back and feared that the Jews would prove stronger. The unlikelihood of non-Jews fearing the military strength of the Jews is just one more of many implausibilities in the book. All of this should be understood in the spirit of the carnivalesque, where reality is turned on its head. Only in a carnivalesque fiction could a small Jewish minority be given such power and privilege.

CHAPTER 9

Riots and Revelry

This chapter connects the events of the story with the holiday of Purim. It turns the story, which may once have existed independent of its Purim connection, into an etiology of Purim, providing the reason for both the origin of the holiday and for its annual celebration. This is most likely the reason that the Book of Esther became popular among the Jews and was taken into the biblical canon.

Chapter 9 portrays scenes of violence and revenge on a massive scale in the form of the massacre by the Jews of over 75,000 non-Jews. To make matters worse, the massacre is replayed a second time. This then becomes an occasion for celebration and merrymaking for all Jews everywhere. It is no wonder that this chapter did not resonate well with later readers, especially Christians, and many Jews, too, are uncomfortable with what they see as heartless and bloodthirsty Jewish revenge. That the massacre is not an act of revenge but is an act of self-defense taken by Jews against their enemies, explicitly stated in 9:2, does not lay their discomfort to rest.

A better way to relate to the events of chapter 9 is to see them as part of the carnivalesque farce that permeates the whole book and defines its genre.[1] Scenes of tumultuous riots and violent mock-destruction are completely at home in farcical and carnivalesque works; in fact, they are their hallmarks. Chapter 9 is the climax of the carnivalesque, the peak of disorder. Exaggeration and irrationality reach new heights, even for this book. But it is all in fun; nothing here is real. It is emotional release at its wildest.

Our reaction to the carnivalesque is a learned reaction. Children are often afraid of clowns and masquerades until they learn to laugh at them. There is, indeed, something dark and scary about the carnivalesque, just barely masked by the fun that surrounds it. The actions of carnival are playfully grotesque acts that would never be condoned in real life. It is in this context of carnivalesque violence that we should understand chapter 9.

The literary critic Eric Bentley makes an apt observation about the psychological nature of farce and about why a negative reaction to it misses the point.

> [I]n farce, as in dreams, one is permitted the outrage but is spared the consequences....

But while dreams are ignored or forgotten, farces incur the censure of professional moralists and amateur psychologists. The thought arises: "The theatre is inciting my children to hate the home, if not to commit murder and arson. We must have more censorship!" It is overlooked that such fantasies are kept for dreams and pictures and plays just because each of us already has within him so strong a censorship, and it is wrongly inferred from the power of the fantasies that people are likely to fail to distinguish between fantasy and reality....

The function of "farcical" fantasies, in dreams or in plays, is not as provocation but as compensation. The violent release is comparable to the sudden relieving hiss of steam through a safety valve. Certainly, the mental energies involved are destructive, and in all comedy there remains something of destructive orgy, farce being the kind of comedy which disguises that fact least thoroughly. But the function of orgies is also that of a safety valve. An orgy...is an essentially temporary truancy from the family pieties, and, like farces, if it has any appreciable effect at all, it helps those pieties to go on existing.[2]

What we have in chapter 9 is the orgy, the riot, the revelry that fits so well with farce and carnival. The violent free-for-all in which the Jews kill their enemies is transmuted into the revelry of the festival. The make-believe victory is the safety valve for Diaspora Jewry that permits the continuation of the belief in the security of their lives and their community. To put the world right, as the Book of Esther does, requires the removal of evil, of the enemy. This is the idea in Ps. 1:6: "For the Lord cherishes the way of the righteous, but the way of the wicked is doomed" and in Ps. 104:35: "May sinners disappear from the earth, and the wicked be no more." It is not a matter of revenge, or even of defense, but a matter of the natural order of things in a perfect, enemy-free, world.

Throughout this Commentary we have taken pains to point out motifs shared by Esther and the Greek historiographers, and this chapter is no exception. The death of the Magi, as told by Herodotus 3.79, has often been compared to Esther because it, too, tells of a festival arising from a victory against an enemy; and like Esther it is violent and bloodthirsty.

> Once they had killed the Magi, the conspirators cut off their heads. They left their wounded comrades where they were, because they were incapacitated and because the acropolis needed guarding. Taking the heads of the Magi with them, they ran out of the palace. They raised the alarm as they went and shouted out their news to all the rest of the Persians, showing them the heads and calling them to arms. Meanwhile, they killed any Magi they came across. When the Persians learnt of the hoax the Magi had practised and realized what the seven had done, they decided to follow their lead; they drew their daggers and began to kill any Magi they could find, and if night had not intervened they would not have left a single one alive. This is now the most important day of the year in the Persian public calendar, and they spend it celebrating a major festival which they call the Magophonia. During the festival, no Magus is allowed to appear outdoors; they have to stay inside their houses all day long.

While the similarities between Esther and the story of the Magi are relevant to the question of shared literary motifs, the differences between them are more instructive because they shed light on the nature of the Book of Esther. Here, as elsewhere, the biblical account is less graphic than the Greek, with much less blood and guts. The Greek writers spare no detail, while the biblical author paints the scene with broad strokes of the brush, giving the main points but leaving the details for the reader to fill in. It is not important *how* the Jews killed their enemies, only that they did so, that they had been authorized to do so (by royal decree and by the rightness of their cause), and that they

9 And so, on the thirteenth day of the twelfth month—that is, the month of Adar—when the king's command and decree were to be executed, the very day on which the enemies of the Jews had expected to get them in their power, the opposite happened, and the Jews got their enemies in their power. [2] Throughout the provinces of King Ahasuerus, the Jews mustered in their cities to attack those who

ט וּבִשְׁנֵים֩ עָשָׂ֨ר חֹ֜דֶשׁ הוּא־חֹ֣דֶשׁ אֲדָ֗ר בִּשְׁלוֹשָׁ֨ה עָשָׂ֥ר יוֹם֙ בּ֔וֹ אֲשֶׁ֨ר הִגִּ֧יעַ דְּבַר־ הַמֶּ֛לֶךְ וְדָת֖וֹ לְהֵעָשׂ֑וֹת בַּיּ֗וֹם אֲשֶׁ֨ר שִׂבְּר֜וּ אֹיְבֵ֤י הַיְּהוּדִים֙ לִשְׁל֣וֹט בָּהֶ֔ם וְנַהֲפ֖וֹךְ ה֑וּא אֲשֶׁ֨ר יִשְׁלְט֧וּ הַיְּהוּדִ֛ים הֵ֖מָּה בְּשֹׂנְאֵיהֶֽם׃ [2] נִקְהֲל֣וּ הַיְּהוּדִ֗ים בְּעָרֵיהֶם֙ בְּכָל־מְדִינוֹת֙ הַמֶּ֣לֶךְ אֲחַשְׁוֵר֔וֹשׁ לִשְׁלֹ֣חַ יָ֔ד בִּמְבַקְשֵׁ֖י

were amazingly successful in their undertaking. Another difference between the Greek and the Hebrew accounts is that the author of Esther is describing Jewish actions for a Jewish audience, while Herodotus is describing Persian actions for a Greek audience. The author's attitude toward his subject, is, therefore, quite different in the two cases. For the Greeks, the Persians were an alien and therefore inferior people; and one may note a tone of detachment tinged with distaste—the narrator is like an anthropologist reporting unsympathetically about the practice of a strange tribe. The biblical account of the battle and the festival is altogether different in tone. The biblical narrator identifies with his subject, and the account is much more celebratory. The narrator approves of the Jews' acts and is cheering them on and enjoying their success. Herodotus may have intended a bit of satire against the Persians, but he was not writing comedy. Farcical comedy can only be directed at one's own society, its customs and values, its wishes and fears. That is one of the major differences between Esther's account of the origin of Purim and Herodotus's account of the massacre of the Magi.

The etiology of Purim dominates the last part of this chapter. An etiology stands outside of the plot of the story, but may be written as part and parcel of the work in which it is contained. By that I mean that the etiology of Purim in chapter 9, at least until verse 29, was probably written at the same time as the rest of the book (see the Commentary to vv. 24–25). I am not saying that the story did not exist independently, in one form or another, prior to its appearance in the Masoretic Text. My point is that I see the present form of the story along with the etiology of Purim as the work of the Masoretic author. This author reshaped the earlier story for use as an explanation of and as encouragement for the perpetual celebration of Purim. Purim needs this type of justification, for it is a "new" holiday, the first new holiday not commanded in the Torah. The reference to more than one Purim letter suggests that Purim may not have been widely celebrated at first and needed the authentication and authority of the book.[3]

1. The day has now arrived on which Haman's decree was to have taken effect— the day on which the enemies of the Jews looked forward to overpowering them. But because of Mordecai's decree, the opposite took place and the Jews triumphed over their enemies. This is the greatest and most important of the many reversals in the story, and it sums up the underlying theme of Jewish security in the Diaspora. The outcome of events is given at the start; it is not a question of whether the Jews will win, but how they will win and how great their victory will be.

2. In their cities In all cities throughout the empire where Jews resided. Jews were a minority in these cities.

to attack those who sought their hurt While some in Persia sided with the Jews (8:17), others were prepared to do them harm, and it is these enemies that the Jews attack.

sought their hurt; and no one could withstand them, for the fear of them had fallen upon all the peoples. ³ Indeed, all the officials of the provinces—the satraps, the governors, and the king's stewards—showed deference to the Jews, because the fear of Mordecai had fallen upon them. ⁴ For Mordecai was now powerful in the royal palace, and his fame was spreading through all the provinces; the man Mordecai was growing ever more powerful. ⁵ So the Jews struck at their enemies with the sword, slaying and destroying; they wreaked their will upon their enemies.

⁶ In the fortress Shushan the Jews killed a total of five hundred men. ⁷ They also killed

Parshandatha,
Dalphon,
Aspatha,

רָעָתָ֑ם וְאִ֙ישׁ֙ לֹא־עָמַ֣ד לִפְנֵיהֶ֔ם כִּֽי־
נָפַ֥ל פַּחְדָּ֖ם עַל־כָּל־הָעַמִּֽים׃ 3 וְכָל־שָׂרֵ֣י
הַמְּדִינ֡וֹת וְֽהָאֲחַשְׁדַּרְפְּנִ֣ים וְהַפַּחוֹת֩ וְעֹשֵׂ֨י
הַמְּלָאכָ֜ה אֲשֶׁ֣ר לַמֶּ֗לֶךְ מְנַשְּׂאִ֖ים אֶת־
הַיְּהוּדִ֑ים כִּֽי־נָפַ֥ל פַּֽחַד־מָרְדֳּכַ֖י עֲלֵיהֶֽם׃
4 כִּֽי־גָד֤וֹל מָרְדֳּכַי֙ בְּבֵ֣ית הַמֶּ֔לֶךְ וְשָׁמְע֖וֹ
הוֹלֵ֣ךְ בְּכָל־הַמְּדִינ֑וֹת כִּֽי־הָאִ֥ישׁ מָרְדֳּכַ֖י
הוֹלֵ֥ךְ וְגָדֽוֹל׃ פ 5 וַיַּכּ֤וּ הַיְּהוּדִים֙ בְּכָל־
אֹ֣יְבֵיהֶ֔ם מַכַּת־חֶ֥רֶב וְהֶ֖רֶג וְאַבְדָ֑ן וַיַּעֲשׂ֥וּ
בְשֹׂנְאֵיהֶ֖ם כִּרְצוֹנָֽם׃
6 וּבְשׁוּשַׁ֣ן הַבִּירָ֗ה הָרְג֤וּ הַיְּהוּדִים֙ וְאַבֵּ֔ד
חֲמֵ֥שׁ מֵא֖וֹת אִֽישׁ׃ 7 וְאֵ֧ת ׀
פַּרְשַׁנְדָּ֖תָא וְאֵ֥ת ׀
דַּֽלְפ֑וֹן וְאֵ֖ת ׀
אַסְפָּֽתָא׃ 8 וְאֵ֥ת ׀

---

fear of them   As in 8:17, fear of the Jews overcame the populace. In this case it weakened the strength of the non-Jewish aggressors so that the Jews were able to defeat them.

3.   The list of high provincial officials includes the overseers of the treasury, *'osei ha-mela'khah,* who were earlier mentioned in connection with Haman's offer of money in 3:9.

showed deference to the Jews   The same word, *n-s-',* was used in the promotion of Haman in 3:1 and its use here reinforces the reversal in status of Mordecai and his people vis à vis Haman. The esteem that these officials showed for the Jews is attributed to their fear of Mordecai, whose power at court was growing. The enemy masses were deterred by fear of the Jewish masses and the officials were deterred by fear of an official.

4.   Mordecai is not called *ha-yehudi,* "the Jew" (8:7) or *'ish yehudi,* "a Jewish man," (2:5) but rather "the man" to call attention to his own personal status. Compare Exod. 11:3: "The man Moses was very great." The word *'ish,* "the man," was also used in the expression in 7:6 referring to Haman, *'ish tzar ve-'oyev,* literally, "man, adversary and enemy" and there may be a contrast here between Haman and Mordecai.[4]

5.   *sword, slaying, and destroying*   The last two terms echo the last two terms of the decree, *la-harog* and *le-'abed.* Compare also verses 6 and 12.

6.   *In the fortress Shushan*   The acropolis, not the lower city. Presumably those killed were members of the court.

7-10.   Singled out by name are the ten sons of Haman. According to the scribal tradition, this list of names is written in two parallel columns, the names in one column and the accusative particle *'et* in the other. This stichography is usually reserved for certain poems, but it is also used for lists (in nonpoetic contexts), as in Josh. 12:9–24 and 1 Sam. 30:27–31. The list of Haman's sons may have been modeled on Josh. 12:9–24, a list of vanquished kings, with the total number in the list recorded at the end.

⁸ Poratha,
Adalia,
Aridatha,
⁹ Parmashta,
Arisai,
Aridai,
and Vaizatha,
¹⁰ the ten sons of Haman son of Hammedatha, the foe of the Jews. But they did not lay hands on the spoil. ¹¹ When the number of those slain in the fortress Shushan was reported on that same day to the king, ¹² the king said to Queen Esther, "In the fortress

פּוֹרָ֖תָא | וְאֵ֥ת
אֲדַלְיָ֖א | וְאֵ֥ת
אֲרִידָ֑תָא: | וְאֵ֥ת ⁹
פַּרְמַ֖שְׁתָּא | וְאֵ֥ת
אֲרִיסַ֖י | וְאֵ֥ת
אֲרִידַ֖י | וְאֵ֥ת
וַיְזָֽתָא: | עֲשֶׂ֨רֶת ¹⁰
בְּנֵ֨י הָמָ֧ן בֶּֽן־הַמְּדָ֛תָא צֹרֵ֥ר הַיְּהוּדִ֖ים הָרָ֑גוּ
וּבַ֨בִּזָּ֔ה לֹ֥א שָׁלְח֖וּ אֶת־יָדָֽם: ¹¹ בַּיּ֣וֹם הַה֗וּא
בָּ֣א מִסְפַּ֧ר הַהֲרוּגִ֛ים בְּשׁוּשַׁ֥ן הַבִּירָ֖ה לִפְנֵ֥י
הַמֶּֽלֶךְ: ס ¹² וַיֹּ֨אמֶר הַמֶּ֜לֶךְ לְאֶסְתֵּ֗ר

The sound of the multisyllabic, foreign-sounding names is amusing, like the names in Esther 1:10 and 14; and the tradition of reading them all out in one breath when the *Megillah* is read publicly on Purim (B. Megillah 16b) adds to the amusement. The killing of Haman's sons, who were mentioned along with his wealth in 5:11, is one more way that Haman's glory is diminished. Their deaths assure the reader that Haman's lineage is now ended forever and the family will present no further threat.

10. *they did not lay hands on the spoil* The decree of Haman permitted the enemies to despoil the Jews and the counter-decree by Mordecai permitted the Jews to take spoil from their enemies. In fact, taking spoil after a victory is normal in ancient warfare. Here and in verses 15 and 16 it is repeatedly noted that the Jews did not take spoil. In addition to showing that the Jewish action was not motivated by economic gain, it strongly reinforces the connection with 1 Samuel 15, the chapter recounting Saul's tribulations against Agag the Amalekite (and ancestor of Haman).[5] In Esther, the Jews of Persia "correct" Saul's error. Saul took booty from the Amalekites although he was forbidden to do so; but the Jews of Persia do not take booty from their enemies even though they are entitled to do so. If the feud between Haman and Mordecai is viewed as an extension of the dispute between Agag and Saul, this reversal in reference to booty wipes away the sin of the house of Saul. There is now nothing to prevent a complete triumph of the descendants of Saul over the descendants of Agag. And indeed, this is what happens in Mordecai's defeat of Haman and in the Jews' defeat of their Haman-inspired enemies.

12–15. The report to the king makes clear to him that Esther's request has been carried out. That he should permit Esther yet another request borders on the ludicrous. But being ludicrous is precisely the point of much in this story. So, for the fourth time, the king offers Esther anything she wants. It has been said that repetition may be the single most important mechanism in comedy, and the repetition often takes the form of a repeated gesture or expression.[6] The expression "what is your request" has by now become the king's byword when he speaks to Esther, and its appearance yet again provokes laughter—it is another sign that the scene is not meant to be taken too seriously.

As the carnivalesque climax approaches we expect more outlandishness, and that is exactly what we get. The opportunity for another request paves the way for further Jewish victories over their enemies and more indignities to the house of Haman. Many things in this story come in pairs, and the repetition of the previous day's events fits that pattern. Haman's sons, who, after all, cannot be killed twice, are impaled just as their father was, with the same dishonor associated with impalement.

Shushan alone the Jews have killed a total of five hundred men, as well as the ten sons of Haman. What then must they have done in the provinces of the realm! What is your wish now? It shall be granted you. And what else is your request? It shall be fulfilled." ¹³ "If it please Your Majesty," Esther replied, "let the Jews in Shushan be permitted to act tomorrow also as they did today; and let Haman's ten sons be impaled on the stake." ¹⁴ The king ordered that this should be done, and the decree was proclaimed in Shushan. Haman's ten sons were impaled: ¹⁵ and the Jews in Shushan mustered again on the fourteenth day of Adar and slew three hundred men in Shushan. But they did not lay hands on the spoil.

הַמַּלְכָּ֜ה בְּשׁוּשַׁ֣ן הַבִּירָ֗ה הָרְגוּ֩ הַיְּהוּדִ֨ים
וְאַבֵּ֜ד חֲמֵ֧שׁ מֵא֣וֹת אִ֗ישׁ וְאֵת֙ עֲשֶׂ֣רֶת
בְּנֵֽי־הָמָ֔ן בִּשְׁאָ֛ר מְדִינ֥וֹת הַמֶּ֖לֶךְ מֶ֣ה עָשׂ֑וּ
וּמַה־שְּׁאֵלָתֵךְ֙ וְיִנָּ֣תֵֽן לָ֔ךְ וּמַה־בַּקָּשָׁתֵ֥ךְ ע֖וֹד
וְתֵעָֽשׂ׃ ¹³ וַתֹּ֤אמֶר אֶסְתֵּר֙ אִם־עַל־הַמֶּ֣לֶךְ
ט֔וֹב יִנָּתֵ֣ן גַּם־מָחָ֗ר לַיְּהוּדִים֙ אֲשֶׁ֣ר בְּשׁוּשָׁ֔ן
לַעֲשׂ֖וֹת כְּדָ֣ת הַיּ֑וֹם וְאֵ֛ת עֲשֶׂ֥רֶת בְּנֵֽי־הָמָ֖ן
יִתְל֥וּ עַל־הָעֵֽץ׃ ¹⁴ וַיֹּ֤אמֶר הַמֶּ֙לֶךְ֙ לְהֵֽעָשׂ֣וֹת
כֵּ֔ן וַתִּנָּתֵ֥ן דָּ֖ת בְּשׁוּשָׁ֑ן וְאֵ֛ת עֲשֶׂ֥רֶת בְּנֵֽי־הָמָ֖ן
תָּלֽוּ׃ ¹⁵ וַיִּקָּהֲל֞וּ הַיְּהוּדִ֣ים אֲשֶׁר־
בְּשׁוּשָׁ֗ן גַּ֡ם בְּי֣וֹם אַרְבָּעָ֣ה עָשָׂר֮ לְחֹ֣דֶשׁ
אֲדָר֒ וַיַּֽהַרְג֣וּ בְשׁוּשָׁ֔ן שְׁלֹ֥שׁ מֵא֖וֹת אִ֑ישׁ
וּבַ֨בִּזָּ֔ה לֹ֥א שָֽׁלְח֖וּ אֶת־יָדָֽם׃

The doubling of the days of fighting may serve an etiological purpose as well as a literary purpose. If the festival predated the book, and if the festival was celebrated for more than one day, or on a different day at different locations, then there would need to be an explanation of how these dates came to be celebrated. These verses provide the reason.

12. *What then must they have done in the provinces of the realm!* Fox and Levenson see in this question a sign of the king's insensitivity and obtuseness—he is more concerned with the death toll than with the deliverance of the Jews. I see this as a funny line, adding to the mock violence. The king has joined the Jews' cheering section. He reflects on the number of dead enemies already presented to him and muses on how many more there might be in the provinces. He will next offer Esther another opportunity for the Jews to kill their enemies.

13. *If it please Your majesty* Esther's words retain the formality of the occasion but are not as flowery as before. She doesn't need to butter up the king any more.

in Shushan The lower city, or the area with a Jewish population (cf. 4:8, 16). This is a different part of the city from the battle recorded on the previous day. The Jews of the lower city will fight for two days. There are three arenas of battle—the fortress Shushan, the provinces, and Shushan (the lower city)—each with its death toll and the notice that no booty was taken.

14. The decree is officially promulgated but this time we are not told of the writing of an edict and its circulation throughout the empire, for the edict was a local one and pertained only to Shushan, so there was no need to publish it widely. We see once again, counter to Haman's accusation, how law-abiding the Jews are; they would not undertake a battle unless it was legally authorized.

Haman's ten sons were impaled In verses 7–10 the sons were killed. Now, after their deaths, they are impaled, to further emphasize the disgrace that comes to Haman's house. I see another reflex here of the Saul story. Just as the bodies of Saul and his sons were impaled in 1 Sam. 31:10, now the enemies of the descendants of Saul are impaled.

15. The battle of 14 Adar takes place in the lower city whereas on 13 Adar it was in the fortress Shushan.

16 The rest of the Jews, those in the king's provinces, likewise mustered and fought for their lives. They disposed of their enemies, killing seventy-five thousand of their foes; but they did not lay hands on the spoil. 17 That was on the thirteenth day of the month of Adar; and they rested on the fourteenth day and made it a day of feasting and merrymaking. (18 But the Jews in Shushan mustered on both the thirteenth and fourteenth days, and so rested on the fifteenth, and made it a day of feasting and merrymaking.) 19 That is why village Jews, who live in unwalled

16 וּשְׁאָ֣ר הַיְּהוּדִ֡ים אֲשֶׁר֩ בִּמְדִינ֨וֹת הַמֶּ֜לֶךְ נִקְהֲל֣וּ ׀ וְעָמֹ֣ד עַל־נַפְשָׁ֗ם וְנ֙וֹחַ֙ מֵאֹ֣יְבֵיהֶ֔ם וְהָרֹג֙ בְּשֹׂ֣נְאֵיהֶ֔ם חֲמִשָּׁ֥ה וְשִׁבְעִ֖ים אָ֑לֶף וּבַ֨בִּזָּ֔ה לֹ֥א שָׁלְח֖וּ אֶת־יָדָֽם׃ 17 בְּיוֹם־שְׁלֹשָׁ֥ה עָשָׂ֖ר לְחֹ֣דֶשׁ אֲדָ֑ר וְנ֗וֹחַ בְּאַרְבָּעָ֤ה עָשָׂר֙ בּ֔וֹ וְעָשֹׂ֣ה אֹת֔וֹ י֖וֹם מִשְׁתֶּ֥ה וְשִׂמְחָֽה׃ 18 והיהודיים וְהַיְּהוּדִ֣ים אֲשֶׁר־בְּשׁוּשָׁ֗ן נִקְהֲלוּ֙ בִּשְׁלֹשָׁ֤ה עָשָׂר֙ בּ֔וֹ וּבְאַרְבָּעָ֥ה עָשָׂ֖ר בּ֑וֹ וְנ֗וֹחַ בַּחֲמִשָּׁ֤ה עָשָׂר֙ בּ֔וֹ וְעָשֹׂ֣ה אֹת֔וֹ י֖וֹם מִשְׁתֶּ֥ה וְשִׂמְחָֽה׃ 19 עַל־כֵּ֞ן הַיְּהוּדִ֣ים

16. The reports thus far have been for the fortress Shushan and Shushan (the lower city). Now we are given the report for the provinces. It responds to Ahasuerus's rhetorical question in verse 12: "What must they have done in the provinces!"

The number of the slain enemies, seventy-five thousand, has troubled the many commentators who take this chapter as serious revenge. But this number should be understood as being just as exaggerated as the other numbers in the story. The unbelievably large number is an additional sign that this "overkill" is not real killing. There is no way that the relatively small Jewish communities in Persia could kill so many people. We are in the realm of carnivalesque fantasy. To be sure, inflated body counts are traditional in Assyrian annals, where they are not carnivalesque. The purpose of the large numbers of dead is to give more glory to the conquering king and his god. The same purpose may be implied in Esther as well: it is to the credit of the Jews (and their unmentioned God) that they were so successful.

they disposed of their enemies The Hebrew contains two phrases, *noaḥ me-'oyveihem,* "rested from their enemies," and *harog be-son'eihem,* "killed their foes." Fox rightly notes that the first is out of place here, being more appropriate in verses 17 and 18 where it refers to the respite after the battles had been concluded. He prefers to read *naḥum me-'oyveihem,* "gaining relief from their enemies." I would go even further and suggest that the phrase does not belong here at all but has crept up from verse 17.

17. Verses 16–17 are somewhat awkward. The date of 13 Adar at the beginning of verse 17 refers to the events in verse 16. The two verses are really one long sentence with two purposes: to continue the story of the battles and to recount the celebration of the first Purim.

a day of feasting Literally, "a party day." Parties are the glue that holds this story together. The royal parties were, in a sense, the foreshadowing of the Purim festivities; and, conversely, the Purim partying re-enacts the events of the story. This verse marks the celebration of the first Purim by the Jews in the provinces, on 14 Adar.

18. The first Purim in Shushan was a day later, on 15 Adar, since they fought there on 13 and 14 Adar.

19. The etiology continues, backtracking a bit to explain the date of Purim in Shushan, which was different from elsewhere.

unwalled towns Originally, according to verses 17–18, the distinction was between the Jews of Shushan, who celebrated on 15 Adar, and all other Jews (including

towns, observe the fourteenth day of the month of Adar and make it a day of merrymaking and feasting, and as a holiday and an occasion for sending gifts to one another.

²⁰Mordecai recorded these events. And he sent dispatches to all the Jews throughout the provinces of King Ahasuerus, near and far, ²¹ charging them to

הַפְּרוֹזִים הַיֹּשְׁבִים֙ בְּעָרֵ֣י הַפְּרָזֹ֔ות
עֹשִׂ֣ים אֵ֡ת יֹ֣ום אַרְבָּעָה֩ עָשָׂ֨ר לְחֹ֜דֶשׁ אֲדָ֗ר
שִׂמְחָ֤ה וּמִשְׁתֶּה֙ וְיֹ֣ום טֹ֔וב וּמִשְׁלֹ֥וחַ מָנֹ֖ות
אִ֥ישׁ לְרֵעֵֽהוּ׃ פ
²⁰ וַיִּכְתֹּ֣ב מָרְדֳּכַ֔י אֶת־הַדְּבָרִ֖ים הָאֵ֑לֶּה
וַיִּשְׁלַ֣ח סְפָרִ֗ים אֶל־כָּל־הַיְּהוּדִים֙ אֲשֶׁר֙
בְּכָל־מְדִינֹות֙ הַמֶּ֣לֶךְ אֲחַשְׁוֵרֹ֔ושׁ הַקְּרוֹבִ֖ים
וְהָרְחוֹקִֽים׃ ²¹ לְקַיֵּם֙ עֲלֵיהֶ֔ם לִהְיֹ֣ות

those in walled cities other than Shushan), who celebrated on 14 Adar. This verse seems to represent a change by which Shushan and all other walled cities are contrasted with unwalled towns. The Septuagint attempts to harmonize verses 17–18 with verse 19, referring to 14 Adar as the holiday for Jews who are "scattered around the country outside of Susa" and 15 Adar as the holiday for Jews who live in large cities. The practice that may be reflected in the Septuagint was codified in the rabbinic tradition, according to which Jews in all cities that had been walled since the time of Joshua were to celebrate Purim on 15 Adar—Shushan Purim—and Jews elsewhere were to celebrate on 14 Adar.

merrymaking, feasting,...sending gifts We can watch the festival take shape, beginning with a one-time day of merrymaking (drinking or feasting) and joy (vv. 17–18); then becoming an annual day of joy, feasting, and sending of gifts (v. 19). In verse 22, Mordecai adds to this list the sending of presents to the poor. We have here the outline of a festival that does not (or cannot) include bringing sacrifices to the Temple; nor does it prohibit work, as in the Torah festivals. The emphasis is on the public display of joy, which includes eating and drinking. Fox suggests that the exchange of *manot,* a term long understood as foodstuff (see the Septuagint), creates a symbolic communal banquet to which everyone is invited. How fitting that a story with so many banquet scenes gives birth to a holiday whose main feature is banqueting. But Esther is not alone in enjoining good eating as a mode of celebration. Neh. 8:10 defines the celebration of the festive day (the first day of the seventh month, Rosh Hashanah) as requiring the eating of rich food, the drinking of sweet drinks, and the giving of *manot,* portions of food, to those who have nothing prepared. Esther 9:22 distinguishes between *manot,* which were given to all, and *mattanot,* "presents," for the poor.

20. In keeping with the story's propensity for written documents published throughout the empire, Mordecai records the events that have occurred and sends the record to Jews far and wide, so that they will continue to celebrate these events each year.

Mordecai recorded these events Rashi takes the Book of Esther to be the record of events that Mordecai wrote down. Modern interpreters prefer to see the summary of events in verses 24–25 as the record that Mordecai wrote.

21. *charging them* Hebrew *le-kayyem* has the sense of "confirm, certify, authorize." See also verses 27 and 31 where the verb is used to indicate that the Jews took upon themselves as binding the celebration of Purim. Mordecai's letter is written in order to authorize or authenticate the perpetual observance of a holiday, which had already been celebrated for the first time after the victory.⁷ The letter serves an important etiological purpose even though it may be just as fictional as the rest of the story; it provides the authorization for a new holiday. The story provides the reason for the holiday and the letter (or letters—see below) provides the authorization for its perpetual celebration.

observe the fourteenth and fifteenth days of Adar, every year—²²the same days on which the Jews enjoyed relief from their foes and the same month which had been transformed for them from one of grief and mourning to one of festive joy. They were to observe them as days of feasting and merrymaking, and as an occasion for sending gifts to one another and presents to the poor. ²³The Jews accordingly assumed as an obligation that which they had begun to practice and which Mordecai prescribed for them.

עֹשִׂים אֵת יוֹם אַרְבָּעָה עָשָׂר לְחֹדֶשׁ אֲדָ֔ר וְאֵת יוֹם־חֲמִשָּׁה עָשָׂר בּוֹ בְּכָל־שָׁנָה וְשָׁנָה: ²²כַּיָּמִים אֲשֶׁר־נָחוּ בָהֶם הַיְּהוּדִים מֵאוֹיְבֵיהֶם וְהַחֹדֶשׁ אֲשֶׁר נֶהְפַּךְ לָהֶם מִיָּגוֹן לְשִׂמְחָה וּמֵאֵבֶל לְיוֹם טוֹב לַעֲשׂוֹת אוֹתָם יְמֵי מִשְׁתֶּה וְשִׂמְחָה וּמִשְׁלוֹחַ מָנוֹת אִישׁ לְרֵעֵהוּ וּמַתָּנוֹת לָאֶבְיוֹנִים: ²³וְקִבֵּל הַיְּהוּדִים אֵת אֲשֶׁר־הֵחֵלּוּ לַעֲשׂוֹת וְאֵת אֲשֶׁר־כָּתַב מָרְדֳּכַי אֲלֵיהֶם:

Levenson suggests a parallel with the events of the Exodus, which culminate in the affirmation of the Israelites at Sinai to accept new obligations.

to observe the fourteenth and fifteenth days of Adar That is, to celebrate whichever of these two days was the appropriate one, depending on whether the celebrant was in an unwalled village or not.

22. relief from their foes The Jews did not commemorate the day of their victorious battle, but the day on which they rested *(noah)* from their enemies. Fox and Levenson connect the word *noah* with *le-haniham* in 3:8, seeing irony in the fact that Haman had wished to deprive the Jews of rest and now they obtain rest from their enemies.

from one of grief and mourning... The Hebrew reads "from grief to joy, from mourning to holiday." Indeed, the mourning of chapter 4 has turned to joy and festivity here. On *yom tov* see 8:17.

presents to the poor With this addition to the list of actions in verse 19, the mode of celebrating Purim is complete. See Neh. 8:10–12 where the sending of *manot* to those who have no prepared food, along with eating and drinking well, constitute the celebration of the holy day [Rosh Hashanah]. These elements were seen by the rabbis as constituting the halakhic requirements for the celebration of Purim.

23. They had begun the celebration of Purim spontaneously after their victorious battles; and then Mordecai enjoined on them the annual celebration of Purim, which they took upon themselves to perpetuate.

24–25. A summary of the story is given, leading to another etiology in verse 26, this time explaining the name of the holiday. These verses may be construed as the contents of Mordecai's letter.

It has often been noted that the summary of the story in these verses differs in some important respects from what we were told in chapters 1–8. The roles played by Esther and Mordecai are completely absent (or almost absent, depending on the interpretation of verse 25), as are the battles between the Jews and their enemies. The king's role is more central. Haman's casting of the lot receives more attention here than in the main story. (It was mentioned in 3:7 but is not crucial to the plot.) These differences have been explained by some scholars as evidence of a later editor;[8] and by others as an intentionally different retelling of the story for the purpose of explaining the holiday. I advocate the second position. Clearly, the emphasis in the retelling is on the villain, not on the heroes. Haman's name and epithet are prominent, as are his scheme and his demise. The retelling revolves

24 For Haman son of Hammedatha the Agagite, the foe of all the Jews, had plotted to destroy the Jews, and had cast *pur*—that is, the lot—with intent to crush and exterminate them. 25 But when [Esther] came before the king, he commanded: "With the promulgation of this decree, let the evil plot, which he devised against the Jews, recoil on his own head!" So they impaled him and his sons on the stake. 26 For that reason these days were named Purim, after *pur*.

In view, then, of all the instructions in the said

24 כִּי הָמָן בֶּן־הַמְּדָתָא הָאֲגָגִי צֹרֵר כָּל־הַיְּהוּדִים חָשַׁב עַל־הַיְּהוּדִים לְאַבְּדָם וְהִפִּיל פּוּר הוּא הַגּוֹרָל לְהֻמָּם וּלְאַבְּדָם: 25 וּבְבֹאָהּ לִפְנֵי הַמֶּלֶךְ אָמַר עִם־הַסֵּפֶר יָשׁוּב מַחֲשַׁבְתּוֹ הָרָעָה אֲשֶׁר־חָשַׁב עַל־הַיְּהוּדִים עַל־רֹאשׁוֹ וְתָלוּ אֹתוֹ וְאֶת־בָּנָיו עַל־הָעֵץ: 26 עַל־כֵּן קָרְאוּ לַיָּמִים הָאֵלֶּה פוּרִים עַל־שֵׁם הַפּוּר עַל־כֵּן עַל־כָּל־דִּבְרֵי הָאִגֶּרֶת הַזֹּאת וּמָה־

around Haman, what he did, and what was done to him. It thereby lets the reader relive the destruction of the enemy. And, as befits the context in which these words are set, Mordecai does not credit himself or Esther, but rather the king. This "official" version of the story is simplified and sanitized.

24. *pur* Haman's casting of the lot is not an important feature of the story, but the similarity in sound between the word *pur,* "lot," and Purim, the name of the holiday, leads to the etiological linking of the two. This may be another reason that the story is retold in this way—the emphasis on Haman leads to the highlighting of the *pur,* which is a play on the name of the holiday.

to crush We might expect the phrase from Haman's edict, "to destroy, massacre, and exterminate" (3:13; 7:4). The use of the word *le-hummam,* "to crush them, to discomfit them," is a pun on the sound of Haman's name (Levenson).

25. The verse is awkwardly worded. It begins with "when she came" but the referent of the feminine pronoun is not obvious. If it refers to Esther, as some exegetes think, then we must supply her name, which is not mentioned at all. An alternative, suggested by Levenson, is to take the pronoun as referring to "his evil plot" (*mahashavto* is grammatically feminine). The phrase would then mean "when it [Haman's plot] came before the king."

he commanded: "With the promulgation of this decree Hebrew *'amar 'im ha-sefer* is enigmatic. It would seem to refer to the document written at the bidding of Mordecai to counteract Haman's decree.

him and his sons Haman and his sons were not impaled together. The verse is compressing the events, as is often done in a summary. The point is that Haman and his sons all came to an ignoble end, signaled by their impalement.

26. *Purim* The name of the holiday is given an etiology. But as Levenson notes, the etiology leaves one with questions, for why is "Purim" in the plural when only one lot was cast, and the casting of the lot was itself of little significance in the story. In our earliest reference to the holiday outside of Esther it is called "The Day of Mordecai" (2 Macc. 15:36), and there is no mention of "Purim." The Greek versions show some confusion about the name of the festival, calling it *phrourai* or *phourdaia.* (The Greek versions show less interest than the Masoretic Text in the etiology of the holiday.) It seems likely, as Levenson and others have suggested, that the holiday and its name originated independently from the book, and that the book is the vehicle through which the holiday was reinterpreted so as to invest it with Jewish significance. It is here that the name of the

letter and of what they had experienced in that matter and what had befallen them, [27] the Jews undertook and irrevocably obligated themselves and their descendants, and all who might join them, to observe these two days in the manner prescribed and at the proper time each year. [28] Consequently, these days are recalled and observed in every generation: by every family, every province, and every city. And these days of Purim shall never cease among the Jews, and the memory of them shall never perish among their descendants.

כז קִיְּמ֣וּ רָא֣וּ עַל־כָּ֔כָה וּמָ֥ה הִגִּ֖יעַ אֲלֵיהֶֽם׃ קִיְּמ֣וּ וְקִבְּל֣וּ הַיְּהוּדִים֩ ׀ עֲלֵיהֶ֨ם ׀ וְעַל־ זַרְעָ֜ם וְעַ֨ל כָּל־הַנִּלְוִ֤ים עֲלֵיהֶם֙ וְלֹ֣א יַעֲב֔וֹר לִהְי֣וֹת עֹשִׂ֗ים אֵ֣ת שְׁנֵ֤י הַיָּמִים֙ הָאֵ֔לֶּה כִּכְתָבָ֖ם וְכִזְמַנָּ֑ם בְּכָל־שָׁנָ֖ה וְשָׁנָֽה׃ כח וְהַיָּמִ֣ים הָאֵ֗לֶּה נִזְכָּרִ֤ים וְנַעֲשִׂים֙ בְּכָל־ דּ֣וֹר וָד֔וֹר מִשְׁפָּחָה֙ וּמִשְׁפָּחָ֔ה מְדִינָ֖ה וּמְדִינָ֑ה וְעִ֣יר וָעִ֑יר וִימֵ֞י הַפּוּרִ֣ים הָאֵ֗לֶּה לֹ֤א יַֽעַבְרוּ֙ מִתּ֣וֹךְ הַיְּהוּדִ֔ים וְזִכְרָ֖ם לֹא־ יָס֥וּף מִזַּרְעָֽם׃ ס

holiday is linked with the story of its origin, through the type of false etymology that is so common in the Bible.

27–28. These verses are concerned with the establishment of Purim for all Jews and for all time. Here the feeling is especially strong that the author is writing from a vantage point removed from his story and is eager to emphasize that this new, non-Torah holiday should take firm hold.

27. *all who might join them* Some have taken this as a reference to the *mityahadim,* those who identified with the Jewish cause, in 8:17. But since a different term, *nilvim,* is used, it is likely that it refers to a different group of people. The same term occurs in Isa. 14:1; 56:3, 6 and is the Late Biblical Hebrew term for converts or those who joined the Jewish community (Levenson). The verse is concerned with the broadest definition of who, in the future, is obligated to celebrate Purim.

irrevocably This translates *lo' ya'avor,* but as I said in my Commentary to 1:19, I do not think that it means that the law or observance cannot be changed. It means, rather, that it cannot be disobeyed, or that there can be no exception to it. The Jews are taking upon themselves to observe the holiday exactly as prescribed, without fail. Or, alternatively, *lo' ya'avor* may refer to the list of observers: Jews, their descendants, and all who join them, without exception, shall observe the holiday. (See Moore.)

these two days It is not a two-day holiday. Each community celebrates on either 14 or 15 Adar, according to whether it is located in an unwalled town or not.

28. This verse emphasizes the permanence of the holiday, in all places and in all periods. As Ibn Ezra says, the holiday is incumbent also on Jews who live in a place where there were no Jews at the time of the events.

Just as we had the impression at the beginning of the book that the story was being told some time after the events had occurred, so here too we have the sense that the narrator is looking back on the origin of the festival and noting how its observance spread throughout all Jewish communities. Looking toward the future, he sees that the festival will be observed forever.

29–32. The second Purim letter. Because of the internal difficulties in these verses and the difficulty in harmonizing them with what went before, in verses 20–28, there is widespread agreement among modern scholars that verses 29–32 constitute a later addition.[9] But even this explanation does not altogether solve the problems of meaning. At best we can say that these verses pile one confirmation on another, thus stressing the

29 Then Queen Esther daughter of Abihail wrote a second letter of Purim for the purpose of confirming with full authority the aforementioned one of Mordecai the Jew. 30 Dispatches were sent to all the Jews in the hundred and twenty-seven provinces of the realm of Ahasuerus with an ordinance of "equity and honesty:" 31 These days of Purim shall be observed at their proper time, as Mordecai the Jew—and now Queen Esther—has obligated them to do, and just as they have assumed for themselves and their descendants the obligation of the fasts with their lamentations.

29 וַתִּכְתֹּב אֶסְתֵּר הַמַּלְכָּה בַת־אֲבִיחַיִל וּמָרְדֳּכַי הַיְּהוּדִי אֶת־כָּל־תֹּקֶף לְקַיֵּם אֵת אִגֶּרֶת הַפֻּרִים הַזֹּאת הַשֵּׁנִית: 30 וַיִּשְׁלַח סְפָרִים אֶל־כָּל־הַיְּהוּדִים אֶל־שֶׁבַע וְעֶשְׂרִים וּמֵאָה מְדִינָה מַלְכוּת אֲחַשְׁוֵרוֹשׁ דִּבְרֵי שָׁלוֹם וֶאֱמֶת: 31 לְקַיֵּם אֶת־יְמֵי הַפֻּרִים הָאֵלֶּה בִּזְמַנֵּיהֶם כַּאֲשֶׁר קִיַּם עֲלֵיהֶם מָרְדֳּכַי הַיְּהוּדִי וְאֶסְתֵּר הַמַּלְכָּה וְכַאֲשֶׁר קִיְּמוּ עַל־נַפְשָׁם וְעַל־זַרְעָם דִּבְרֵי הַצֹּמוֹת וְזַעֲקָתָם:

authoritative establishment of the holiday. It would seem that, Purim being the first newly instituted holiday not mentioned in the Torah, the need to legitimize this innovation was great. Chapter 9, and indeed the entire book, were designed to serve this purpose.

The main problem, as will become evident below, is: Who wrote this letter? Was it Esther and Mordecai or Esther alone?

29. The Hebrew says that both Esther and Mordecai wrote this letter, but many exegetes excise Mordecai because it is awkward for Mordecai to write his own letter and then join Esther in a second letter confirming the first one. The JPS translation has moved "Mordecai the Jew" to the end of the verse to make Esther's letter a confirmation of Mordecai's. Levenson (130), sticking more closely to the Hebrew, suggests that the wording means to say that "Queen Esther and Mordecai the Jew, invoking the full authority of their respective offices, wrote a second letter to confirm the observance of Purim."

with full authority   With the authority of Esther's (and perhaps also Mordecai's) position. This is another intimation about the need to authorize the new holiday. The phrase is slightly awkward and adds to the impression that something is wrong with the verse.

30. Dispatches were sent   Hebrew: "he sent dispatches." The impersonal (often translated by a passive) is usually third-person masculine plural, not singular as here. The word "he" could refer back to Mordecai in verse 29, but that again makes him a co-author of this letter.

"equity and honesty"   Shalom ve-'emet. The phrase is also found, in inverted order, in Zech. 8:19, strengthening the link between verses 30–31 and the Zechariah passage (see the Commentary to v. 31). In contrast, the same phrase, in the same order as in our verse, also occurs in Isa. 39:8 and Jer. 33:6 and it may simply be a common expression.

31. just as they have assumed for themselves and their descendants the obligation of the fasts with their lamentations   One line of interpretation sees the fasts mentioned here as referring to the fasting of the Jews and of Esther in 4:3, 16. If so, the point being made in our verse would be that just as the Jews had fasted in their time of trouble, so should they celebrate joyfully in commemoration of their deliverance. But our verse is emphasizing the permanent institution, for all future generations, of the celebration, and there is no sense that the fasts of chapter 4 were to be permanently instituted. They were, rather, one-time occurrences in an emergency. (The Fast of Esther on 13 Adar is a later institution).[10]

³²And Esther's ordinance validating these observances of Purim was recorded in a scroll.

וּמַאֲמַר אֶסְתֵּר קִיַּם דִּבְרֵי הַפֻּרִים הָאֵלֶּה ³²
וְנִכְתָּב בַּסֵּפֶר: פ

A better explanation, favored by Ibn Ezra and many modern exegetes, sees in our verse an allusion to Zech. 8:19.[11] Zech. 8:19 says: "The fast of the fourth month, the fast of the fifth month, the fast of the seventh month, and the fast of the tenth month shall become occasions for joy and gladness, happy festivals for the House of Judah; but you must love honesty [*'emet*] and integrity [*shalom*]." The fasts listed here are post-Torah fasts, commemorating events leading to the destruction of the Temple. As Ibn Ezra explains (at Esther 9:31 and Zech. 8:19), just as the Jews had adopted these fasts that had not been commanded by the Torah, so they will here, for the first time, adopt a new non-Torah holiday commemorating their deliverance. In other words, the author of Esther has found in the Zechariah passage a precedent for the institution of a new festival.[12]

32. Esther's ordinance If we assume that Esther is the sole author of the letter in verse 29, then this ordinance would refer to that letter. If, however, verse 29 speaks of a letter written by Esther and Mordecai, then this ordinance is a third document, composed by Esther alone. In either case, it is the authority of Esther that has the last word in inscribing the authorization for Purim.

recorded in a scroll As Clines (22) has noted, and as we have observed earlier, the Book of Esther is obsessed with the writing of documents for this is how events become official and laws become legal. Nothing is real until it is written down and publicized. While this is a feature of the bureaucratic practices of the Persian period, and is evident also in Ezra and Daniel, one may see the roots in earlier parts of the Bible, beginning with Moses and continuing with other prophets. There is the recording of events, of letters, of official documents, of wisdom instructions, and so forth.[13] While Esther may exaggerate the writing of documents (as it exaggerates so many other things), it constantly draws on the practices of its own time and of the themes of the traditional literature of the Jewish community.

CHAPTER 10

All's Well That Ends Well

Chapter 9 focused on the establishment of the festival of Purim. Now, in chapter 10 we return to the end of our story, and a happy end it is. This chapter sums up the accomplishments of the great king Ahasuerus and his Jewish courtier, Mordecai. The king is more powerful than ever, and, as Persian kings did, he demonstrates his control over his empire by imposing taxation and tribute. Mordecai, the Jewish courtier in the foreign court, has triumphed over his rival, has achieved the highest position possible, and has gone on to do many great deeds. Most of all, Mordecai's Jewishness is underscored. He is beloved by his people and continues to work for their benefit. The ending brings a sense of satisfaction, for we see that the Jews have overcome the threat of destruction and have prospered in the Diaspora.

The ending of the book, like its beginning, gives the sense that this is a story written in a quasi-historical style some time after the events. In an echo of the Book of Kings, we are told of the recording in the official annals of the accomplishments of Ahasuerus's reign, including the elevation of Mordecai.

10 King Ahasuerus imposed tribute on the mainland and the islands. ²All his mighty and powerful acts, and a full account of the greatness to which the king advanced Mordecai, are they not

י וַיָּ֩שֶׂם֩ הַמֶּ֨לֶךְ אחשרש אֲחַשְׁוֵר֧וֹשׁ ׀ מַ֛ס
עַל־הָאָ֖רֶץ וְאִיֵּ֥י הַיָּֽם: ² וְכָל־מַעֲשֵׂ֤ה תָקְפּוֹ֙
וּגְב֣וּרָת֔וֹ וּפָרָשַׁת֙ גְּדֻלַּ֣ת מָרְדֳּכַ֔י אֲשֶׁ֥ר גִּדְּל֖וֹ
הַמֶּ֑לֶךְ הֲלוֹא־הֵ֣ם כְּתוּבִ֗ים עַל־סֵ֙פֶר֙ דִּבְרֵ֤י

A few scholars have found the chapter to be anticlimactic or out of place, and, in fact, it is omitted in the Greek Alpha-text. But the chapter serves an important narrative function. It is a "coda" and as such it is in exactly the right place, at the very end of the book.[1]

The coda completes the telling of the story by making a transition from the time of the main narrative to some time after its action has finished, possibly the time of the audience. It is the counterpart of the prologue, which draws the audience from its own time into the time of the story. Verse 1 of this chapter is indeed a nice counterpart to 1:1; both verses present an overview of Ahasuerus and his empire, one before the events of the story and one after. The rest of the coda follows the main character, Mordecai, beyond the events of the main plot. In so doing, it rounds out the story of Mordecai and serves as a bridge in time. Our coda also "verifies" the story and its aftermath by telling the reader, by means of a literary fiction, that "this is a true story." The "proof" is that the events of the main story, and everything else that Mordecai did, were recorded in an official state document, the Annals of the Kings of Media and Persia. This does not mean that the story is historically true, or even that the author was trying to make the audience believe that it was historically true. Rather, the author is using a literary device to confirm that the story is complete, its loose ends have been tied up, and that it is valid—that the story is of great consequence to the reader.

1. tribute The king's ability to levy a tax or tribute on so great an empire speaks to his power and to the prosperity of his realm. It may also be an indirect echo of the Joseph story, in which Joseph's actions brought wealth to Pharaoh (Fox). Ehrlich suggests that this is a reversal of the tax remission granted by the king at the coronation of Esther in 2:18.

the mainland and the islands A merismus for the whole inhabited world; compare Isa 42:4, 10.[2]

Now Ahasuerus's control extends beyond the 127 provinces of Chapter 1. The phrase is reminiscent of Herodotus's statement about Darius (3.96): "This was the tribute Darius levied from Asia and a few places in Libya. Later, further revenue was raised from the Aegean islands and from settlements in Europe as far as Thessaly." This is yet another indication that Ahasuerus should not be equated with the historical Xerxes, or even with the Greek view of him, for Xerxes' historical claim to fame is that he failed to expand his empire as he had hoped to do.

2. There is no modesty in the description of Mordecai. His greatness is exaggerated as much as anything in the book.

greatness...advanced The Hebrew *g-d-l* is the same verb used in 3:1 for the promotion of Haman. The same root appears in 10:3, where Mordecai is "highly regarded by the Jews." Mordecai has achieved greatness in the world of the Persian court and in the Jewish community.

are they not written in the book The phrase echoes the summary statement after many kings in the Book of Kings, for example 1 Kings 14:29; 15:31.

written in the book of the chronicles of the kings of Media and Persia. 3 For Mordecai the Jew ranked next to King Ahasuerus and was highly regarded by the Jews and popular with the multitude of his brethren; he sought the good of his people and interceded for the welfare of all his kindred.

הַיָּמִ֔ים לְמַלְכֵ֖י מָדַ֥י וּפָרָֽס׃ 3 כִּ֣י ׀ מׇרְדֳּכַ֣י הַיְּהוּדִ֗י מִשְׁנֶה֙ לַמֶּ֣לֶךְ אֲחַשְׁוֵר֔וֹשׁ וְגָדוֹל֙ לַיְּהוּדִ֔ים וְרָצ֖וּי לְרֹ֣ב אֶחָ֑יו דֹּרֵ֥שׁ טוֹב֙ לְעַמּ֔וֹ וְדֹבֵ֥ר שָׁל֖וֹם לְכׇל־זַרְעֽוֹ׃ *

v. 3. סכום הפסוקים של ספר 167 (אף על פי שכתוב 168 בכתב היד שלנו) וחציו 5.7

תם ונשלם תהילה לאל בורא עולם

book of the chronicles of the kings of Media and Persia   Presumably the same annals mentioned in 6:1. At last, the annals contain full information about Mordecai, and he is immortalized by his inclusion in them. The Book of Esther, like other books of this period (Ezra and Nehemiah, for example), shows much concern for official written documents.

But these annals should not be confused with actual Persian records. These annals are no more real than the edicts in the story. As explained earlier, they are part of the coda, and they serve as a bridge between the time of the story's events and the time of the reader. They stand simultaneously inside the story and outside of it. As objects outside the story, these annals are the fictive proof that this is a "true" story. Like Mordecai's letters, and like the book as a whole, these documents give lasting authority to the events recounted.

3.   *ranked next to King Ahasuerus*   Mordecai has been raised to a position as high or higher than the one Haman had. The phrase is reminiscent of Joseph, who, in Gen. 41:43, rides in the "chariot of the second-in-command." Mordecai's position may be that of the Persian *hazarapatish*, rendered by the Greeks as chiliarch. This official was second to the king in rank and was chief of the central state chancellory. He reported to the king concerning all visitors, and no one was admitted to the king's presence without his consent.[3]

In this position Mordecai is well-placed to be a spokesman for his people. As Fox mentions, this role has been played by many high-ranking Jews throughout history. But according to Zadok, the highest administrative positions in Achaemenid Babylonia were held by Persians and sometimes Medes, with Babylonians occupying lower positions and members of other ethnic groups sparsely represented. The few Jews who held positions were mostly minor functionaries.[4]

We may assume that the same was true in Susa and elsewhere. So Mordecai's royal station, like Esther's, is more in keeping with Jewish Diaspora storytelling than with reality.

As with his introduction and throughout the story, so here at the end, Mordecai's Jewishness is emphasized, as is his popularity in the Jewish community and his concern for his people. Mordecai is a model of Jewish success in the Diaspora. The ending of the Book of Esther assures Jewish readers that the Jewish community will endure and that its place in the world is secure.

NOTES TO THE COMMENTARY

Chapter 1

1. Alexander, 89.

2. *ANET*, 560. The description of the banquet is preceded by a description of the palace, which bears some resemblance to Ahasuerus's palace. The palace at Calah had seven beautiful halls with expensive wooden beams and doors, bronze decorations, painted walls, and lapislazuli-colored glazed bricks. The royal garden had many exotic plants and irrigation weirs.

3. See Briant, "Table du roi" and Sancisi-Weerdenburg, "Gifts in the Persian Empire."

4. Wills, *Jewish Novel*, 51.

5. The Greek portrait of Cyrus, like the biblical portrait of Cyrus, is much more positive. The Bible's portrayal of Cyrus should also be seen in this broader context of shared motifs.

6. See Fox, 171–77, for a fuller discussion.

7. Targum Rishon, Esther Rabbah 1:1 and elsewhere.

8. Laniak, 38.

9. See Briant, *Histoire*, 503 and compare Ezra 5:8: *yehud medinta*, "the province of Yehud." *Yehud* was not a satrapy, but a district within the satrapy of *Beyond the River*.

10. Wills, *Jewish Novel*, 64, comes to a similar conclusion about the 120 satrapies in Daniel.

11. According to M. Miller, 114.

12. H. Sancisi-Weerdenburg, "Gifts in the Persian Empire," 133.

13. *ANET*, 558–60.

14. See Oppenheim, "On Royal Gardens in Mesopotamia" and Stronach, "The Garden as a Political Statement."

15. Compare Briant, "Social and Legal Institutions," 523 and *Histoire*, 527.

16. M. Simon, 8.

17. See B. Megillah 12b and Segal, *The Babylonian Esther Midrash*, I, 255–58.

18. Segal, *The Babylonian Esther Midrash*, I, 251, prefers this reading to "Rava," which appears in the printed edition.

19. This statement is followed by an obscure proverb that seems to suggest that both the king and the queen had licentious motives. See Segal, *The Babylonian Esther Midrash*, I, 253 and Lachs, "Sexual Imagery," 246–47. Segal also notes that in Josephus's account, the party is held in Vashti's own palace.

20. Compare Radday and Brenner, 70–72.

21. For more discussion of the rabbinic view of Vashti see Bronner, "Esther Revisited."

22. See Fox, 164–70 for a discussion of Vashti's characterization.

23. See Spycket, "Women in Persian Art."

24. Frye, "Minorities," 464.

25. Duchesne-Guillemin, "Les noms des eunuques d'Assuärus."

26. Laniak, 54–55.

27. Ehrlich, 111.

28. Bardtke, 284–85.

29. Gordis, "Studies in the Esther Narrative," 46–47. He translates: "And the noblewomen of Persia and Media will say this very day that they heard what the queen had said in the presence of all the king's lords...."

A fourth explanation was suggested to me by Sol Cohen, who takes *ʾ-m-r* to mean "to be lofty, elevated" (cf. Barth, 5–6 and Koehler and Baumgartner, I, 67. It occurs in the *hitpaʿel* form in this sense in Ps. 94:4 and perhaps in Isa. 61:6. If we can

apply this meaning to our phrase (which is not in the *hitpaʿel*), it would yield "the ladies of Persia and Media will boast."

30. Paton, 156; Clines, 32.

31. Walfish, *Esther in Medieval Garb*, 246, note 66, observes that while many of the medieval commentaries accept this interpretation, some do not.

32. For a good description see Graf, "The Persian Royal Road System." See also Herodotus 5.52–53; 8.98; Xenophon, *Cyropaedia* 8.6.17.

33. *ANET*, 316.

34. Greenfield, "Aramaic in the Achaemenian Empire," 708, says of our verse and of 3:12 and 8:9: "Since most of the provinces in the Achaemenian empire had no script of their own, the use of Aramaic 'read out' in the local tongue must be meant by these verses."

35. Bergey, *The Book of Esther*, 68.

36. Or, as Frye, "Minorities," 463, puts it, "land together with its people."

37. Gerleman, 70.

38. Gerleman, 70. Gaster, "Esther 1:22," suggests that just as local governors were empowered to use their own language, so each man will be like a governor in his own house and use his own language.

Chapter 2

1. Wills, *Jew in the Court*, 189.

2. Brown, 342.

3. Zadok, *The Jews in Babylonia*, 2 and 4.

4. Bickerman, *Four Strange Books*, 209.

5. See Walfish, *Esther in Medieval Garb*, 122–26.

6. In his discussion of a cosmetic burner dating from the Persian period, W. F. Albright raises the possibility that perfumes were released into the air through burning, much like incense, and would then adhere to persons near the burner. See Albright, "The Lachish Cosmetic Burner and Esther 2:12" in Moore, *Studies*, 361–68.

7. See Berlin, 63, 69, 125–27.

8. See also Clines, 105.

9. Paton, 190.

10. See also Levenson, 41.

11. Gordis, "Studies in the Esther Narrative," 47–48. Bickerman, *Four Strange Books*, 178, notes that in Greek sources "the royal gate" means the court of the Persian king.

12. Heltzer, "The Book of Esther," 29.

13. Dandamaev and Lukonin, 111. C. L. Seow finds references to these officials in Eccles. 10:20 and in the *Proverbs of Ahiqar* 35 and 341. Dandamaev and Lukonin, 119.

14. Dandamaev and Lukonin, 119.

15. See also Westbrook, "Punishments and Crimes," 546–56, especially 555. For additional references see Tigay, 383 note 60.

16. See Thornton, "The Crucifixion of Haman and the Scandal of the Cross" and G. O'Collins, "Crucifixion."

Chapter 3

1. Stolper, 519–21. But cf. Zadok, "Notes on Esther," 107.

2. Bush, 384, finds a chiastic order in the use of the two appellatives, with the climactic use of both in 9:24.

3. See Fretz, 89–90.

4. Fox, 42–46, summarizes recent views. See also Levenson, 67–68.

5. Bickerman, *Four Strange Books,* 180; cf. 220–21.

6. Among the passages often cited on this issue are the following.

> Plutarch, *Themistocles* 27.4–5: Whereupon the Chiliarch [of Persia, Artabanus] replied [to Themistocles]: "O, Stranger, men's customs differ; but all honor the exaltation and maintenance of their own peculiar ways. Now you Hellenes are said to admire liberty and equality above all things; but in our eyes, among many fair customs, this is the fairest of all, to honor the King, and to pay obeisance to him *[proskynesis]* as the image of that god who is the preserver of all things. If, then, you approve our practice and will pay obeisance, it is in your power to look upon and address the King; but if you are otherwise minded, you will need to employ messengers to him in your stead, for it is not a custom of this country that the King give ear to a man who has not paid him obeisance."

> Herodotus 1.134: There is a way of telling whether or not two Persians who meet on the street are of the same social standing. If they are, then instead of saying hello to each other, they kiss each other on the lips; if either of them is from a slightly lower rank, they kiss each other on the cheeks; and if one of them is the other's inferior by a long way, he falls to the ground and prostrates himself in front of the other person.

7. Briant, *Histoire,* 235. See also Frye, "Gestures of Deference to Royalty in Ancient Iran" and Bickerman, "A propos d'un passage de Chares."

8. Josephus calls Mordecai wise, as he does for other biblical figures, because Jews had been accused by Apion (*Against Apion* 2,135) of not having produced men like Socrates. It is part of Josephus's apologetic stance to show that the Jews had wise men like the Greeks. Josephus is also concerned to show that Jews were law-abiding. Therefore he mentions that Mordecai obeyed the laws of his own country (Israel), even if that meant he had to go against Persian law. See Feldman, 516 and 547.

9. Moore, *Daniel, Esther, and Jeremiah,* 189, thinks the religious reasons are mere speculation, but we can see how they might have developed from the earlier Greek abhorrence of bowing. What was originally ethnically unpalatable became religiously unpalatable.

10. Clines, 105.

11. On point of view in biblical narrative see Berlin, 43–82.

12. See Hallo, "The First Purim."

13. Schäfer, 15–21.

14. Schäfer, 208.

15. Levenson, "The Scroll of Esther."

16. See also Segal, *Babylonian Esther Midrash,* 2:114–130, for a discussion of the rabbinic and related material; Berman, "Aggadah and Anti-Semitism"; and Walfish, *Esther in Medieval Garb,* 143–55.

17. Frye, "Minorities."

18. Briant, *Histoire,* 526.

19. *ANET,* 316.

20. Simon, 195. Levenson also refers to Gen. 37:24–25 in this connection.

21. Paton, 211; see Fox, 280.

Chapter 4

1. Anderson, *A Time to Mourn, A Time to Dance.*

Chapter 5

1. See Sefati, 132–41. I thank Paul Delnero for this reference.

2. S. Cohen would propose a grammatical explanation instead of a rhetorical one. He finds the same type of alternation of pronouns in several cases when referring to a dual antecedent, the most famous being Gen. 1:27: "in the image of God He created him; male and female He created them." See S. Cohen, 59–61.

3. See Joüon and Muraoka, 559.

Chapter 6

1. U. Simon, 219.

2. Sancisi-Weerdenburg, "Exit Atossa," 29. Gera, 222, note 116, echoes this sentiment.

3. Barrick, "The Meaning and Usage of RKB in Biblical Hebrew."

4. As seen by Grottanelli, "Honour," and Heltzer, "Mordekhai and Demaratos."

5. Reardon, *Collected Ancient Greek Novels,* 55. See also Quintus Curtius, 4.10.34 and 10.5.24.

6. Bakhtin, 148.

7. Bentley, xx, notes that the swift tempo of farce is not merely a technical, literary, or theatrical fact, but has the psychological effect of making the actions seem abstract and automatic.

Chapter 7

1. Sol Cohen has noted this motif in his unpublished dissertation on the Sumerian text, *Enmerkar and the Lord of Aratta* (University of Pennsylvania, 1973), 244–45, and J.-M. Dentzer, *Le Motif du Banquet Couché,* has documented it extensively in later periods.

2. Bickerman, *Four Strange Books, 182.*

3. See Waltke and O'Connor, 603, for active infinitives with a passive sense.

4. On the general sense of "slave" see Westbrook, "The Female Slave," 230. Briant, *Histoire,* 335–37, discusses the term *bandaka* and its Greek rendering, *pistis,* "fidelity, loyalty."

5. Greenberg, 180.

6. Bar-Efrat, 45, suggests that the repetition in Gen. 22:7 "represents irresolution, perhaps nervousness. Isaac wants to ask the question which is bothering him . . . but he is unsure, begins speaking, then hesitates."

7. The structure of this dialogue may have been determined at least in part by the fact that biblical narrative never represents a three-way conversation. Only two parties may interact verbally. Nevertheless, the silencing of Haman is used to good effect.

Chapter 8

1. Fox and Levenson are representative of the moderns; among the medievals are Joseph Kara and especially Abraham Saba. See Walfish, *Esther in Medieval Garb,* 63–65.

2. Clines, 101.

3. Fox, *Redaction,* 118–19.

4. Klingbeil, "R-K-SH and Esther 8,10.14."

5. Bergey, *The Book of Esther,* 163–64. The occurrence in 1 Sam. 25:8 is in connection with sheep shearing and is not a technical usage.

6. As Williamson argues in "Review of *The Esther Scroll,*" 148.

Chapter 9

1 Jones, "Two Misconceptions," 177–81 also finds humor in this chapter although he does not relate it to the carnivalesque.

2. Bentley, xiii. Certain medieval Purim practices were, like chapter 9, violent and hostile to non-Jews (Christians). For these practices and the embarrassment they caused later scholars see Horowitz, "The Rite to Be Reckless."

3. See Tabory, *Moʿadei Yisraʾel,* 324.

4. Levenson, 121, contrasts the words introducing Mordecai in 2:5, *ʾish yehudi,* "a Jewish man," with his designation here, suggesting that this reflects a contrast between his status as a mere exile with his high status here.

5. With Fox and Levenson and against McKane, "A Note on Esther XI and I Samuel XV."

6. Charney, 82.

7. See Fox and especially Fox, *Redaction,* 123–24. Fox compares the rigid and hierarchical manner in which Persian laws are made with the communal, almost democratic way that the law of Purim is made. He explains that *kayyem* "refers not to the imposition of one's will on others or to the prescription of new ordinances, but rather to the fulfillment or regularization of a decision or an existing intention."

8. A number of scholars have seen evidence of a later addition in all or part of chapter 9. Clines advocates that 9:1–10:3 is by a different hand or hands from the first part of the book (*The Esther Scroll,* 39–63). Others think that the additions begin at 9:20 or 9:29. Fox, *Redaction,* 96–126, responds to these arguments and concludes that, while the Masoretic Text drew on earlier versions of the story, the Masoretic Text as it now stands can be explained as the work of one author.

9. Fox is reluctant to conclude that the redundancy signifies a later addition, suggesting that the redundancy is an intentional reconfirmation. He is, nevertheless, aware of the problems posed in these verses (*Redaction,* 106).

10. Fox, 126, note 74 mentions that tractate Soferim 21:1 knows of a three-day fast following Purim. The Fast of Esther on 13 Adar is first attested in the eighth century, in the Sheʾiltot of R. Aḥa of Shabha. It is also discussed in Maimonides, *Yad Ha-ḥazaqah,* Taʿanit 5:5. See also Loewenstamm, 75.

11. See the commentaries by Fox, Hakham, and Levenson. The point is discussed by Loewenstamm, 74–77, by Fishbane, 503–5, and by Fox, *Redaction,* 105–6.

12. The Malbim (nineteenth-century Jewish commentator) clarifies the comparison by stating that one can take upon oneself fasts or commemorative celebrations as a type of vow, which need not be mentioned in the Torah.

13. See *TDOT* VII, 371–82.

Chapter 10

1. See Berlin, 107–110.

2. A merismus is a figure of speech in which the whole is represented by its parts at either extreme. For example, "from head to toe" means "the entire body" and "heaven and earth" means the entire world.

3. Dandamaev and Lukonin, 111.

4. Zadok, *The Jews of Babylonia,* 87. Zadok notes that Nehemiah, who held a senior position, was an exception.

BIBLIOGRAPHY

Abrams, M. H. *A Glossary of Literary Terms.* 4ᵗʰ ed. New York: Holt, Rinehart and Winston, 1981.

Abramsky, S. "Shivah le-malkhut sha'ul bi-megilat 'ester uve-divrei ha-yamim." *Milet* 1 (1983): 39–63.

Ackroyd, P. R. "The Biblical Portrayal of Achaemenid Rulers." In *Achaemenid History V: The Roots of the European Tradition.* Edited by H. Sancisi-Weerdenburg and J. Drijvers, pp. 1–16. Leiden: Nederlands Instituut voor het Nabije Oosten, 1990.

——. "Problems in the Handling of Biblical and Related Sources in the Achaemenid Period." In *Achaemenid History III: Method and Theory.* Edited by A. Kuhrt and H. Sancisi-Weerdenburg, pp. 33–54. Leiden: Nederlands Instituut voor het Nabije Oosten, 1988.

Alexander, S. M. "The Influence of Achaemenian Persia on the Jewellry of the Migrations Period in Europe." In *Ancient Persia: The Art of an Empire.* Edited by D. Schmandt-Besserat, pp. 87–94. Malibu, CA: Undena, 1980.

Alter, R. "Biblical Imperatives and Literary Play." In *"Not in Heaven": Coherence and Complexity in Biblical Narrative.* Edited by J. Rosenblatt and J. Sitterson, pp. 13–27. Bloomington, IN: Indiana University Press, 1991.

Amiet, P. *Art of the Ancient Near East.* New York: H. N. Abrams, 1980.

——. *Suse: 6000 ans d'histoire.* Paris: Monographs du Musée du Louvre. Éditions de la Réunion des Musées Nationaux, 1988.

Anderson, G. *A Time to Mourn, A Time to Dance: The Expression of Grief and Joy in Israelite Religion.* University Park, PA: The Pennsylvania State University Press, 1991.

Anchor Bible Dictionary. Edited by D. N. Freedman. New York: Doubleday, 1992.

Azarpay, G. "Crowns and Some Royal Insignia in Early Iran." *Iranica Antiqua* 9 (1972): 108–15.

Bakhtin, M. *Rabelais and His World.* Bloomington, IN: Indiana University Press, 1984.

Bal, M. "Lots of Writing." *Semeia* 54 (1991): 77–102.

Balcer, J. M. *The Persian Conquest of the Greeks 545–450 B.C.* Konstanz: Universitätsverlag Konstanz, 1995.

——. *A Prosopographical Study of the Ancient Persians Royal and Noble C. 550–450 B.C.* Lewiston, ME: Edwin Mellen, 1993.

——. *Sparda by the Bitter Sea: Imperial Interaction in Western Asia.* Chico, CA: Scholars Press, 1984.

Barber, C. L. *Shakespeare's Festive Comedy.* Princeton, NJ: Princeton University Press, 1959.

Bardtke, H. *Das Buch Esther.* KAT 17/5. Gütersloh: Mohn, 1963.

Bar-Efrat, S. *Narrative Art in the Bible.* Sheffield, England: Almond, 1989.

Barrick, B. "The Meaning and Usage of RKB in Biblical Hebrew." *JBL* 101 (1982): 481–503.

Barth, J. *Wurzeluntersuchungen zum hebräischen und aramäischen Lexicon.* Leipzig, 1902.

Baumgarten, A. "Scroll of Esther." *EJ* 14: 1047–57.

Bazak, A., ed. *Hadassah hi' 'ester.* Alon Shevut: Tevunot, 5759.

Beal, T. K. *The Book of Hiding: Gender, Ethnicity, Annihilation, and Esther.* London and New York: Routledge, 1997.

Beckwith, R. *The Old Testament Canon of the New Testament Church and Its Background in Early Judaism.* Grand Rapids, MI: Eerdmans, 1985.

Beiner, G. *Shakespeare's Agonistic Comedy: Poetics, Analysis, Criticism.* Rutherford, NJ: Fairleigh Dickinson University Press; London and Toronto: Associated University Presses, 1993.

Bentley, E. "The Psychology of Farce." In *Let's Get a Divorce! and Other Plays,* pp. vii–xx. New York: Hill and Wang, 1958.

Berg, S. B. "After the Exile: God and History in the Books of Chronicles and Esther." *The Divine Helmsman: Studies on God's Control of Human Events, Presented to Lou H. Silberman.* Edited by J. Crenshaw and S. Sandmel, pp. 107–27. New York: Ktav, 1980.

——. *The Book of Esther.* Missoula, MT: Scholars Press, 1979.

Bergey, R. L. "The Book of Esther—Its Place in the Linguistic Milieu of Post-Exilic Biblical Hebrew Prose: A Study in Late Biblical Hebrew." Ph.D. diss., Dropsie College, Philadelphia, 1983.

——. "Late Linguistic Features in Esther." *JQR* 75 (1984): 66–78.

Berlin, A. *Poetics and Interpretation of Biblical Narrative.* Sheffield, England: Almond, 1983.

Berman, J. "Aggadah and Anti-Semitism: The Midrashim to Esther 3:8." *Judaism* 38 (1989): 185–96.

Berquist, J. *Judaism in Persia's Shadow.* Minneapolis: Fortress, 1995.

Bickerman, E. "The Colophon of the Greek Book of Esther." *JBL* 63 (1944): 339–62. Reprinted in Moore, *Studies,* 529–52.

——. *Four Strange Books of the Bible.* New York: Schocken, 1967.

——. "A propos d'un passage de Chares de Mytilene." *La Parola del Passato* 91 (Naples, 1963): 241–55.

Blumenthal, D. R. "Where God Is Not: The Book of Esther and Song of Songs." *Judaism* 44 (1995): 80–92.

Boardman, J. et al. *The Cambridge Ancient History IV: Persia, Greece and the Western Mediterranean.* Second Edition. Cambridge: Cambridge University Press, 1988.

Brenner, A., ed. *A Feminist Companion to Esther, Judith and Susanna.* Sheffield, England: Sheffield Academic Press, 1995.

Briant, P. "Ctesias." *ABD* I, 1211–12.

——. *From Cyrus to Alexander: A History of the Persian Empire.* 2 vols. Translated by P. Daniels. Winona Lake, IN: Eisenbrauns. Forthcoming.

——. "Herodote et la société perse." In *Hérodote et les peuples non Grec.* Edited by W. Burkert et al., pp. 69–113. Geneva: Vandoeuvres, 1990.

——. *Histoire de l'empire perse: de Cyrus à Alexandre.* Paris: Fayard, 1996. (*Achaemenid History X*).

——. "Histoire et idéologie: Les Grecs et la 'décadence perse.'" In *Mélanges Pierre Lévêque.* Edited by M. Mactoux and E. Geny, pp. 33–47. Paris: Annales Littéraires de l'Université de Besançon, 1989.

——. "Institutions perses et histoire comparatiste dans l'historiographie grecque." In *Achaemenid History II: The Greek Sources.* Edited by H. Sancisi-Weerdenburg and A. Kuhrt, pp. 1–10. Leiden: Nederlands Instituut voor het Nabije Oosten, 1987.

——. "Persian Empire." *ABD* V, 236–44.

——. "Social and Legal Institutions in Achaemenid Iran." In *Civilizations of the Ancient Near East,* vol. I. Edited by J. M. Sasson, pp. 517–28. New York: Charles Scribner's Sons/ Macmillan, 1995.

——. "Table du roi, tribut et redistribution chez les Achéménides." In *Le tribut dans l'empire Perse: Actes de la Table ronde de Paris, 12–13 Décembre 1986.* Edited by P. Briant and C. Herrenschmidt, pp. 35–44. Louvain and Paris: Peeters, 1989.

Bronner, L. L. "Esther Revisited: An Aggadic Approach." In *A Feminist Companion to Esther, Judith, and Susanna.* Edited by A. Brenner, pp. 176–97. Sheffield, England: Sheffield Academic Press, 1995.

Brosius, M. *Women in Ancient Persia.* Oxford: Clarendon, 1996.

Brown, J. P. *Israel and Hellas.* Berlin and New York: Walter de Gruyter, 1995.

Broyde, M. J. "Defilement of the Hands, Canonization of the Bible, and the Special Status of Esther, Ecclesiastes, and Song of Songs." *Judaism* 44 (1995): 64–79.

Brulé, P. "Des femmes au miroir masculin." *Mélanges Pierre Lévêque.* Edited by M. Mactoux, and E. Geny, pp. 49–61. Paris: Annales Littéraires de l'Université de Besançon. 1989.

Buber, S. *Sifrei De-'agadta'.* Vilna: Ram, 1886.

Buber, S., ed. *'Aggadat 'Ester.* Lwow, 1897.

Burkert, W. "Herodot als Historiker Fremder Religionen." In *Hérodote et les peuples non Grec.* Edited by W. Burkert et al., pp. 1–39. Geneva: Vandoeuvres, 1990.

——. *The Orientalizing Revolution: Near Eastern Influence on Greek Culture in the Early Archaic Age.* Cambridge, MA: Harvard University Press, 1992.

Bush, F. *Ruth, Esther.* Word Biblical Commentary. Waco, TX: Word, 1996.

Calmeyer, P. "Greek Historiography and Achaemenid Reliefs." In *Achaemenid History II: The Greek Sources.* Edited by H. Sancisi-Weerdenburg and A. Kuhrt, pp. 11–26. Leiden: Nederlands Instituut voor het nabije Oosten, 1987.

Cameron, G. G. "Ancient Persia." In *The Idea of History in the Ancient Near East.* Edited by R. Dentan, pp. 77–97. New Haven and London: Yale University Press, 1955.

——. "The Persian Satrapies and Related Matters." *JNES* 32 (1973): 47–56.

Caputi, A. *Buffo: The Genius of Vulgar Comedy.* Detroit: Wayne State University Press, 1978.

Charney, M. *Comedy High and Low: An Introduction to the Experience of Comedy.* New York: Oxford University Press, 1978.

Clines, D. J. A. *The Esther Scroll: The Story of the Story.* Sheffield, England: JSOT Press, 1984.

——. "In Quest of the Historical Mordecai." *VT* 41 (1991): 129–36.

Cohen, A. "'Hu Ha-goral': The Religious Significance of Esther." *Judaism* 23 (1974): 87–94.

Cohen, S. "A Note on the Dual in Biblical Hebrew." *JQR* 73 (1982): 59–61.

Collins, N. "Did Esther fast on the 15th Nisan?" *Revue biblique* 100 (1993): 533–61.

Craig, K. *Reading Esther: A Case for the Literary Carnivalesque.* Louisville, KY: Westminster John Knox, 1995.

Crüsemann, F. "'. . . und de Gesetze des Königs holten sie nicht' (Est 3,8): Widerstand und Recht im Alten Testament." *Wort und Dienst. Jahrbuch der Kirchlichen Hochschule Bethel.* NF 17 (1983): 9–25.

Dandamaev, M. *A Political History of the Achaemenid Empire.* Leiden: Brill, 1989.

Dandamaev, M., and V. Lukonin. *The Cultural and Social Institutions of Ancient Iran.* Cambridge: Cambridge University Press, 1989.

Daube, D. *Esther.* Oxford: The Yarnton Trust for the Oxford Centre for Postgraduate Hebrew Studies, 1995.

——. "The Last Chapter of Esther." *JQR* 37 (1946–1947): 139–47.

Davies, W. D., and L. Finkelstein, eds. *The Cambridge History of Judaism. Volume One. Introduction; The Persian Period.* Cambridge: Cambridge University Press, 1984.

Davis, J. M. *Farce.* London: Methuen, 1978.

Day, L. *Three Faces of a Queen: Characterization in the Books of Esther.* Sheffield, England: Sheffield Academic Press, 1995.

De Troyer, K. "On Crowns and Diadems from Kings, Queens, Horses and Men." In *IX Congress of the International Organization for Septuagint and Cognate Studies, Cambridge 1995.* Edited by B. Taylor, pp. 355–67. Atlanta: Scholars, 1997.

Deem, A. "*Megillah* maḥteret." *Bizaron* 24–25 (5745): 49–52.

Deem-Goldberger, A. "Hatashtit ha'amanutit bamegillat 'ester." *Biqoret ufarshanut* 11–12 (1978): 285–97.

Del Medico, H. E. "Le cadre historique des fêtes de Hanukkah et de Púrîm." *VT* 15 (1965): 238–70.

Dentzer, J.-M. "L'iconographie iranienne du souverain couché et le motif du banquet." *Annales Archéologiques Arabes Syriennes* 21 (1971): 39–50.

——. *Le Motif du Banquet Couché dans le Proche-Orient et le Monde Grec du VIIᵉ au IVᵉ Siècle avant J.-C.* Rome: École Française de Rome, 1982.

Dommershausen, W. *Die Estherrolle: Stil und Ziel einer alttestamentlichen Schrift.* Stuttgart: Katholisches Bibelwerk, 1968.

——. *Ester.* Stuttgart: Echter Verlag, 1980.

Doniach, N. S. *Purim or the Feast of Esther.* Philadelphia: Jewish Publication Society, 1933.

Dorothy, C. V. *The Books of Esther: Structure, Genre and Textual Integrity.* Sheffield, England: Sheffield Academic Press, 1997.

Drews, R. *The Greek Accounts of Eastern History.* Washington, DC: Center for Hellenic Studies, 1973.

Duchesne-Guillemin, J. "Les noms des eunuques d'Assuérus." *Le Muséon* 66 (1953): 105–8. Reprinted in Moore, *Studies,* 273–76.

Ego, B. "Targumization as Theologization: Aggadic Additions in the Targum Sheni of Esther." In *The Aramaic Bible: Targums in Their Historical Context.* Edited by D. Beattie and M. McNamara, pp. 354–59. JSOT Supplement Series 166. Sheffield, England: Sheffield Academic Press, 1994.

Ehrlich, A. B. *Randglossen zur hebräischen Bibel.* Leipzig: J. C. Hinrichs, 1908–1914.

Eissfeldt, O. "Rechtskundige und Richter in Esther 1, 13–22." In *Festschrift für Wilhelm Eilers,* pp. 164–66. Wiesbaden: Otto Harrassowitz, 1967.

Encyclopaedia Judaica. Jerusalem: Keter, 1972.

Epstein, S. "The 'Drinking Banquet' (Trink-Siyde): A Hasidic Event for Purim." *Poetics Today* 15:1 (1994): 133–52.

Eskenazi, T. "Out from the Shadows: Biblical Women in the Postexilic Era." *JSOT* 54 (1992): 25–43.

Feldman, L. H. *Studies in Josephus' Rewritten Bible.* Leiden: Brill, 1998.

Fisch, H. *Poetry with a Purpose.* Bloomington, IN: Indiana University, 1988.

——. "Reading and Carnival: On the Semiotics of Purim." *Poetics Today* 15:1 (1994): 55–74.

Fishbane, M. *Biblical Interpretation in Ancient Israel.* Oxford: Oxford University Press, 1985.

Foster, B. R. "Humor and Wit in the Ancient Near East." In *Civilizations of the Ancient Near East.* Vol. 4. Edited by J. M. Sasson, pp. 2459–69. New York: Charles Scribner's Sons/ Macmillan, 1995.

Fox, M. V. *Character and Ideology in the Book of Esther.* Columbia, SC: University of South Carolina, 1991.

——. *The Redaction of the Books of Esther.* Atlanta: Scholars, 1991.

——. "The Redaction of the Greek Alpha-Text of Esther." In *Shaʿarei Talmon: Studies in the Bible, Qumran, and the Ancient Near East Presented to Shemaryahu Talmon.* Edited by M. Fishbane et al., pp. 207–20. Winona Lake, IN: Eisenbrauns, 1992.

——. "Religion in the Book of Esther." *Judaism* 39 (1990): 254–55.

——. "The Structure of Esther." In *Isaac Leo Seeligmann Volume.* Edited by A. Rofé and Y. Zakovitch, pp. 291–304. Jerusalem: Rubenstein, 1983.

Fretz, M. J. "Agagite." *ABD* I, 89–90.

Frisch, A. "Bein megilat 'ester le-sefer melakhim." *Meḥqerei ḥag* 3 (1992): 25–35.

Frye, N. *Anatomy of Criticism*. Princeton, NJ: Princeton University Press, 1957.

Frye, R. N. "Gestures of Deference to Royalty in Ancient Iran." *Iranica Antiqua* 9 (1972): 102–7.

——. *The History of Ancient Iran*. Munich: Beck, 1983.

——. "Minorities in the History of the Near East." In *A Green Leaf: Papers in Honour of Professor Jes P. Asmussen. Acta Iranica* 28. Edited by J. Duchesne-Guillemin et al., pp. 461–71. Leiden: Brill, 1988.

Gamble, H. Y. "Canon." *ABD* I, 837–61.

Gammie, J. G. "Herodotus on Kings and Tyrants: Objective Historiography or Conventional Portraiture?" *JNES* 45 (1986): 171–95.

Gan, M. "Megilat ʾester be-ʾaspaqlariyat qorot yosef be-mitzrayim." *Tarbiz* 31 (1961–1962): 144–49.

Gardner, A. E. "The Relationship of the Additions to the Book of Esther to the Maccabean Crisis." *Journal for the Study of Judaism in the Persian, Hellenistic and Roman Period* 15 (1984): 1–8.

Gaster, T. H. "Esther 1:22." *JBL* 69 (1950): 381.

——. *Purim and Hanukkah in Custom and Tradition*. New York: Schuman, 1950.

Gehman, H. "Notes on the Persian Words in the Book of Esther." *JBL* 43 (1924): 321–28.

Gendler, M. "The Restoration of Vashti." In *The Jewish Woman*. Edited by E. Koltun, pp. 241–47. New York: Schocken, 1976.

Georges, P. *Barbarian Asia and the Greek Experience: From the Archaic Period to the Age of Xenophon*. Baltimore and London: The Johns Hopkins University Press, 1994.

——. "The Persians in the Greek Imaginations, 550–479 B.C." Ph.D. diss., University of California, Berkeley, 1981.

Gera, D. L. *Xenophon's* Cyropaedia: *Style, Genre, and Literary Technique*. Oxford: Clarendon, 1993.

Gerleman, G. *Esther*. Biblischer Kommentar. Neukirchen-Vluyn: Neukirchener, 1973.

Gershevitch, I., ed. *The Cambridge History of Iran*. Vol. 2, *The Median and Achaemenian Periods*. Cambridge: Cambridge University Press, 1985.

Gevaryahu, H. "Esther is a Story of Jewish Defense, Not a Story of Jewish Revenge." *Jewish Bible Quarterly* 21 (1993): 3–12.

Ginsberg, H. L. "Introductions." In *The Five Megilloth and Jonah*. 2nd rev. ed. Philadelphia: Jewish Publication Society, 1974.

Ginzberg, L. *Legends of the Jews*. Philadelphia: Jewish Publication Society, 1913–1938.

Goldman, S. "Narrative and Ethical Ironies in Esther." *JSOT* 47 (1990): 15–31.

Goodman, P. *The Purim Anthology*. Philadelphia: Jewish Publication Society, 1949.

Gordis, R. *Megillat Esther with Introduction, New Translation and Commentary*. New York: Rabbinical Assembly, 1974.

——. "Religion, Wisdom and History in the Book of Esther: A New Solution to an Ancient Crux." *JBL* 100 (1981): 359–88.

——. "Studies in the Esther Narrative." *JBL* 95 (1976): 43–58.

Grabbe, L. *Judaism from Cyrus to Hadrian*. 2 vols. Minneapolis: Fortress, 1992.

Graf, D. F. "The Persian Royal Road System." In *Achaemenid History VIII: Continuity and Change*. Edited by H. Sancisi-Weerdenburg et al., pp. 167–89. Leiden: Nederlands Instituut voor het Nabije Oosten, 1994.

Greenberg, M. *Ezekiel 1–20*. Garden City, NY: Doubleday, 1983.

Greenfield, J. "Aramaic in the Achaemenian Empire." In *The Cambridge History of Iran*. Vol. 2. Edited by I. Gershevitch, pp. 698–713. Cambridge: Cambridge University Press, 1985.

——. "The Aramaic Legal Texts of the Achaemenian Period." *Transeuphratène* 3 (1990): 85–92.

Greenstein, E. L. "A Jewish Reading of Esther." In *Judaic Perspectives on Ancient Israel*. Edited by J. Neusner, pp. 225–43. Philadelphia: Fortress, 1987.

——. "The Scroll of Esther: A New Translation." *Fiction* 9:3 (1990): 52–81.

Grossfeld, B. *The First Targum to Esther: According to the MS. Paris Hebrew 110 of the Bibliotèque Nationale*. New York: Sepher-Hermon, 1983.

——. *The Targum Sheni to the Book of Esther: A Critical Edition Based on MS. Sassoon 282 with Critical Apparatus*. New York: Sepher-Hermon, 1994.

——. *The Two Targums of Esther, Translated, with Apparatus and Notes*. Collegeville, MN: Liturgical Press/Michael Glazier, 1991.

Grottanelli, C. "Honour, Women and Sanctuary at the Persian Court (Plutarc. *Themist.* 29–31 and *Esther* 6–8)." *Dialoghi di Archeologia* 6: 2 (1988): 135–38.

Hakham, A. "'Ester." In *Hamesh megilot*. Da'at Miqra'. Jerusalem: Mosad Harav Kook, 1990.

Halbertal, M. *People of the Book: Canon, Meaning, and Authority*. Cambridge, MA: Harvard University Press, 1997.

Hallo, W. W. "The First Purim." *BA* 46 (1983): 19–26.

Hanhart, R., ed. *Esther*. Göttingen: Vandenhoeck & Ruprecht, 1966.

Haran, M. *Ha-'asufah ha-miqra'it*. Jerusalem: Mosad Bialik and Magnes Press, 1996.

Harrelson, W. "Textual and Translation Problems in the Book of Esther." *Perspectives in Religious Studies* 17 (1990): 197–208.

Harris, M. "Purim: The Celebration of Dis-order." *Judaism* 26 (1977): 161–70.

Hartog, F. *The Mirror of Herodotus: The Representation of the Other in the Writing of History*. Berkeley: University of California Press, 1988.

Heinz, K. "Religion und Politik in Vorderasien im Reich der Achämeniden." *Klio* 69 (1987): 317–25.

Heltzer, M. "The Book of Esther." *Bible Review* 8 (1992): 24–30, 41.

——. "Mordekhai and Demaratos and the Question of Historicity." *Archaeologische Mitteilungen aus Iran* 27 (1994): 119–21.

Herion, G. A. et al. "Humor and Wit." *ABD* III, 325–33.

Herodotus. *The Histories*. Translated by R. Waterfield. Oxford: Oxford University Press, 1998.

Herst, R. "The Purim Connection." *Union Seminary Quarterly Review* 28 (1972–1973): 139–45. Reprinted in Moore, *Studies,* 220–26.

Hirsch, S. W. "1001 Iranian Nights: History and Fiction in Xenophon's *Cyropaedia*." In *The Greek Historians: Literature and History. Papers Presented to A. E. Raubitschek*, pp. 65–85. Saratoga, CA: ANMA Libri and Department of Classics, Stanford University, 1985.

Hoffner, H. "Text, Artifact, and Image: Revealing Ancient Israelite Religion." Center for Judaic Studies, University of Pennsylvania, 27–29 April 1998.

Hofmann, I., and A. Vorbichler. "Herodot und der Schreiber des Esther-Buches." *Zeitschrift für Missionswissenschaft und Religionswissenschaft* 66 (1982): 294–302.

Horowitz, C. M., ed. *'Aguddat 'Aggadot*. Berlin, 1881.

Horowitz, E. "The Rite to Be Reckless: On the Perpetration and Interpretation of Purim Violence." *Poetics Today* 15:1 (1994): 9–54.

Humphreys, W. L. "A Life-Style for the Diaspora: A Study of the Tales of Esther and Daniel." *JBL* 92 (1973): 211–23.

——. "The Story of Esther and Mordecai." In *Saga, Legend, Tale, Novella, Fable*. Edited by G. Coats, pp. 97–113. Sheffield, England: JSOT Press 1985.

Jacobs, L. "Purim." *EJ* 13:1390–95.

Jarden, D. *Shirei Ha-qodesh le-Rabi Yehuda Ha-levi*. Vol. 1. Jerusalem: 1978.

Jobes, K. *The Alpha-Text of Esther: Its Character and Relationship to the Masoretic Text.* Atlanta: Scholars, 1996.

Johnson, M. D. *The Purpose of the Biblical Genealogies.* 2nd ed. Cambridge: Cambridge University Press, 1988.

Jones, B. W. "The So-called Appendix to the Book of Esther." *Semitics* 6 (1978): 36–43.

———. "Two Misconceptions about the Book of Esther." *CBQ* 39 (1977): 171–81. Reprinted in Moore, *Studies,* 437–47.

Josephus Flavius. *The Works of Josephus.* Translated by W. Whiston. N.P.: Hendrickson, 1987. First pub. 1736.

Joüon, P., and T. Muraoka. *A Grammar of Biblical Hebrew.* Rome: Pontifical Biblical Institute, 1993.

Jump, J. D. *Burlesque.* London: Methuen, 1972.

Koehler, L., and W. Baumgartner. *The Hebrew and Aramaic Lexicon of the Old Testament.* Vol. 1. Translated by M. E. J. Richardson. Leiden, 1994.

Klein, L. "Esther's Lot." *Currents in Research: Biblical Studies* 5 (1997): 111–45.

Klein, Y., M. Heltzer, and Y. Avishur, eds. "'Ester." In *'Entziqlopediyah 'olam ha-tanakh* 16b, pp. 62–109. Ramat Gan: Revivim, 1988.

Klingbeil, G. A. "*R-K-SH* and Esther 8,10.14: A Semantic Note." *ZAW* 107 (1995): 301–3.

Knox, B. M. "Athenian Religion and Literature." *Cambridge Ancient History V: The Fifth Century B.C.* Edited by D. M. Lewis, pp. 268–86. Cambridge: Cambridge University Press, 1992.

Kurht, A. *The Ancient Near East c. 3000–330 B.C.* London and New York: Routledge, 1995.

Lachs, S. T. "Hadassah That Is Esther." *Journal for the Study of Judaism* 10 (1979): 219–20.

———. "Sexual Imagery in Three Rabbinic Passages." *Journal for the Study of Judaism* 23 (1992): 244–48.

LaCocque, A. "The Different Versions of Esther." *Biblical Interpretation* 7 (1999): 301–22.

———. *The Feminine Unconventional: Four Subversive Figures in Israel's Tradition.* Minneapolis: Fortress, 1990.

———. "Haman in the Book of Esther." *HAR* 11 (1987): 207–22.

Laniak, T. *Shame and Honor in the Book of Esther.* SBL Dissertation Series 165. Atlanta: Scholars Press, 1998.

Lebram, J. C. H. "Purimfest und Esterbuch." *VT* 22 (1972): 208–22. Reprinted in Moore, *Studies,* 205–19.

Lehman, M. "The Literary Study of Esther." *Biblical Viewpoint* 26 (1992): 85–95.

Leiman, S. Z. *The Canonization of Hebrew Scripture: The Talmudic and Midrashic Evidence.* New Haven, CT: Connecticut Academy of Arts and Sciences, 1976.

Levenson, J. D. *Esther, A Commentary.* Old Testament Library. Louisville, KY: Westminster John Knox, 1997.

———. "The Scroll of Esther in Ecumenical Perspective." *Journal of Ecumenical Studies* 13 (1976): 440–52.

Levit-Tawil, D. "The Enthroned King Ahashuerus at Dura in Light of the Iconography of Kingship in Iran." *BASOR* 250 (1983): 57–78.

Lewis, D. M., ed. *The Cambridge Ancient History V: The Fifth Century.* Cambridge: Cambridge University Press, 1992.

———. "The Kings' Dinner (Polyaenus IV 3.32)." In *Achaemenid History II: The Greek Sources.* Edited by H. Sancisi-Weerdenburg and A. Kuhrt, pp. 79–87. Leiden: Nederlands Instituut voor het Nabije Oosten, 1987.

——. "Persians in Herodotus." In *The Greek Historians: Literature and History. Papers Presented to A. E. Raubitschek,* pp. 101–17. Saratoga, CA: ANMA Libri and Department of Classics, Stanford University, 1985.

Lewy, J. "The Feast of the 14th Day of Adar." *HUCA* 14 (1939): 127–51. Reprinted in Moore, *Studies,* 160–84.

Littman, R. "The Religious Policy of Xerxes and the Book of Esther." *JQR* 65 (1974–1975): 145–55.

Loader, J. A. "Esther as a Novel with Different Levels of Meaning." *ZAW* 90 (1978): 417–21.

Loewenstamm, S. E. "Esther 9:29–32: The Genesis of a Late Addition." *HUCA* 42 (1971): 117–24.

Loretz, O. "*šʿr hmlk*—Das Tor des Königs (Est 2,19)." *Die Welt des Orients* 4 (1967): 104–8.

Lubitch, R. "A Feminist's Look at Esther." *Judaism* 42 (1993): 438–46.

Magonet, J. "The Liberal and the Lady: Esther Revisited." *Judaism* 29 (1980): 167–76.

McBride, W. T. "Esther Passes: Chiasm, Lex Talio and Money in the Book of Esther." In *"Not in Heaven": Coherence and Complexity in Biblical Narrative.* Edited by J. Rosenblatt and J. Sitterson, pp. 211–23. Bloomington, IN: Indiana University Press, 1991.

McKane, W. "A Note on Esther IX and 1 Samuel XV." *JTS* 12 (1961): 260–1. Reprinted in Moore, *Studies,* 306–7.

Meinhold, A. "Die Gattung der Josephsgeschichte und des Esterbuches: Diasporanovelle, I." *ZAW* 87 (1975): 306–24; II. *ZAW* 88 (1976): 72–93.

Metzler, D. "Stilische Evidenz für die Benutzung Persischer Quellen durch Griechische Historiker." *Achaemenid History II: The Greek Sources.* Edited by H. Sancisi-Weerdenburg and A. Kuhrt, pp. 89–91. Leiden: Nederlands Instituut voor het Nabije Oosten, 1987.

Midrash Rabbah. Esther. Translated by Maurice Simon. London: Soncino, 1939.

Midrash Shoḥer Tov. Jerusalem: Midrash, 1968.

Millard, A. R. "The Persian Names in Esther and the Reliability of the Hebrew Text." *JBL* 96 (1977): 481–88.

Miller, C. H. "Esther's Levels of Meaning." *ZAW* 92 (1980): 145–48.

Miller, M. C. *Athens and Persia in the Fifth Century B.C.: A Study in Cultural Receptivity.* Cambridge: Cambridge University Press, 1997.

Miroschedji, P. de. "Susa." *ABD* VI, 242–45.

Momigliano, A. *Alien Wisdom: The Limits of Hellenization.* Cambridge: Cambridge University Press, 1975.

——. "Eastern Elements in Post-Exilic Jewish, and Greek, Historiography." In *Essays in Ancient and Modern Historiography,* pp. 25–35. Middletown, CT: Wesleyan University Press, 1977.

——. *Essays on Ancient and Modern Judaism.* Chicago and London: University of Chicago Press, 1994.

Moore, C. A. *Daniel, Esther, and Jeremiah: The Additions.* Anchor Bible. Garden City, NY: Doubleday, 1977.

——. "Eight Questions Most Frequently Asked about the Book of Esther." *Bible Review* 3 (1987): 16–21.

——. *Esther.* Anchor Bible. Garden City, NY: Doubleday, 1971.

——. "Esther, Additions to." *ABD* II, 626–33.

——. "Esther, Book of." *ABD* II, 633–43.

——. "Esther Revisited: An Examination of Esther Studies over the Past Decade." In *Biblical Studies in Honor of Samuel Iwry.* Edited by A. Kort and S. Morschauser, pp. 163–172. Winona Lake, IN: Eisenbrauns, 1985.

——. "Esther Revisited Again: A Further Examination of Certain Esther Studies over the Past Ten Years." *HAR* 7 (1983): 169–86.

——, ed. *Studies in the Book of Esther.* New York: Ktav, 1982.

Moreen, V. "The 'Iranization' of Biblical Heroes in Judeo-Persian Epics: Shahin's *Ardashīr-nāmah* and *'Ezrā-nāmah.*" *Iranian Studies* 29 (1996): 321–38.

Morgan, J. R., and R. Stoneman, eds. *Greek Fiction: The Greek Novel in Context.* London and New York: Routledge, 1994.

Murray, O. "Herodotus and Oral History." *Achaemenid History II: The Greek Sources.* Edited by H. Sancisi-Weerdenburg and A. Kuhrt, pp. 93–115. Leiden: Nederlands Instituut voor het Nabije Oosten, 1987.

Neusner, J. *Esther Rabbah I: An Analytical Translation.* Atlanta: Scholars, 1989.

Niditch, S. "Legends of Wise Heroes and Heroines." In *The Hebrew Bible and Its Modern Interpreters.* Edited by D. A. Knight and G. M. Tucker, pp. 445–63. Philadelphia/Chico, CA: Fortress/Scholars, 1985.

——. "Short Stories: The Book of Esther and the Theme of Women as a Civilizing Force." In *Old Testament Interpretation Past, Present, and Future: Essays in Honor of Gene M. Tucker.* Edited by J. L. Mays et al., pp. 195–209. Nashville: Abingdon, 1995.

——. *War in the Hebrew Bible.* New York and Oxford: Oxford University Press, 1993.

Noss, P. A. "A Footnote on Time: The Book of Esther." *The Bible Translator* 44 (1993): 309–20.

O'Collins. G. "Crucifixion." *ABD* I, 1207–10.

Oppenheim, A. L. "On Royal Gardens in Mesopotamia." *JNES* 24 (1965): 328–33. Reprinted in Moore, *Studies,* 350–55.

Paton, L. B. *A Critical and Exegetical Commentary on the Book of Esther.* ICC. New York: Scribner, 1908.

Perrot, J. "Shoshan Ha-birah." *Eretz Israel* 20 (1989): 155*–60*.

Pirkê de Rabbi Eliezer. Translated by G. Friedlander. New York: Hermon, 1965.

Polzin, R. *Late Biblical Hebrew: Towards a Typology of Biblical Hebrew Prose.* Missoula, MT: Scholars Press, 1976.

Porada, E. *The Art of Ancient Iran.* New York: Crown, 1965.

Pritchard, J. *Ancient Near Eastern Texts Relating to the Old Testament.* Princeton, NJ: Princeton University Press, 1969.

"Purims, Special." *Encyclopedia Judaica* 13:1396–1400.

Radday, Y. T., and A. Brenner, eds. *On Humour and the Comic in the Hebrew Bible.* Sheffield, England: Almond, 1990.

Reardon, B. P. *The Form of Greek Romance.* Princeton, NJ: Princeton University Press, 1991.

Reardon, B. P., ed. *Collected Ancient Greek Novels.* Berkeley: University of California Press, 1989.

Ringgren, H. "Esther and Purim." *Svensk exegetisk Årsbok* 20 (1955): 5–24. Reprinted in Moore, *Studies,* 185–204.

Root, M. C. *The King and Kingship in Achaemenid Art.* Leiden: Brill, 1979.

Rubenstein, J. "Purim, Liminality, and Communitas." *AJS Review* 17/2 (1992): 247–77.

Ruether, R., ed. *Religion and Sexism.* New York: Simon and Schuster, 1974.

Russell, J. R. "Zoroastrian Elements in the Book of Esther." In *Irano-Judaica II: Studies Relating to Jewish Contacts with Persian Culture Throughout the Ages.* Edited by S. Shaked and A. Netzer, pp. 33–40. Jerusalem: Ben Zvi Institute, 1990.

Sáenz Badillos, A. *A History of the Hebrew Language.* Cambridge: Cambridge University Press, 1993.

Salvesen, A. "*KTR* (Esther 1:11; 2:17; 6:8) 'Something to do with a Camel'?" *Journal of Semitic Studies* 44 (1999): 35–46.

Sancisi-Weerdenburg, H. "Decadence in the Empire or Decadence in the Sources? From Source to Synthesis: Ctesias." *Achaemenid History I: Sources, Structures and Synthesis*. Edited by H. Sancisi-Weerdenburg, pp. 33–45. Leiden: Nederlands Instituut voor het Nabije Oosten, 1987.

——. "Exit Atossa: Images of Women in Greek Historiography on Persia." In *Images of Women in Antiquity*. Edited by A. Cameron and A. Kuhrt, pp. 20–33. Detroit: Wayne State University Press, 1983.

——. "The Fifth Oriental Monarchy and Hellenocentrism." In *Achaemenid History II: The Greek Sources*. Edited by H. Sancisi-Weerdenburg and A. Kuhrt, pp. 117–31. Leiden: Nederlands Instituut voor het Nabije Oosten, 1987.

——. "Gifts in the Persian Empire." *Le tribut dans l'empire Perse: Actes de la Table ronde de Paris, 12–13 Décembre 1986*. Edited by P. Briant and C. Herrenschmidt, pp. 129–45. Louvain and Paris: Peeters, 1989.

Sasson, J. M. "Esther." In *The Literary Guide to the Bible*. Edited by R. Alter and F. Kermode, pp. 335–42. Cambridge, MA: Belknap, 1987.

Sato, S. "*Dāta*: King's Law in the Persian Empire" (in Japanese with English summary). *Orient. Bulletin of the Society for Near Eastern Studies in Japan* 28 (1985): 1–16.

Schäfer, P. *Judeophobia: Attitudes toward the Jews in the Ancient World*. Cambridge, MA: Harvard University Press, 1997.

Schauss, H. *The Jewish Festivals*. Cincinnati: Union of American Hebrew Congregations, 1938.

Scheftelowitz, I. *Arisches im Alten Testament I*. (Inaugural-Dissertation zur philosophischen Fakultät der Albertus-Universität zu Königsberg i. Pr.) Königsberg: Hartungsche Buchdruckerei, 1901.

Schmandt-Besserat, D., ed. *Ancient Persia: The Art of an Empire*. Malibu, CA: Undena, 1980.

Schwartz, M. "The Religion of Achaemenian Iran." In *The Cambridge History of Iran*. Vol. 2, pp. 664–97. Cambridge: Cambridge University Press, 1985.

Segal, E. *The Babylonian Esther Midrash*. 3 vols. Atlanta: Scholars Press, 1994.

——. "Human Anger and Divine Intervention in Esther." *Prooftexts* 9 (1989): 247–56.

Seow, C. L. *Ecclesiastes*. Anchor Bible. New York: Doubleday, 1997.

Shaked, S. "Iranian Functions in the Book of Esther." *Irano-Judaica: Studies Relating to Jewish Contacts with Persian Culture Throughout the Ages*. Edited by S. Shaked, pp. 292–303. Jerusalem: Ben Zvi Institute, 1982.

Shuv, S. "Megillat ʾester: megillah shel karnival." *Meḥqerei ḥag* 2 (5730): 31–43.

Simon, M. D. "'Many Thoughts in the Heart of Man...': Irony and Theology in the Book of Esther." *Tradition* 31: 4 (1997): 5–27.

Simon, U. *Reading Prophetic Narratives*. Bloomington, IN: Indiana University Press, 1997.

Spycket, A. "Women in Persian Art." In *Ancient Persia: The Art of an Empire*. Edited by D. Schmandt-Besserat, pp. 43–45. Malibu, CA: Undena, 1980.

Stern, E. *Material Culture of the Land of the Bible in the Persian Period, 538–332 B.C.* Jerusalem: Israel Exploration Society, 1982.

Stolper, M. "A Paper Chase after the Aramaic on *TCL* 13 193." *JAOS* 116 (1996): 517–21.

Streidl, H. "Untersuchung zur Syntax und Stilistik des hebräischen Buches Esther." *ZAW* 55 (1937): 73–108.

Stronach, D. "The Garden as a Political Statement: Some Case Studies from the Near East in the First Millennium B.C." *Bulletin of the Asia Institute* 4 (1990): 171–80.

Tabory, J. *Moʿadei Yisraʾel bi-tequfat ha-mishnah ve-ha-talmud*. Jerusalem: Magnes, 1995.

——. "Review of Eliezer Segal, *The Babylonian Esther Midrash: A Critical Commentary*." *JQR* 88 (1997): 113–20.

Talmon, S. "Ha-'im nod'ah megilat 'ester be-qerev 'adat 'ba'ei ha-berit ha-ḥadashah'?" *Eretz Israel* 25 (1996): 377–82.

——. "Was the Book of Esther Known at Qumran?" *DSD* 2 (1995): 249–67.

——. "'Wisdom' in the Book of Esther." *VT* 13 (1963): 419–55.

Thornton, T. C. G. "The Crucifixion of Haman and the Scandal of the Cross." *JTS* 37 (1986): 419–26.

Tigay, J. *Deuteronomy* (The JPS Torah Commentary). Philadelphia: Jewish Publication Society, 1996.

Tov, E. "The 'Lucianic' Text of the Canonical and the Apocryphal Sections of Esther: A Rewritten Book." *Textus* 10 (1982): 1–25.

Tuplin, C. *Achaemenid Studies.* Stuttgart: Franz Steiner, 1996.

——. "Persian Decor in *Cyropaedia:* Some Observations." In *Achaemenid History V: The Roots of the European Tradition.* Edited by H. Sancisi-Weerdenburg and J. W. Drijvers, pp. 17–29. Leiden: Nederlands Instituut voor het Nabije Oosten, 1990.

Unterman, Jeremiah. "The Influence of Daniel on Esther." Paper presented at the Association for Jewish Studies, Boston, 22 December 1997.

——. "The Influence of Kings on Esther." (unpublished paper).

Vogelsang, W. J. *The Rise and Organization of the Achaemenid Empire: The Eastern Iranian Evidence.* Leiden: Brill, 1992.

Waldbaum, J. "Early Greek Contacts with the Southern Levant, ca. 1000–600 B.C.: The Eastern Perspective." *BASOR* 293 (1994): 53–66.

——. "Greeks *in* the East or Greeks *and* the East? Problems in the Definition and Recognition of Presence." *BASOR* 305 (1997): 1–17.

Walfish, B. D. *Esther in Medieval Garb.* Albany, NY: State University of New York, 1993.

——. "The Two Commentaries of Abraham ibn Ezra on the Book of Esther." *JQR* 79 (1989): 323–45.

Waltke, B. and M. O'Connor. *Biblical Hebrew Syntax.* Winona Lake, IN: Eisenbrauns, 1990.

Wechsler, M. "The Purim-Passover Connection: A Reflection of Jewish Exegetical Tradition in the Peshitta Book of Esther." *JBL* 117 (1998): 321–27.

Weisman, Z. *Political Satire in the Bible.* Atlanta: Scholars, 1998.

Weiss, R. "Leshonah ve-signonah shel megilat 'ester." *Maḥanayim* 104 (1966): 56–63.

Welles, C. B. "The Hellenistic Orient." In *The Idea of History in the Ancient Near East.* Edited by R. Dentan, pp. 133–67. New Haven and London: Yale University Press, 1955.

Westbrook, R. "The Female Slave." In *Gender and Law in the Hebrew Bible and the Ancient Near East.* Edited by V. Matthews et al., pp. 214–38. Sheffield, England: Sheffield Academic Press, 1998.

——. "Punishments and Crimes." *ABD* V, 546–56.

Whedbee, J. W. *The Bible and the Comic Vision.* Cambridge: Cambridge University Press, 1998.

White, S. A. "Esther: A Feminine Model for Jewish Diaspora." In *Gender and Difference in Ancient Israel.* Edited by P. Day, pp. 161–77. Minneapolis: Fortress, 1989.

——. "Esther." In *The Women's Bible Commentary.* Edited by C. Newsom and S. Ringe, pp. 124–29. Louisville, KY: John Knox, 1992.

White Crawford, S. "Has *Esther* Been Found at Qumran? *4QProto-Esther* and the *Esther* Corpus." *Revue de Qumran* 17 (1996): 307–25.

Wiebe, J. M. "Esther 4:14: 'Will Relief and Deliverance Arise for the Jews from Another Place'?" *CBQ* 53 (1991): 409–15.

Williamson, H. G. M. "Review of *The Esther Scroll*, by D. J. A. Clines." *JTS* 37 (1986): 146–52.

Wills, L. M. *The Jew in the Court of the Foreign King.* Minneapolis: Fortress, 1990.

——. *The Jewish Novel in the Ancient World.* Ithaca, NY: Cornell University Press, 1995.

——. "The Jewish Novellas." In *Greek Fiction: The Greek Novel in Context*. Edited by J. R. Morgan and R. Stoneman, pp. 223–38. London and New York. Routledge, 1994.

Wiseman, D. J. "Mesopotamian Gardens." *Anatolian Studies* 33 (1983): 137–44.

Wolski, J. "L'hellenisme et l'Iran." In *Mélanges Pierre Lévêque*. Edited by M. Mactoux and E. Geny, pp. 439–46. Paris: Annales Littéraires de l'Université de Besançon 1989.

Yamauchi, E. M. "Ahasuerus." *ABD* I, 105.

——. "Mordecai, the Persepolis Tablets, and the Susa Excavations." *VT* 42 (1992): 272–75.

——. *Persia and the Bible*. Grand Rapids, MI: Baker, 1990.

Zadok, R. *The Jews in Babylonia During the Chaldean and Achaemenian Periods According to the Babylonian Sources*. Haifa: University of Haifa, 1979

——. "Notes on Esther." *ZAW* 98 (1986): 105–110; *ZAW* 99 (1987): 156.

——. "On Five Biblical Names." *ZAW* 89 (1977): 266–68.

——. "On Five Iranian Names in the Old Testament." *VT* 26 (1976): 246–47.

——. "On the Historical Background of the Book of Esther." *Biblische Notizen* 24 (1984): 18–23.

——. *The Pre-Hellenistic Israelite Anthroponymy and Prosopography*. Leuven: Uitgeverji Peeters, 1988.